CANADA'S CHEESE AND WINE LOVERS' COOKBOOK

Shari Darling

D1413662

Macmillan Canada
Toronto

Canadian Cataloguing in Publication Data

Darling, Shari, date.
    Canada's Cheese and Wine Lovers' Cookbook

Includes index.
ISBN 0-7715-9058-X

1. Cookery (Cheese).   2. Cookery (Wine).   3. Cheese   4. Wine and winemaking. I. Title.
TX759.D37 1994   641.3′73   C94-931488-9
1 2 3 4 5 TR 98 97 96 95 94

Cover design by Andrew Smith

Cover illustration by Linda Montgomery

Interior illustrations by Agnes Aru

Macmillan Canada wishes to thank the Canada Council, the Ontario Ministry of Culture and Communications and the Ontario Arts Council for supporting its publishing program.

Macmillan Canada
A Division of Canada Publishing Corporation
Toronto, Ontario, Canada

Printed in Canada

CONTENTS

A MESSAGE FROM THE VINTNERS QUALITY ALLIANCE

PERHAPS NO TWO ITEMS IN THE WORLD are as inextricably linked as wine and cheese. Over centuries and civilizations, peasants and aristocrats alike have consumed wine and cheese, and in all but the harshest of circumstances, have taken time to reflect upon them.

Wine and cheese, it would seem, are partners not only on the table, but in the hearts and minds of those with a passion for life and an appreciation of the earth's largesse. And where there is passion, there must be quality, so not surprisingly, generations of cheese and wine makers have striven for excellence and diversity in their trade.

This quest for perfection and authenticity had its origins in ancient times. The Egyptians, Greeks and Romans made some of the greatest advances in the production of wine and cheese, initiating trade and even creating the word "tyrophile" to describe one who loves cheese. As true connoisseurs, they improved grape quality through pruning and fertilization, and developed a plethora of cheeses, from fresh, smoked and dried versions to cheeses basted in wine and flavoured with marjoram, mint and coriander.

In modern times this commitment to quality has culminated in international laws and regulatory bodies that govern all aspects of wine and cheese production. In 1935, France introduced the "Appellation d'Origine Controlé" to set standards for the production of wine and spirits, and the standards remain today. Italy created the "Denominazione di Origine Controllata" designation for wine, and an abundance of designations for cheese, though all on a local level.

At home, the past decade has seen the development of the Vintners Quality Alliance (VQA), establishing strict standards for Canadian fine wine production. The VQA's principles specify the finest grape varieties, delimit the geographical areas where the grapes may be grown, and dictate how the wine must be made. Experience has shown that certain grapes and certain vineyard areas, because of their favoured soils, exposure and microclimate, produce the best wines year after year. By designating the grape varieties and the appellation of origin on the label, vintners offer wine lovers a guide to their superior products.

Safeguards in the dairy industry have secured Canada's international renown for cheeses such as Ermite, Trappist, Oka and Cheddar.

Our wine, cheese and culinary industries are coming of age, and the future holds the promise of refinement, innovation and uniqueness. Helping shape this future, while chronicling the Canada's successes, is author Shari Darling.

Shari's love of Canada's rich and diverse agricultural bounty has inspired her food and wine writing and challenged the artisans — chefs, winemakers and cheesemakers alike — whose creations grace her pages. In this cookbook Shari has fused the colours and textures, aromas and flavours of our multicultural heritage with those of our distinctive regions. The recipes reveal the passion of this country's culinary artists in a form that may be shared, that may endure.

Peter J. Gamble
Executive Director, VQA,
Director, Wines of Canada

CANADIANS HAVE MUCH TO CELEBRATE when it comes to cheese and wine. Thanks to our dairy farmers and wine growers, our cheesemakers and winemakers, we have domestic products that are distinctive, ethnically diverse and often of exceptional quality.

We have domestic Colby and pasteurized cow's milk feta for those who prefer something mild in flavour, and eight-year-old Cheddar for those with a seasoned palate. Ermite, Oka and Trappist are cheeses distinctive to Canada, all developed more than a century ago at monasteries in Quebec and Manitoba. In fact, Ermite is still being produced by L'Abbaye de Saint-Benoît-du-Lac in Saint-Benoît-du-Lac, Quebec, and Trappist at Our Lady of the Prairies Abbey in Holland, Manitoba. Some of our cheeses are handmade as well, making them unique in size and shape as well as taste.

As for ethnic diversity, the list is nearly endless. More than a hundred varieties of cheese are made in Canada, from the raw and pasteurized milk of Holstein and Jersey cows and a few species of goats. Across the country, large factories and farmhouse cheesemakers are producing cheeses in styles native to Holland, Switzerland, England, France, Italy, Greece, Portugal, Germany and Austria, to name a few. Then there are cheeses for kosher dietary laws, for religious and lacto vegetarians and for those following an organic diet.

I have noticed that all cheesemakers share a common trait — a desire to express their art form mixed with a willingness to experiment. This dedication to their heritage and passion for their craft have spelled global success for Canadian cheese. Our Cheddar, brick and Montasio are a few of the cheeses that win top prizes at international competitions. And competitions at the national level — at the Pacific National Exhibition, Royal Winter Fair, British Empire Dairy Show, Le Concours du Lys d'Or and Mammoth Cheese competitions — give Canada's cheesemakers the opportunity to share knowledge and express ideas about their art. As a result the quality of Canadian cheeses improves every year.

Just as domestic cheese is diverse, distinctive and of world-class quality, so too is Canadian wine. Our winemakers are also artists who are proud of their heritage and draw upon it to produce wines in a variety of styles. In British Columbia, for example, Divino Estate Winery concentrates on Italian grape varieties; Gehringer Brothers and Gray Monk Cellars on the German ones. CedarCreek does wines in the French style but offers variety as well. Organic wines are also made in British Columbia at such wineries as Summerhill Estate Winery in Kelowna and Hainle Vineyards in Peachland. Ontario's wineries are just as eclectic.

Distinctiveness is yet another reason why Canadian wineries are celebrating success. The geography of Ontario's and British Columbia's designated wine regions and specific areas of Quebec and Nova Scotia make wine growing possible. The Okanagan Valley, lying at the same latitude as the Rhine Valley in Germany and the Champagne region of France, benefits from a mild microclimate, consisting of intense sunlight, minimal rainfall, low humidity and cool nights. These climatic conditions, combined with the region's distinctive soils, are ideally suited to European grape varieties with intense flavours and good acidity.

The Niagara Peninsula, as another example, is more southerly than all the wine areas of France. The peninsula is nestled between Lake Ontario to the North and the Niagara Escarpment to the south. The lake moderates temperatures in the vineyards year-round, cooling the summer air so grapes ripen slowly and in the winter warming the air, delaying the first frost and extending the growing season. The escarpment contributes to this microclimate by acting as a barrier against potentially harmful continental trade winds. Sloping gently toward Lake Ontario, the escarpment also offers excellent water drainage. This is crucial, since grape vines prefer to keep their feet dry. Add to this a variety of soil types, and Niagara is able to produce a wide range of European varieties, praised for their delicate nature and outstanding character. Two of these are Chardonnay and Pinot Noir.

What's more fascinating is that even within one designated wine region, a grape variety can vary in character because of the climate and soil conditions found in sub-appellations, even in separate vineyards. Riesling is a good example. Grapes grown near the Niagara River just outside Niagara-on-the-Lake result in a wine with lots of body, tropical fruit character, medium acidity and good ageing potential. Those grown on the first shelf of the Niagara Escarpment (called the bench) are characterized by their citrus character and steely acidity, which gives the wines great ageing potential.

Canadian wines are being celebrated not only at home but also abroad. Our winemakers are winning countless gold and silver medals at international competitions such as VinExpo, VinItaly and InterVin and are being praised by wine writers, wine authorities and wine lovers around the globe. Much of this success can be attributed to the implementation of the VQA (Vintners Quality Alliance) in 1988. "The VQA is an Appellation of Origin system by which consumers can identify wines of Ontario and British Columbia based on the origin of the grapes from which they are produced. The new VQA medallion is awarded to wines of the highest distinction, as selected by a panel of experts," says Peter Gamble, Executive Director of the VQA. Since its inception, Ontario and British Columbia winemakers have had an uncompromising focus on quality. Each year most of their wines surpass the strict regulations and standards set out by the VQA.

The diversity, distinctiveness and high quality of Canadian cheeses and wines makes it possible to serve a range of dishes for all occasions, which is the theme of this cookbook. I gathered recipes from many of Canada's cheese factories and a selection of specialty cheese shops and delis. Still other recipes were created by chefs who work with Canadian cheeses daily. Quite a number of these mouth-watering recipes were developed for — and won prizes in — the annual Foodservice Awards sponsored by the Dairy Bureau of Canada. These recipes were created by award-winning chefs, cooks, foodservice operators and student chefs.

Cheese is featured in the recipes in sauces and toppings, and in stuffings and fillings. The recipes range from fast and simple everyday meals to time-consuming and complex gourmet fare. (No need to be intimidated, though: all recipes are easy to follow.)

Most recipes are accompanied by a Canadian wine. I married the wines to the dishes in one of four ways. The food and the wine may be a traditional match, or they may share corresponding aromas, flavours or textures. Other partnerships are based on the offset of those characteristics, bringing harmony to the palate. And sometimes I chose a wine for no other reason than because it cleans the palate to make way for another scrumptious bite.

Vintage dates and VQA trademarks have been excluded from the tasting notes. This is to restrict you less when you are buying wine. Do keep in mind that, although you do not see the VQA medallion shown on page v, most of the wines listed do reach — even surpass — VQA status every year. If you can't find the wine suggested in the tasting notes, ask your wine merchant to suggest a Canadian substitute of the same grape variety and style. (The wines were chosen according to their typical "varietal" character.)

In most cases the cheese and wine suggestions correspond with the recipe's origin. When profiling an Ontario cheese factory or cheese shop, for instance, I suggested an Ontario wine as a match.

Both the cheese and wine suggestions are meant to help you in your selections, not hamper your imagination, creativity or urge to experiment. Because so many domestic cheeses are interchangeable — Camembert and Brie, Cheddar and Cheshire, mozzarella and Fior di Latte, cream cheese and Quark — this cookbook offers endless possibilities that are sure to please you and your guests for many years.

CHAPTER ONE

CHEESEMAKING

HAVE YOU EVER WONDERED how plain, simple milk can end up as so many types of cheeses, each having its own unique character?

THE ANIMAL

The biggest influence on cheese is the animal from which the milk is obtained. In Canada, milk for cheesemaking comes from mostly Holstein and Jersey cows and from a few species of goats, mainly Nubian. Each breed produces milk with its own special attributes. Jersey milk, for example, is richer in butterfat and protein than Holstein milk, giving Jersey Cheddars a creamy texture. Goat's milk cheeses, renowned for their tangy flavour, are generally higher in protein, calcium, phosphorus and vitamins A and B-complex and lower in cholesterol and lactose than most cow's milk varieties.

THE ENVIRONMENT

The enviromental conditions (climate and soil) under which animal feed is grown and the nature of the feed, be it grass, grain, corn or some combination, determine the quality of the milk and some of the character of the cheese. Most of our domestic cheeses are made from a blend of milk obtained from many herds, so any special characteristics are not noticeable. However, a handful of cheeses are made from the milk produced by one herd that grazes on a specific piece of land. Two examples are Trappist cheese from Our Lady of the Prairies Abbey in Holland, Manitoba, and feta from Kawartha Goat Cheese in Indian River, Ontario. The season when the animal is milked is also important. Louis Paron, of Paron Dairy, uses only winter milk to produce his award-winning Black Parmesan. The reason is that winter milk is higher in calcium and protein and contains less water, thereby producing a Parmesan with richer flavour.

THE CHEESEMAKING PROCESS

Although the cheesemaking process is essentially the same around the globe and consists of four basic steps — curdling, draining, pressing and ripening — various measures can be undertaken before and during the process to produce a variety of results.

MILK: Pasteurized, Heat Treated or Unpasteurized? Today, the majority of the world's cheeses are made from pasteurized milk. This means the milk is heated to a temperature of 72°C to 76°C and maintained for 16 seconds to partly sterilize it and kill potentially bad bacteria, such as *listeria*. Some cheesemakers believe the process destroys important enzymes that aid in the flavour and ageing of the cheese, and they opt for heat-treated milk instead. With heat treatment, the temperature of the milk is raised to approximately 65°C for 16 seconds to kill bad bacteria. This method is said to preserve more of the important enzymes. Still other cheesemakers insist on using unpasteurized milk. Unpasteurized cheeses are no longer a health risk, for factories are regulated under strict health codes. Bad bacteria are killed by the cheesemaking process and through a natural pasteurization that occurs when the raw-milk cheeses are aged for at least 60 days. All three types of milk are used to make domestic cheese.

Any number of agents are added to the heated milk, all producing different effects in the cheese. For example, mould spores promote blue veining. Adding a propionic acid bacteria creates the large holes in a cheese during the ripening process.

CURDLING: When a bacterial culture high in lactic acid is added to the vat of milk, souring begins, with an increase in acidity. Small grains called curds begin to form. When the curds have obtained a desired temperature and acid level, the cheesemaker adds rennet. Rennet is an enzyme taken from the stomach lining of calves, lambs or goats. (A microbial enzyme of plant origin is used in some cheeses for vegetarian markets.) Rennet stimulates the coagulation of all the curds into a large mass, which separates from the whey. The curds consist of the water-insoluble elements in milk, such as casein (protein) and fat. The whey is made up of the water-soluble components, such as carbohydrate, salts and other proteins.

CUTTING, STIRRING, DRAINING, COOKING: The coagulated mass is cut in various ways, depending on the cheese to be made. Cutting expels more whey. Depending on the desired texture and acid level, the curds may be ladled into moulds to drain naturally. Or they may be stretched in hot water until they take on an elastic-like texture (pasta filatas). Some cheeses are made by cooking the curds in the whey. Generally speaking, a lower temperature produces cheeses with a high moisture level and a high temperature brings about a low moisture content in the cheese. During the process the curds may be gently agitated (for making soft cheeses) or rapidly stirred at a high temperature (for making firm or hard types). Stirring keeps the curds from forming a tough skin.

MILLING, SALTING, PRESSING: Once drained, some curds are milled — cut into smaller cubes — to expel more whey and to fit into a perforated mould of a desired shape. The perforations allow even more whey to drain away. At this point the curds can be dry-salted for flavouring, heated or pressed. Firm varieties, for example, Cheddar, undergo a heavy pressing for several hours.

RIPENING: Ripening is the final stage in cheesemaking. Rinds are formed by introducing the cheese to various elements. Caciocavallo is dipped into a brine solution to form its rind; Brie and Camembert are sprayed with a *Penicillium* culture to form a white bloomy rind. Every variety must be cured under specific conditions of temperature, humidity and oxygen level to produce the desired texture, flavour and quality. Trappist cheese, for example, is sponged daily with a salt solution to slow the ripening process.

Under all the right conditions, the cheese will slowly change its molecular structure, becoming surface ripened (Brie, Oka) or interior ripened (Saint Paulin). Through this age-old method, cheeses acquire interesting characteristics. Emmenthal develops holes; Ermite, blue veins; Cheddar, a crumbly texture and nippy flavour.

CHAPTER TWO

UNDERSTANDING WINE

BALANCE IS A TERM OF HIGH PRAISE given to wines whose elements are in proportion and produce harmony on the palate. In whites, desirable elements are acids, fruit and alcohols and sometimes sugars for sweeter wines; in reds, acids, fruit, alcohols and tannin. Each of the elements has a specific function.

Being aware of the elements will help you to find words to describe what you are sensing and help you to gain a better understanding of what makes one wine different from another.

ACIDITY

Acidity gives wine its crisp, fresh quality. It also enhances the fruit character, contributes to the wonderful lasting aftertaste called the finish and aids in extending the lifespan of a wine. Wine has many acids, some found naturally in the grape, such as tartaric, malic and citric acid, others, such as lactic and acetic acid, produced by the winemaking process. Tartaric acid is harsh tasting. Citric acid gives wine a lemony or citric quality, and malic acid tastes like tart green apples. When red and white wines are too high in malic acid, they undergo a secondary malolactic fermentation. Basically, the process converts about half of a wine's malic acid to the softer, milky lactic acid, thereby softening the wine. Acetic acid is the main acid in vinegar. If a wine contains certain bacteria and is exposed to air, it will form large amounts of acetic acid and ethyl acetate and turn to vinegar.

FRUIT CHARACTER

Depending on the grape variety used and the region, soil and vintage in which it is grown, a wine will display an aroma and taste of fresh fruit. Whites can have characteristics reminiscent of tropical fruit (pineapple, mango, melon, banana), hard fruit (pears, apples, quince), exotic fruit (gooseberries) or citrus fruit (lemon, grapefruit). Red wines have characteristics that fall into the soft fruit category such as blackcurrant, blackberry, raspberry, plum, cherry and strawberry.

SWEETNESS

When tasting wine, sweetness is the first sensation you discover, because it is detected by the tip of the tongue. A wine's sweetness is determined by its main fruit sugars, glucose and fructose. However, the alcohol glycerol, better known as glycerine, is present in all wines and although it is colourless and tasteless, it enhances the perception of sweetness in the fruit character while adding body. The temperature of fermentation determines the amount of glycerine in a wine. Reds, fermented at higher temperatures than whites, usually have more glycerine. Glycerine is one of the main components that form the legs or tears (film) on the inside of the wine glass.

ALCOHOLS

Wine has many alcohols. The most noteworthy is ethanol, referred to simply as alcohol. It, too, influences character and enhances the sweetness of a wine. Being volatile, it helps to carry the wine's aromas upward so they can be identified by the nose. As an antibacterial agent, it also contributes to a wine's longevity by killing bacteria that may cause spoilage. Generally speaking, the higher the alcohol content, the longer the life of a wine. (Even then, cellar ageing does not benefit all wines.)

TANNIN

Tannin is found in the stems, skins and pips of the grape and in the wood barrels used to ferment or age wines. To make red wines, the colourless juice is fermented with the grape skins, which release colour and tannin. The amount of tannin in a wine is determined by the grape variety used, the length of time a wine is fermented on its skins, the degree to which the grapes are pressed and the length of time a wine spends in the wood barrels during fermentation or ageing. Tannin, like the other elements, must be present in the right amount to produce a balanced wine. Wines with too much tannin are referred to as "hard" because they are astringent and make the mouth pucker. This is acceptable in some young red wines that are meant to be aged over an extended period, for the tannin helps to extend the wine's life expectancy. As the wine ages, the tannin will precipitate and soften, bringing the wine into harmony.

OAK

Wines can be aged in wood barrels. A wine's character can be enhanced by oak ageing, as the wood imparts colour, tannin, aromas and flavours. Barrel-fermented and/or barrel-aged Chardonnays, for example, are often described as having toasty, oaky tones in the aromas, vanilla and spicy notes in the flavour. Barrel-fermented and/or barrel-aged reds may also display smoky, vanilla or spicy character. The size, shape and type of wood used (new or old, French or American) and the length of time a wine remains in the barrel are strictly up to the winemaker's artistic judgement. However, an exceptional barrel-fermented and/or barrel-aged wine is one whose oaky character is balanced with all other elements.

CHAPTER THREE

BUYING AND STORING CHEESE

BUYING CHEESE

Just like wine, cheese is a "living" substance, and so requires special attention when you are buying it. Nowadays supermarkets offer a wide selection of cheese, both domestic and imported. Supermarket cheese is usually prepackaged, which means you'll have to judge the cheese not by taste but by how it looks and feels.

If you are buying cheese for a particular recipe or to serve at a wine and cheese function, a cheese shop is your best bet for several reasons. Here you'll find a wider range of the best and tastiest cheeses available. Cheese proprietors are educated about their products and will share information on each cheese, its maker and its storage requirements. Most will also offer serving suggestions, recommend brands or types, answer questions and keep you abreast of incoming products.

Above all, you can sample cheeses at a cheese shop. This helps you determine quality and character. Every cheese has its own distinctive character that results, in part, from how long it has been ripened. As a cheese ripens it moves through several stages, from mild to strong or from crumbly to soft and sensuous. Do you like a young Brie with a mild mushroom flavour? Or do you prefer a ripened version that offers more depth of flavour?

Buy only as much cheese as you need and eat it within a day or so. Here are a few buying tips to help you in your selection:

FRESH CHEESES: When buying cottage, Quark, ricotta and Baker's cheeses, check the expiry date and buy as fresh as possible. They should have a sweet aroma, light colour and be moist but not sloppy.

PASTA FILATA CHEESES: Fresh pasta filata cheeses (Fior di Latte, mozzarella) are white and moist with an elastic-like texture. Cheese that is too old has a tough texture. A rancid smell is a sign of spoilage.

SURFACE-RIPENED SOFT CHEESES: Brie, Camembert and double-cream and triple-cream Brie have a white bloomy rind, are soft to the touch and have a mild mushroom aroma. If hard and bland, the cheese may be unripened. In this case, leave it, wrapped, at room temperature for a couple of hours. (A hard texture or discoloration may also mean the cheese was improperly wrapped and has dried out.) If you buy ripened Brie, plan to eat it within a day. An ammonia odour and bitter taste indicate over-ripening.

RIND CHEESES: Besides the bloomy rind cheeses, there are three types of rinds or coatings — the washed rind, the natural rind and waxed. Some cheeses are washed with brine or wine during the ripening process to form a rind. Saint Paulin and Oka are examples of these. Other cheeses are not washed but are simply brushed to slow the ripening process and allow the cheese to develop a natural rind. Trappist and Parmesan both have natural rinds and are ripened slowly. On these cheeses, cracked or swollen rind could be a sign of improper ripening, bitterness or spoilage. Dried-out Parmesan and Romano may also have a grainy texture, rancid odour or bitter taste. Lastly, waxed cheeses have to be judged according to their interior. (The wax coating may look enticing, even though the rind beneath it is cracked.) So buy wedges of waxed cheese (some Cheddars, Gouda). The interior should be a consistent colour throughout.

FIRM CHEESES: Cheddar, Colby, brick, Friulano, Emmenthal, marble and farmer's are only some of the many firm cheeses made in Canada. When choosing these varieties, look for a consistency of colour. A deepened colour near the edges could indicate the cheese has dried out. Cracks and white spots are also signs of improper ripening, bitterness or spoilage.

HARD CHEESES: Romano and Old Bra are judged according to colour. Discolouring or white spots could mean the cheese has a strong or more intense, piquant taste — a flavour you may or may not like.

BLUE-VEINED CHEESES: Blue cheeses are in a class of their own, some creamy like gorgonzola, others crumbly like Ermite. All should have a zesty but not sharp smell and be well marbled with blue. A sticky wrapper, rancid odour or streaks of black are signs of overageing or poor quality.

GOAT CHEESES: Fresh goat cheese has a fresh aroma and creamy consistency. Bloomy-rind Brie made from goat's milk should be subtle to the touch. A firm interior could mean the cheese is underripe. An ammonia odour, yellow colour or bitter taste may be a sign of spoilage. Those packed in their whey (such as feta) should be firm enough to cut and have a clear whey. A milky whey and a soft texture probably mean the cheese is of poor quality.

STORING CHEESE
Cheese is susceptible to oxygen, humidity and temperature fluctuations, and so requires proper storage.

Fresh cheeses such as ricotta and Quark have a high moisture content, and thus need refrigeration in an airtight container. Even with proper storage, they deteriorate quickly, so check the expiry date before you buy and eat soon. Store the container upside down. This keeps the surface air from developing bacteria too quickly. Brie and Camembert have less moisture and so ripen quickly. Therefore, buy small quantities and eat them within a day or so. If storing them, tightly wrap each in plastic wrap and refrigerate. Firm and hard cheeses, which have the least amount of moisture, last longer when refrigerated. But they, too, will lose moisture and dry out if not individually wrapped. Wipe the cheese with a paper towel to remove excess moisture to prevent the development of mould, wrap tightly in plastic wrap and refrigerate. If mould forms on these varieties, simply cut it off. If you've already grated the Parmesan or Romano, add a chunk of bread to the container to prevent clumping. As for rind cheeses, wrap only the cut area to allow the rest of the cheese to breathe.

THE MOULD ISSUE

Cheese can pick up bacteria from the air and begin to mould. Therefore, all individually wrapped pieces of cheese should be stored together in an airtight container. Store the container in the warmest part of the refrigerator. Colder areas may cause the cheese to crystallize, which alters its texture. If mould does form, cut away about one-half inch (1 cm) of the cheese that surrounds the mould. If Brie or Camembert form mould, discard them altogether.

FREEZING CHEESE

Every cheese, because of its moisture, salt content and age, freezes differently. Generally, low-moisture and aged types (such as Parmesan) freeze well, whereas high-moisture ones, such as cottage and cream cheese, do not freeze well at all. In every case, the flavour will probably be retained but the texture will be altered, making the cheese useful as a cooking ingredient only. If you must freeze cheese, do so only up to eight weeks. Cut large slabs into pieces weighing less than 1 lb (500 g) and no more than an inch (2.5 cm) thick. Wrap in an airtight container to prevent drying. Thaw the cheese in the refrigerator for 24 hours and use immediately.

CHAPTER FOUR

BUYING AND STORING WINE

BUYING WINE

The local wine shop need not be an intimidating place if you apply a few basics when purchasing wine.

First, consider the occasion, the type of food the wine will be served with and its price. A casual meal calls for a simple, less expensive wine, just as a formal dinner is enhanced by a varietal wine with a definite personality. Marrying food and wine, like life itself, should be an adventure. Use your imagination to build an interesting, harmonious partnership.

LEARNING THE GRAPE VARIETIES: You can improve your chances of developing harmony on the palate by becoming familiar with the major grape varieties used in wine production. New world countries, including Canada, label their wines by grape varieties. Each grape variety, despite where it is grown and the style in which it is fermented, displays a basic personality that can usually be identified in a blind tasting.

Canada's wine regions, like those of Europe and the United States, grow two families of grapes, called Vitis vinifera and French hybrids, for wine. Both families consist of red and white grape varieties.

Viniferas, the noble grapes of Europe, include such varieties as Chardonnay, Riesling, Gewürztraminer, Pinot Noir, Merlot and Cabernet Sauvignon. They are a sensitive bunch that need ideal weather conditions, proper vineyard management and excellent winemaking skills to produce a decent yield of grapes. The wines are worth the hard work, however, as they have finesse and display wonderful aromas, textures and flavours.

Hybrids are a genetic cross between American and Vitis vinifera varieties. The first hybrids were developed by French botanists as an experiment to produce vines that could resist fungus and disease. In the early 1930s Harry Hatch, then owner of Brights Wines, sent his research director, Adhemar de Chaunac, on an expedition through Europe to collect vine clippings. De Chaunac returned with several dozen French hybrid varieties and a hundred various viniferas. The hybrid family consists of varieties such as Vidal, Seyval, Baco Noir, Maréchal Foch and de Chaunac. They are winter hardy and produce higher yields of early ripening grapes. The wines are more assertive than viniferas but offer more consistency of quality from year to year.

- SAMPLE BEFORE YOU BUY: By sampling before you buy, you'll always be satisfied with the wine you choose. All of Canada's wineries operate an on-site wine boutique where samples of specific wines are available each day. Most independent shops offer the same service. If you are purchasing wine at a liquor store that does not provide this service, ask to see the wine consultant's tasting notes to help you in your selection.
- CHOOSE CAREFULLY: Be sure to purchase only those bottles that have been stored on their sides, allowing the cork to remain in contact with the wine. (If the bottle has been stored upright for a long time, the cork may have dried out. This can cause the wine to be oxidized, which spoils it.) Heat and light can also cause a wine to age before its time, so stay away from bottles used in window displays or those stored under bright lights. Also, avoid wines with soiled labels, leaking capsules and protruding corks.

STORING WINE

If you are keeping your wine for any length of time, proper storage is important. Lay bottles on their sides and cellar them in a cool, dark place where the temperature is constant and free of vibrations. A fruit cellar is ideal, although any corner in the basement will do. Apartment dwellers can set up a cellar in a bedroom closet or a dark corner away from heating vents and air conditioning units. Attractive and practical as it may seem, wine should not be stored in the kitchen, where daylight and constant temperature fluctuations from the refrigerator and oven can spoil it.

Here is a list of Canada's most popular grape varieties. Do not let this list hamper your imagination when describing wines. Wine tasting and evaluation is a subjective art.

RED VITIS VINIFERAS:

Cabernet Sauvignon:
CHARACTER: medium to full bodied, when young tannic with blackcurrant character. When aged, the wine has notes of cedar, sweet pepper, olives, soft tannin.
FOOD MATCH: beef, lamb, duck, tomato-based sauces

Cabernet Franc:
CHARACTER: medium bodied and vigorous with raspberry, herbaceous and sometimes spicy character, soft tannin and low acidity.
FOOD MATCH: beef, lamb

Merlot:
CHARACTER: medium to full bodied with blackberry fruit, sometimes spicy
FOOD MATCH: beef, sausage, pheasant, liver

Pinot Noir:
CHARACTER: light bodied with strawberry, cherry or red plum character
FOOD MATCH: partridge, pheasant, roast chicken

Gamay Noir:
CHARACTER: When fermented in the Beaujolais style, the wines are light with strawberry fruit.
FOOD MATCH: hamburgers, grilled white meat, all picnic foods

WHITE VITIS VINIFERAS:

Chardonnay:
CHARACTER: Can be fermented in many ways. When stainless steel fermented, the wines are light to medium bodied with apple and/or pear aromas and flavours. When barrel-fermented and/or -aged, the wines are usually full bodied with toasty character enhancing the apple fruit.
FOOD MATCH:
> *Light Chardonnays:* white meat, fish, appetizers, light soups, salads
> *Heavy Chardonnays:* lobster and crab, cream/butter-based sauces, chowders

Pinot Blanc:
CHARACTER: medium to full bodied with pear and/or apple character and sometimes a hint of spice (if aged in oak)
FOOD MATCH: white meat, fish, light soups

Auxerrois:
CHARACTER: medium bodied with an apricot/peach character
FOOD MATCH: shrimp and scallops, meaty fish

Riesling:
CHARACTER: medium to full bodied, dry, semi-dry. Can be made into late harvest and Icewines. Can be citrus or tropical in character but always with good to excellent acidity.
FOOD MATCH:
> *Dry Riesling:* vinaigrettes, fish, cream/butter-based sauces and soups
> *Semi-dry Riesling:* meaty fish, shrimp, scallops, white meat, cream/butter-based sauces and soups, pork
> *Late Harvest and Icewines:* fruit-based desserts

Ehrenfelser:
CHARACTER: medium to full bodied with tropical and citrus fruit, good acidity
FOOD MATCH: meaty fish, shrimp and scallops, white meat, cream/butter-based sauces and soups

Gewürztraminer:
CHARACTER: medium to full bodied, dry or semi-dry with a perfumy or lychee nose and tropical fruit, apple or citrus character, often a spicy finish
FOOD MATCH: Thai and Asian foods

RED HYBRIDS:

Baco Noir:
CHARACTER: full bodied with raspberry, blackberry, some tannin, can be spicy and smoky (if barrel-aged)
FOOD MATCH: red meat, tomato-based sauces, pork

Maréchal Foch:
CHARACTER: full bodied with raspberry or red berry, some tannin
FOOD MATCH: red meat, tomato-based sauces, pork

Chancellor:
CHARACTER: full bodied with raspberry, peppery character
FOOD MATCH: beef, lamb, pork

WHITE HYBRIDS:

Seyval:
CHARACTER: light bodied with subtle apple, citrus, vegetative, spicy (if barrel-aged)
FOOD MATCH: light soup, oysters, mussels, salads

Vidal:
CHARACTER: dry or semi-dry, light to full bodied. Also made into late harvest and Icewines. Character ranges from gooseberries to citrus or tropical.
FOOD MATCH:
> Dry Vidal: light soup, oysters, mussels, salads
> Semi-dry Vidal: butter/cream-based sauces, meaty fish
> Icewine: fruit-based desserts

CHAPTER FIVE

HOSTING A CHEESE & WINE PARTY

MOST OF US ENTERTAIN FAMILY, friends and clients a few times a year. The candlelight evening with aperitifs, appetizers and after-dinner drinks is always a thrill for guests, but preparations can be costly and time consuming for the host.

If you have no time to plan a gourmet affair, consider holding a cheese and wine gathering. As basic as it sounds, this event is informal and easy to prepare. It also is an exciting journey of the senses that your guests will remember long after they've left.

BUYING CHEESE FOR THE EVENT

When you are planning this event, remember that a little forethought and creativity will go a long way. First of all, you must know how many guests are attending to calculate the amount of cheese you need. For a party of five or less buy three varieties (one hard, one soft and one blue). For more than five guests, you'll need approximately five to eight cheese varieties, all varying in texture, aroma and taste. Buy about 3/4 lb (375 g) of each variety, which works out to 6 oz (175 g) of cheese altogether per person over the course of an evening.

Then head to your local cheese shop. (When cooking with cheese, supermarket products are fine. Cheese is usually fresh because it sells quickly.) To host a successful cheese and wine party, you'll need to be able to smell, feel and taste the cheeses before you buy them. Why? Because the aroma, texture and taste of one variety can vary considerably between producers. Brie and Cheddar are good examples of this. (See chapter 3 for cheese-buying hints.)

BUYING WINE FOR THE EVENT

Avoid bag-in-the-box and screw top bargains at all cost. Special events deserve a little style. Choose reasonably priced wines that will serve as excellent partners to your cheeses. In fact, it's silly to buy expensive vintages when conversation is the focus of the event. Don't be too shy to ask the wine merchant for advice. Most are well trained and will be more than happy to help you choose. For five or fewer guests, three wines will do — a red, a white and a port. If entertaining more than eight, buy five wines, such as a full-bodied red (Cabernet Sauvignon), a light-bodied red (Pinot Noir) or a fruity red (Gamay), a dry white (Chardonnay), a medium-dry white (Gewürztraminer or Riesling) and a port, sherry, late harvest or dessert wine.

PRESENTATION

Presentation is important not only to the aesthetics of the event but to the flavour of the cheese. If, for example, you are featuring a creamy Camembert with a crumbly Ermite, their opposing aromas, textures and flavours will enhance one another. Also, think in terms of contrasting colours. Saint Paulin's orange rind stands out beside white Cheddar.

The appearance of a cheese can prepare the palate for a gastronomic adventure. The fastest method is to have your local cheese shop cut and prepare the cheese trays for you. If you are doing the work yourself, do not cut the cheese into tiny cubes, and leave rinds intact. Small rounds should be wedged; large wedges and blue-veined cheeses can be cut into single serving-wedges. When cutting wedges of Brie, make sure the rind and centre are served in proportionate amounts. Log-shaped cheeses, such as an aged goat cheese, can be sliced into individual rounds. Cut square and rectangular cheeses with a rind (such as some Muensters) from the centre of the block to keep the ends fresh for another use.

Remove cheeses from the refrigerator about one hour before serving to allow them to warm to room temperature. To prevent the cheeses from drying out, cover the tray with a damp cloth. Keep an eye on the Camembert and Brie; if too warm, they'll begin to run from their crust. Choose a variety of platters because different shapes and colours will entice your guests to try all the cheeses available. Serve two cheese varieties per platter, separated by fresh fruit and vegetables. Provide a knife for each cheese. Place baskets of crisp, chewy breads and crackers between each platter.

Make sure you have plenty of wine glasses on hand, all the same size and made of thin, transparent glass or crystal and with a long stem. Rinse the glasses with cool water so they are free of spots and odours. Place a couple of filled water jugs and spittoon (large empty containers) around the room so your guests can rinse their glasses from the water jug and pour it into the spittoon before sampling another wine. Display wine bottles next to the cheese platters. Whites should be served in ice buckets; light, fruity reds should be cool. Full-bodied reds can be served in decanters to enhance their aromas and flavours.

The purpose of this event is to allow your guests to experiment with the different texture, aroma and taste sensations created by matching each cheese with a particular wine. During the course of the evening you may want to suggest a few perfect combinations, such as blue cheeses, extra-old Cheddars and gorgonzola with Cabernet Sauvignon. Gamay is excellent with Brie.

The following chart will help you choose cheese and wine combinations for your party:

PAIRING CANADIAN-MADE CHEESES
WITH DOMESTIC WINES

Cheese	Wine
young Brie, young Camembert	dry Riesling, dry Vidal, Seyval, dry Kerner
ripened Brie, ripened Camembert	Gamay, Cabernet Sauvignon, Chancellor, Cabernet Franc, Baco Noir
Double-/or Triple-Cream Brie	barrel-fermented and/or -aged Chardonnay

Cheese	*Wine*
mozzarella, Scamorza, Fior di Latte, Monterey Jack, ripened goat's milk feta	Merlot, Maréchal Foch, de Chaunac
Alpina, casata, Muenster, Saint Paulin, Tomme	Chardonnay, Pinot Blanc
Burrini, Oka, Trappist	barrel-fermented and/or -aged Chardonnay, semi-dry Riesling
Havarti, Serra, cow's milk feta	dry Riesling, dry Vidal, Seyval, dry Kerner
Limburger	Cabernet Sauvignon, Chancellor, Cabernet Franc, Baco Noir
Caciocavallo, brick, Colby, farmer's, Gouda, Fontina, Friulano Montasio, Tilsit, Gruyère-types	Pinot Noir, Gamay Noir, light, fruity Chardonnay
Gouda with cumin seed	dry or semi-dry Gewürztraminer, Trebbiano, Scheurebe
mild Cheddar	semi-dry Riesling, semi-dry Vidal, semi-dry Bacchus, semi-dry Kerner
medium Cheddar	Pinot Noir, Gamay Noir
old Cheddar	Merlot, Maréchal Foch, de Chaunac, Late Harvest Vidal or Late Harvest Riesling
extra-old Cheddar	Cabernet Sauvignon, Chancellor, Cabernet Franc, Baco Noir, Icewine
Emmenthal, provolone, raclette, Swiss	Chardonnay, Pinot Blanc
Parmesan, Romano	Merlot, Maréchal Foch, de Chaunac
Cambozola types	Pinot Noir, Gamay Noir
Ermite	Cabernet Sauvignon, Chancellor, Cabernet Franc, Baco Noir
Ermite (after dinner)	port, Icewine, Optima B.A., Riesling B.A., Late Harvest Riesling, Late Harvest Vidal, Late Harvest Ehrenfelser
Gorgonzola types	Cabernet Sauvignon, Chancellor, Cabernet Franc, Baco Noir
fresh goat cheese	Sauvignon, dry Riesling, Pinot Noir, Gamay
ripened goat cheese	Cabernet Sauvignon, Chancellor, Cabernet Franc, Baco Noir

CHAPTER SIX

COOKING WITH CHEESE & WINE

COOKING WITH CHEESE

Cheese is an excellent ingredient, as it performs countless functions when cooked. Among its many uses, cheese acts as a topping, as a flavouring agent and as a stuffing and a filling in dishes. Cheese also thickens and flavours soups and sauces, improves the smoothness of certain dishes and can act as a buffer by neutralizing acidic flavours.

Because so many varieties exist, it's hard to apply any hard-and-fast rules to cooking with cheese. There are, however, a few tricks of the trade that chefs and home cooks use when developing recipes with cheese.

- Cheese melts more easily and evenly when first diced, crumbled or shredded.
- When cooking with more than one cheese, work with the hardest version first (Parmesan and Romano) and grate. Next, add shredded firm cheese, followed by semi-soft, soft, then fresh.
- Always cook cheese slowly and over low heat. Otherwise the proteins and fat will separate and the cheese will become hard and lumpy.
- Today, most soups and sauces are thickened by reduction. However, if a cheese soup or sauce needs binding or thickening, remove it from the heat and whisk in an egg yolk. Make sure the pan is off the burner or the yolk will cook and separate.
- When incorporating cheese with alcohol, lemon juice, apple juice or any acid-based ingredient, such as in a fondue or sauce, always cook over medium to low heat and stir constantly until all ingredients are well incorporated.
- Hard, well-aged cheeses (Parmesan, Romano) can tolerate more heat, but take longer to cook in order to smooth their grainy texture.
- Taste the dish before flavouring with salt, as cheese is salty.
- When making a sauce with Brie or Camembert, add the rind for additional flavour. Strain the sauce to remove lumps of rind before serving.
- Cheeses that can easily develop ammonia aromas and flavours (Brie, Camembert) do not work well with the iodine in fish and can create an unpleasant taste.
- When using fresh cheeses in pastries and desserts, mix the sugar and cheese first before combining with other ingredients. Sugar absorbs some of the cheese's liquid, thus acting as a binding agent.

COOKING WITH WINE

Wine has a valuable place in the chef's repertoire. Marinating, basting, glazing, deglazing and flaming are but some of its many functions.

When using wine in your culinary preparations, remember that a wine's quality or lack of it will be revealed in the dish, so stay away from cooking wines, thin wines and wines past their prime, which will give your dish a bitter taste. Use only young wines with body and flavour to ensure excellent results. If featuring wine with dinner, it makes sense to use a little of it in the food preparation. But if you intend to serve an expensive vintage with dinner, save every drop for your wine glasses and buy something less expensive to cook with, such as a blended wine or house wine. To store leftover wine, simply pour a thin film of olive oil on top; this will keep the wine from oxidizing too quickly.

Red and white wines are basically interchangeable in cooking. Reds do offer more depth of flavour and colour than whites, making them a better choice for heavier dishes containing meat and game. Seafood and fish are delicate foods, thus deserving of a delicate white. White sauces need a white wine in order to retain their colour. Sweet wines work well in pastries and desserts, while those with just a touch of sweetness enhance sweet meats like pork. Champagne loses its bubbles in cooking and basically functions as a white. If the dish takes several hours to cook, add the wine halfway through so its qualities will not be lost.

Wine does not enhance all dishes. Vinegar-based dishes or those with heavy citrus character overshadow any flavour imparted by a wine. Asparagus, artichokes and spinach are enemies of the fermented grape both in the pan and on the table. As for chocolate — brandy, rum and liqueurs are a better choice.

Add wine to the recipe according to its use. If it's acting as a tenderizer or marinade, use it at the beginning of meal preparation. If its aroma and flavour are to predominate, add it at the end. Just be sure to add a little at a time. Above all, add wine only to one element of the meal, otherwise its wonderful effect will be lost.

CHAPTER SEVEN

THE CHEESE FONDUE

COST-EFFECTIVE, DELICIOUS and a form of entertainment, fondues are perfect for short-notice social gatherings.

Even those who suffer from a lack of culinary creativity can make a tasty fondue. All you need is suitable fondue equipment. Most useful is the traditional fondue pot, called a caquelon. But any enamel-lined heatproof pot will do, so long as it has a handle and is deep. You'll also need a spirit lamp to melt the cheese; the most useful ones use alcohol, butane gas or electric heat. Long-handled fondue forks, a bread basket, individual serving plates and small glasses are necessary, too. The forks can be used for fondue friture (raw beef in hot oil) and fondue bouillon (raw meat and vegetables in hot broth). Small glasses are used to serve the kirsch. You may want to serve kirsch at the beginning of the meal, so your guests can dip their bread into it. Kirsch adds a stronger flavour and higher alcohol content to a fondue. Traditionally, it is served halfway through the meal.

It takes only minutes to melt the cheese, so first cut the bread into cubes, leaving crusts on two sides. French and Italian breads are the best for fondues; they absorb the cheese and are crusty enough to hold their shape during dunking.

The main ingredient? Cheese, of course. Three types are generally used. The classic fondue recipe calls for Emmenthal or Gruyère or a combination of these. Emmenthal makes the mildest fondue, Gruyère makes the strongest-tasting fondue. Canada's cheesemakers produce a variety of Swiss-style cheeses (Miranda, Vacherin, raclette) that are excellent for fondues. The more unconventional but delicious fondue types include Cheddar, Montasio, Brie and Camembert.

Now for the wine. In most cases, a dry white with good acidity is preferred. High acidity allows the cheese to melt more rapidly and smoothly while adding incredible flavour. If the wine lacks acidity, add 1 1/2 tsp (7 mL) lemon juice for every 1/2 lb (250 g) of cheese. Our Canadian winemakers produce a wide range of wines suitable for fondues — dry Riesling, Sauvignon and Seyval. For added flavour you can season the fondue with freshly ground pepper, grated nutmeg, salt, curry or dill. Don't be shy about experimenting.

After cubing the bread, shred the cheese so it will melt quickly and smoothly. Set aside.

Begin the fondue in the kitchen over the stove. Rub the inside of the pot all over with a cut clove of garlic. Pour in the wine and heat it gently until air bubbles form. Never let the wine

THE CHEESE FONDUE | 19

boil, or this will cook the cheese and make it hard and lumpy. Add the cheese, about 1/2 cup (125 mL) at a time, stirring constantly in a figure eight pattern. Melt each batch of cheese completely before adding another to the pot. If the fondue is too thin, blend in a little cornstarch or flour. About 2 tbsp (25 mL) of kirsch will also add flavour.

Allow the fondue to bubble gently while you stir. Transfer the fondue pot to the spirit lamp. Continue stirring. If the fondue becomes too thick, add a little warmed wine.

If you plan to have more than five guests for dinner, be sure to have two fondue pots going at the same time. Near the end of the meal, when the pot is almost empty, you'll see rich brown crusts on the bottom, crusts that fell from all the forks during the course of the meal. Do not discard these. They're a much sought-after delicacy!

MOZZARELLA AND ROASTED RED PEPPER BRUSCHETTA

SERVES FOUR   Shari Darling — Toronto, Ontario

Lang Vineyards Pinot Noir Naramata Dry

Naramata, British Columbia

Located in south Okanagan Valley, Lang Vineyards is owned and operated by winemaker Guenther Lang. Using 100 percent of a specific grape variety, Lang's varietals are produced according to VQA standards. In 1993 he won a bronze medal for his Pinot Noir Naramata at the Okanagan Wine Festival. Exhibiting a ruby robe, ripe cherry aromas and flavours, Lang Vineyards Pinot Noir has enough weight to match the heavy, elastic texture of mozzarella, but does not overshadow its soft, milky taste.

Other Choices:
Ontario Pinot Noir

Tre Stelle Mozzarella

Made by National Cheese

1	large sweet red pepper	1
8	brine-cured black olives	8
½ cup	olive oil	125 mL
2	cloves garlic, minced	2
8	slices Italian bread	8
1 cup	finely chopped fresh basil	250 mL
1 lb	mozzarella cheese, thinly sliced	500 g

1 Cut pepper in half; do not remove seeds. Lay peppers on a baking sheet, cut sides down. Grill about 5 inches (12 cm) from heat, turning every 2 to 3 minutes to blister and char all sides, about 25 minutes total. Cover peppers with plastic wrap and let cool. **2** Peel peppers, beginning at stem end; cut off tops and discard seeds and ribs. Dice; set aside. **3** In a blender or food processor, blend olives, oil and garlic to smooth paste; set aside. **4** Grill one side of Italian bread slices until golden. Brush untoasted side with olive paste. Top with diced roasted peppers and basil. Cover with sliced mozzarella. Grill until mozzarella is melted and bread is golden. Serve hot.

ROLLED PROSCIUTTO AND MELON WITH BURRINI

SERVES FOUR | Chef Ronald Saint-Pierre — Vancouver, British Columbia

THIS SPECTACULAR APPETIZER calls for Burrini cheese. Available in most cheese shops, this mild cheese has a pale yellow or ivory rind and a ball of butter tucked inside.

Calona Wines 1984 LBV Port Proprietor's Reserve

Kelowna, British Columbia

One of B.C.'s largest wineries, Calona Wines makes a spectrum of varietals (such as Chardonnay, Gewürztraminer, Chenin Blanc), ports, sherries and fruit wines. The LBV Port Proprietor's Reserve has forward cherries on the nose with plums and nuts on the palate. It is a late bottled vintage port, meaning the wine was made from a single year of grapes and aged for an extended period in wood before bottling. Being a rich wine, it is an appropriate choice for this rich appetizer. Cellar ageing will not improve its character.

Other Choices:
Ontario port

CALONA VINEYARDS

Burrini

Made by International Cheese

2 tsp	olive oil	10 mL
1/3 cup	diced mushrooms	75 mL
1/2	sweet red pepper, diced	1/2
	Salt and pepper to taste	
2 tsp	lemon juice	10 mL
1/2 lb	Burrini cheese	250 g
1/3 cup	diced honeydew melon	75 mL
1/3 cup	diced cantaloupe	75 mL
1 tsp	finely chopped fresh oregano	5 mL
1 tsp	finely chopped fresh chives	5 mL
1 tsp	finely chopped lemon balm leaves	5 mL
4	thin slices prosciutto (2" x 6"/5 cm x 15 cm)	4

1 In a small skillet or sauté pan over medium heat, heat oil. Sauté mushrooms and red pepper until pepper is soft; stir in salt and pepper. Increase heat to medium-high and deglaze pan with lemon juice, scraping up brown bits. Set aside to cool. **2** Slice cheese in half and remove ball of butter from inside. In a large bowl, whip butter until doubled in volume. Dice Burrini cheese and add to butter. Stir in melon, cantaloupe, oregano, chives, lemon balm, and mushroom and red pepper mixture; mix well. **3** Lay out each prosciutto slice on a square of waxed paper. Spread filling about 1/4 inch (5 mm) thick evenly over prosciutto. **4** Carefully roll prosciutto lengthwise into a cylinder, peeling back the waxed paper as you go. Refrigerate for 1 hour to allow butter to firm up. **5** With a warm, dry knife, cut rolled prosciutto into 1/2-inch (1 cm) slices.

BRIE EN CROUTE

SERVES SIX TO EIGHT   Fromagerie Clement Inc. — Saint-Damase, Quebec

CLAUDE BONNET, OF FROMAGERIE CLEMENT, began his long, successful career in cheesemaking in Meaux, France. Inheriting the family cheese plant, established in 1915, Claude went on to become president of the Master Cheese-Makers of the Brie region in France. In 1985 Claude and his two sons immigrated to Saint-Damase, Quebec, and following family tradition opened Fromagerie Clement. The Bonnets make soft ripened and unripened cheese, whey cheese and yogurt. Although their Damafro Brie and Damafro Camembert are made from pasteurized milk, the Bonnets consider them to taste as good as and even better than their rivals from France.

 Château des Charmes Paul Bosc Estate Cabernet Sauvignon

Niagara-on-the-Lake, Ontario
Available in Quebec (La Maison des Vins)
Available in Ottawa (Château des Charmes Wine Boutique, Minto Place, Laurier Ave., 613-783-2410)

This Cabernet Sauvignon is a gem, made from 100 percent Cabernet Sauvignon grown on the Paul Bosc Estate Vineyard in St. David, Ontario. Aged in Nevers oak, this red is deep purple, medium to full bodied with sweet cigar tobacco and green peppers with some berry fruit on the nose. The palate is well balanced and swirling with cigar tobacco, blackberries and just a tinge of chocolate in the background. The blackberry fruit and austere tannin add delightful contrast to the mushroom taste and rich, creamy texture of Brie.

Other Choices:
 B.C. Baco Noir

"Transportation from Europe," says Claude, "can alter the quality of the cheese." One thing is for sure: Fromagerie Clement's cheeses are enjoyed by many in Quebec and Ontario.

1	loaf (1 lb/ 500 g) frozen bread dough, thawed	1
1 lb	Brie, rind removed	500 g
1	egg yolk, beaten	1

1 Divide dough in half. On a lightly floured work surface, roll each half into a 7-inch (18 cm) circle. Place one circle on a greased baking sheet. Mould cheese into a ball; place in centre of dough. Brush edge of dough with water. **2** Place remaining circle over cheese ball, pressing firmly on edges of dough to seal. Brush dough with egg yolk. **3** Place a pan of hot water in bottom of oven to create steam that keeps the crust tender. Bake bread at 375°F (190°C) for 25 to 30 minutes or until golden. Cool 5 minutes and cut in wedges.

Damafro Brie

Made by Fromagerie Clement

FRIULANO AND MUSHROOM TARTLETS

MAKES TWENTY-FOUR   International Cheese Company Ltd. — Toronto, Ontario

FAMOUS FOR ITS TRADITIONAL Italian-style cheeses — ricotta, bocconcini, Caciocavallo, Romano, mozzarella and Friulano, Burrini, Scamorza and hot provolone (aged for at least six months) — International Cheese has satisfied Toronto's Italian neighbourhoods since 1966. You need not travel to the city's Mediterranean districts to find these palatable products, however. International's cheeses are distributed to specialty food shops in Ontario, such as Buon Appetite Deli & Fine Foods in Scarborough and the Cheese Boutique & Deli in Toronto's Bloor West Village.

Pastry:

4 cups	sifted all-purpose flour	1 L
2 tsp	salt	10 mL
2/3 cup	vegetable shortening	150 mL
1/4 cup (approx)	cold water	50 mL

Filling:

2 tbsp	extra virgin olive oil	25 mL
1/4 cup	minced onion	50 mL
1 tbsp	minced garlic	15 mL
1 1/2 lb	button mushrooms, thinly sliced	750 g
3/4 cup	ricotta cheese	175 mL
1 tsp	finely chopped fresh sage	5 mL
Dash	hot pepper sauce	Dash
Pinch	freshly ground black pepper	Pinch
1/4 cup	finely chopped fresh parsley	50 mL
1/2 cup	shredded Friulano cheese	125 mL

*Inniskillin Wines
Pinot Noir*

Niagara-on-the-Lake, Ontario

Inniskillin Wines brought worldwide attention to the Canadian wine industry by capturing a gold medal for their 1991 Pinot Noir Private Reserve in the 1993 VinItaly International Wine Competition. Inniskillin's Pinot Noir is bursting with cherry aromas and flavours that create a perfect marriage with the soft, tangy flavour of Friulano cheese.

Other Choices:

B.C. Gamay Noir

1 To make pastry, in a large bowl combine flour and salt. Cut in shortening with a fork. Add water a few drops at a time, tossing mixture with fork to combine evenly. The dough should be moist enough to hold together but not too wet. Form into a ball, wrap in plastic wrap and chill for at least 15 minutes. **2** On a lightly floured work surface, roll out pastry to 1/8 inch (3 mm) thick. Using a 4-inch (10 cm) cookie cutter, cut out rounds; fit into tart pans, making 24 tart shells. Bake at 400°F (200°C) for 10 to 12 minutes or until golden. Remove shells from pans and cool on a rack. **3** To make filling, in a medium saucepan over medium heat, heat oil. Sauté onion for 2 minutes or until soft. Add garlic and cook another minute. Add button mushrooms. Simmer, uncovered, stirring occasionally, for 10 to 12 minutes or until almost all liquid has evaporated. **4** Stir in ricotta, sage, hot pepper sauce and pepper. Reduce heat to low and simmer, stirring occasionally, for 12 minutes or until mixture is thick. Stir in parsley. Cool slightly. **5** Spoon 1 heaping tsp (5 mL) of warm filling into each shell; sprinkle generously with Friulano. Place tarts on a cookie sheet; grill until cheese has melted, about 3 minutes. Serve warm.

Ricotta and Friulano

International Cheese

BALDERSON'S WHITE CHEDDAR AND SHERRY SPREAD

SERVES FOUR　　　　　　　　　　　　Shari Darling — Toronto, Ontario

London Wines Pale Dry Sherry

London, Ontario

London Wines Pale Dry Canadian Sherry is a blend of dry Flor sherry and baked sherry, aged and blended in a white oak barrel solera system. Excellent on its own or with old Cheddar, provolone and Swiss cheeses. Naturally, it's the only partner for this appetizer.

Other Choices:
B.C. sherry

London Winery Limited

Quark (cream-based)

Made by Pinneau Dairy
Old White Cheddar

Made by Balderson Cheese

½ lb	old white Cheddar cheese	250 g
8 oz	Quark cheese, cream-based	250 g
1 tsp	sugar	5 mL
1 tbsp	finely chopped fresh parsley	15 mL
½ cup	London Wines Pale Dry Sherry	125 mL

1 In a food processor or blender, blend all ingredients until smooth. **2** Chill for 2 hours. Serve with thin slices of rye bread.

GRILLED CHEDDAR DOLMATHES

SERVES FOUR   Black River Cheese Co. Ltd. — Milford, Ontario

JOHN KELLY, CHEESEMAKER at Black River since 1986, follows the same cheesemaking process that has been employed at this company since 1901. As in the making of all cheddars, John must employ the cheddaring process. This means the curds are packed together to form one mass that is cut into narrow slabs. The slabs are repeatedly turned and piled on each other to expel additional whey. Next is milling the curds — sending them through a mill to be cut into 5/8 by 4-inch cubes, which reduces moisture and eliminates even more whey. Finally, John salts and forks the curds, stirring them from the sides of the vat toward the centre to evenly distribute the salt. The curds are hooped, or shovelled into stainless steel moulds, and pressed overnight. Black River's standard hoop is a 40-lb block. In the morning John vacuum-seals the Cheddars and sends them to the cold storage room for ageing. Black River Cheddars range in age from three weeks (a mild version) to three years (Extra, Extra Old). Most can be found in specialty cheese shops and independent supermarkets throughout Eastern Ontario.

Hillebrand Estates Collector's Choice Cabernet-Merlot

Niagara-on-the-Lake, Ontario

Working with more than 45 wine growers in the Niagara region, Hillebrand has a notable reputation for their varietal wines and Mounier Brut Champagne, produced by their on-site sister company. The Collector's Choice Cabernet-Merlot is a perfect example of quality grapes plus skilled winemaking abilities. With a deep purple appearance, forward raspberry aromas backed up by faint cedar and berry fruit on the mouth, this medium-bodied blend tastes wonderful with nippy Cheddar.

Other Choices:
B.C. Merlot

20	large marinated vine leaves*	20
1 lb	extra-old, white Cheddar cheese, cut into 20 1-inch (2.5 cm) cubes	500 g

Grape leaves packed in bottles can be found in many specialty food stores. Or use kale leaves. Shock kale in boiling salted water for 5 minutes, then plunge in ice water to stop cooking.

1 Rinse as much salt as possible from vine leaves. Pat dry.
2 Spread out one leaf with the underside up and the stem end toward you; cut off the stem. Place a Cheddar cube at the stem end; fold sides of leaf over the cube. Roll up tightly in a jelly-roll fashion. Continue with remaining leaves and cheese cubes. **3** Place dolmathes on a well-greased baking sheet, seam side down. Grill for 5 to 6 minutes or until leaves are crisp. Turn dolmathes and grill other side. Serve warm.

Extra, Extra Old Cheddar

Made by Black River Cheese

EMMENTHAL-FILLED PARATHAS

MAKES SIXTEEN   Shari Darling — Toronto, Ontario

A POPULAR SWISS-STYLE CHEESE, Canadian Emmenthal is made from pasteurized cow's milk and comes in large wheels weighing anywhere from 150 to 200 lb. It is light gold or ivory, has large holes or "eyes" and has a sweet, nutty flavour. An excellent cheese for fondues, au gratin dishes, cheese trays and for cooking in general.

4 cups	sifted whole wheat flour	1 L
¾ tsp	salt	4 mL
2 tbsp	poppy seeds	25 mL
1 cup	water	250 mL
1 lb	Emmenthal cheese, cut in 16 slices	500 g

1 In a large mixing bowl combine flour, salt and poppy seeds. Blend in water gradually until a soft dough is formed. Knead dough until pliable and smooth. Cover with plastic wrap and refrigerate for 30 minutes. **2** Divide dough into 16 balls. On a lightly floured work surface, roll out each ball into a 6-inch (15 cm) circle. Place a slice of Emmenthal on half of each round. Fold the rounds twice to form a triangle. Roll out the parathas to 5 inches (12 cm). **3** Brush one side of parathas with oil. In a skillet over medium-high heat, fry parathas, oiled side down, for 30 to 60 seconds or until small specks appear on bottom. **4** Brush oil on top, turn parathas, and fry another 30 to 60 seconds. **5** Drain on paper towels; keep warm. Continue with remaining parathas.

Domaine de Chaberton Blanc (House Blend)

Langley, British Columbia

This farm-gate winery in the Fraser Valley concentrates on white wines, such as Bacchus and Ortega. Chaberton Blanc is pale straw, light bodied and refreshingly crisp, with melon and apple aromas and peach-like flavours. A suitable match for this light appetizer featuring the delicate, nutty flavour of Emmenthal cheese.

Other Choices:
Ontario dry Vidal

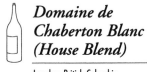

Domaine de Chaberton Estates Limited

Anco Emmenthal

Made by Agropur

ERMITE BLUE PARCELS WITH BLACKBERRY CHUTNEY

SERVES FOUR TO SIX   The Cheese Cupboard — Mississauga, Ontario

AMID MISSISSAUGA'S GENERAL POPULATION is a colony of fervent cheese lovers who visit The Cheese Cupboard frequently. Steve Stewart has owned the shop since 1988 and offers a medley of imported and Canadian cheeses. Gourmet catering and specialized gift baskets are also an integral part of the shop's repertoire.

Konzelmann Estate Winery Late Harvest Zweigelt

Niagara-on-the-Lake, Ontario

Owner and winemaker Herbert Konzelmann was the first to introduce Vertico vine training to Canada, a method that offers good sun exposure and allows the wind to travel through the vines, drying off morning dew and rain. One of the Austrian hybrid varieties grown at Konzelmann Estates is Zweigelt. Blackberry aromas and flavours demand attention. Medium-bodied, this cherry-coloured wine is a perfect match for the blue cheese parcels while complementing the blackberry chutney.

Other Choices:
B.C. Chancellor

Chutney:

1 1/2 cups	fresh blackberries	375 mL
1/4 cup	brown sugar	50 mL
1/4 cup	raspberry vinegar	50 mL
1/4 cup	Konzelmann Estate Zweigelt (red wine)	50 mL
	Juice of 1/2 lemon	
1/4 tsp	pepper	1 mL
Pinch	salt	Pinch
1/4 cup	blackberry jelly	50 mL

Ermite Blue Parcels:

1 cup	crumbled blue cheese (Ermite)	250 mL
3 oz	Neufchatel cheese	75 g
2	egg yolks	2
2 tsp	finely chopped fresh parsley	10 mL
1	clove garlic, minced	1
	Seasoned flour for dredging	
	Eggwash (1 egg beaten with 1 tsp/5 mL water)	
	dry bread crumbs for dredging	
3 cups (approx)	vegetable oil for deep-frying	750 mL

1 To make chutney, in a medium saucepan combine all chutney ingredients except blackberry jelly. Bring to a boil. Reduce heat and simmer, uncovered, for 40 minutes, stirring occasionally. Remove from heat and stir in jelly. Refrigerate until needed. **2** To make parcels, in a medium bowl cream together blue cheese, Neufchatel cheese, egg yolks, parsley and garlic. **3** Line an 8-inch (20 cm) pie plate with waxed paper. Spread parcel mixture on waxed paper; refrigerate for 4 hours or until mixture is firm. **4** Cut mixture into thin wedges. **5** Dredge each wedge in seasoned flour, dip in egg-wash and dredge in bread crumbs. **6** In a deep saucepan over moderate heat, heat oil until smoking. Deep-fry wedges for 2 to 3 minutes or until golden. Drain on paper towels. Serve warm with chilled chutney.

Ermite
Made by L'Abbaye de Saint-Benoît-du-Lac
Baron Roula Neufchatel
Made by Fromagerie Cayer

CAMEMBERT CHEESE PÂTÉ

SERVES FOUR TO SIX — House of Cheese — Ottawa, Ontario

CHEFS AND HOME COOKS ALIKE pretty much agree that the local farmers' market is where one finds specialty ingredients and fresh produce, not to mention natural cheeses cut to order. In Ottawa, food enthusiasts swear by the Byward Farmers' Market, in Byward Square, where the House of Cheese has specialized in Canadian and imported cheese for more than 16 years. It's hard to say what will impress you more about this shop — that owner Omer Hamway's extensive stock consists of 600 cheeses or that 200 of these are domestic.

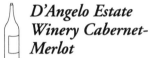

D'Angelo Estate Winery Cabernet-Merlot

Amherstburg, Ontario

Owner and winemaker Sal D'Angelo has made a name for himself in Ontario's wine industry by producing this excellent blend that combines Cabernet and Merlot grown on the estate vineyard. On the nose there are forward nutty and smoky tones, followed by berry-like flavours, making this blend an excellent choice for Camembert's nutty flavours. Full weight makes it a match for heavy garlic.

Other Choices:
B.C. Merlot

L'Extra Camembert
Made by Agropur

4	unpeeled cloves garlic	4
1 tbsp	finely chopped fresh rosemary	15 mL
¼ cup	olive oil	50 mL
½ tsp	pink peppercorns	2 mL
1 tbsp	hot water	15 mL
1 lb	cold Camembert, rind removed, cubed	500 g*

*To remove the rind use a cheese plane or vegetable peeler.

1 Wrap garlic cloves tightly in aluminum foil. Roast at 300°F (150°C) for 1 hour. Cool to room temperature. **2** Peel cloves. In a blender or food processor, chop garlic, turning motor on and off. Add rosemary, olive oil, peppercorns and water. Blend for 30 seconds. Set aside. **3** Place Camembert in the top of a double boiler set over low heat; soften. **4** In a bowl combine Camembert with garlic mixture. Whip with a fork until well blended. Transfer pâté to a crock. Serve hot with melba toasts or water crackers.

CHEDDAR SAUSAGES WITH THAI DIPPING SAUCE

SERVES FOUR　　　　　　　　　　　　Maple Dale Cheese — Plainfield, Ontario

MAPLE DALE CHEESE has survived and flourished for more than a hundred years. Opened as a co-operative, the company is now privately owned by Keith Henry and son Paul. Although they make a wide range of cheeses, such as marble, Colby, farmer's, brick and mozzarella, Maple Dale is famed for its Cheddars — low in moisture, with a firm but crumbly body and sharp acidity. Not commonly made today, this style of Cheddar is preferred by a select group of consumers. It takes a talented and experienced cheesemaker to make good low-moisture Cheddars because so much can go wrong in the cheesemaking process. The curds can develop too much acid, making the Cheddar bitter, or too little acid, giving the Cheddar a flat-tasting texture. Extensive ageing is another reason why Maple Dale Cheddars are popular. Their four-year-old version has a flavour so nippy it almost bites back. The Henrys' continued success can be attributed to their focused attitude. "We'll always remain true to our cheesemaking recipe," Paul says, "because, above all, it garners success." Recently added to their line of products is a creamy Stilton Cheddar.

Pelee Island Winery Scheurebe

Kingsville, Ontario

Though the wines are produced in Kingsville, Ontario, Pelee Island has a gorgeous tasting pavilion on the island itself. This straw-coloured Scheurebe, with its tangerine and pineapple aromas and flavours, hint of sweetness and lingering spice on the finish, contrasts with the nippy Cheddar sausages and the very spicy, very tart sauce, thus bringing balance to the palate.

Other Choices:

B.C. off-dry Gewürztraminer

PELEE ISLAND WINERY

Sauce:

½ cup	freshly squeezed lime juice	125 mL
2 tbsp	oyster sauce	25 mL
3	large cloves garlic, minced	3
1	small dried Thai chili, ground*	1

Sausages:

1 ½ cups	shredded 4-year-old Cheddar cheese	375 mL
1 ½ cups	fresh bread crumbs	375 mL
¾ tsp	dry mustard	4 mL
Pinch	pepper	Pinch
1 tsp	finely chopped fresh rosemary	5 mL
1	large egg, lightly beaten	1
2	egg whites	2
Pinch	salt	Pinch
1 cup	dry bread crumbs	250 mL

	Vegetable oil for frying

Dried Thai chilies are available in Asian supermarkets. Grind them between your fingers. Be sure to wash your hands afterwards.

1 To make sauce, in a food processor or blender blend lime juice, oyster sauce, garlic and chili. Refrigerate until needed.
2 To make sausages, in a large bowl combine Cheddar

cheese, fresh bread crumbs, mustard, pepper, rosemary and egg; set aside. **3** In separate bowl, beat 2 egg whites with salt until stiff. **4** Make 12 to 16 sausages about 2 inches (5 cm) long and 1 inch (2.5 cm) wide. Roll sausages in egg whites, then roll in dry crumbs until well coated. **5** Thinly coat a large skillet with oil. Over high heat, fry the sausages, turning often, until crisp and golden on all sides. Serve warm or cold with dipping sauce.

4-year-old Cheddar

Made by Maple Dale Cheese

BABA GANOUJI WITH FETA

SERVES SIX TO EIGHT   Shari Darling — Toronto, Ontario

CedarCreek Estate Winery Chardonnay

Kelowna, British Columbia

CedarCreek makes one of the best Chardonnays in B.C. Ann Sperling is the artist and award-winning winemaker behind their labels. Barrel-fermented and aged in three types of oak, the Estate Chardonnay is a big wine with full body, forward aromas of vanilla backed up by apples, a palate of toffee and apples and a lingering spice to the finish. Its outgoing personality makes it a suitable choice for this highly flavourful spread.

Other Choices:
Ontario barrel-fermented and/or -aged Chardonnay

Feta

Made by Woolwich Dairy

2	medium eggplants	2
2	cloves elephant garlic, minced	2
1 cup	crumbled feta cheese	250 mL
	Olive oil as needed	

1 Cut eggplant in half and place cut side down on a greased baking sheet. Roast at 375°F (190°C) for 40 to 45 minutes or until tender. Allow to cool for 5 minutes. Scoop out flesh. **2** In a food processor or blender purée garlic cloves, eggplant flesh and feta. Add enough olive oil to bring mixture to a smooth paste. **3** Chill until needed. Spread on pita bread or on wedges of toast.

PORK AND CHEDDAR STEAMED DUMPLINGS

MAKES THIRTY-FIVE   Eldorado Cheese Limited — Eldorado, Ontario

JUST SIX MILES NORTH OF MADOC, Eldorado Village is renowned as the site of Ontario's first gold find, in 1856. This discovery brought gold diggers to the area, many of whom drifted away when gold fever subsided. Some stayed to work the land and build the community. The region's fertile hills and valleys also made dairy farming possible and profitable, and over time many small dairy factories were built. In 1952 four of these amalgamated to form a dairy co-operative on the site where Eldorado Cheese now stands. Then, a co-operative was simply a place where the dairy workers gathered to process all the milk supplied by the town's cows. Today, Eldorado is privately run, though many of the original co-op members are still supplying milk to the factory. Cheddars are Eldorado's forte, with the Gold Brand being the oldest (two years) and most favoured.

Stonechurch Vineyards Morio Muscat

Niagara-on-the-Lake, Ontario

Stonechurch wines are made from 100 percent estate-grown grapes. Each has its own distinctive taste provided by the climate and soil conditions of the vineyard. Normally, Cheddar goes better with reds than whites. In this dish, however, the Cheddar takes the background to the pork and spice. Therefore, this appetizer goes great with a white showing a lot of spice — like Morio Muscat. A fabulous aperitif or food partner, the wine is dry, light and refreshing, with full orange aromas and flavours and lots of spicy character.

Other Choices:
B.C. dry Gewürztraminer

Filling:

¾ cup	ground pork	175 mL
2	shiitake mushrooms, diced	2
1¼ cups	shredded extra-old Cheddar cheese	300 mL
½ tsp	maple syrup	2 mL
1 tbsp	soy sauce	15 mL
Pinch	pepper	Pinch
1 tsp	finely chopped fresh chives	5 mL
1	dried Thai chili, ground*	1
Pinch	salt	Pinch
1 tbsp	sesame oil	15 mL
1½ tsp	cornstarch	7 mL

Dumplings:

1¾ cups	sifted all-purpose flour	425 mL
Pinch	salt	Pinch
1 cup	boiling water	250 mL
2 tbsp	all-purpose flour	25 mL

Dried Thai chilies are available in Asian supermarkets. Grind them between your fingers. Be sure to wash your hands afterwards.

Stonechurch
vineyards

1 *To make filling,* in a large saucepan over medium heat, fry ground pork until meat is no longer pink. Add mushrooms; cook until mushrooms are soft. Drain fat from pan. In a large bowl combine pork, mushrooms, Cheddar cheese, maple syrup, soy sauce, pepper, chives, chili and salt. Stir in oil and cornstarch. Set aside. **2** *To make dumplings,* in a large bowl combine sifted flour and salt. Add boiling water and knead quickly until dough is formed. If dough is too sticky, add more flour. Cover bowl with plastic wrap and let stand at room temperature for 30 minutes. **3** Knead dough for 2 to 3 minutes. Divide into 35 balls. On a work surface sprinkled lightly with cornstarch, roll out each ball to a 2-inch (5 cm) circle. **4** Divide filling into 35 equal portions. Place 3/4 tsp (4 mL) filling in centre of each circle. **5** Blend 2 tbsp (25 mL) flour with a few drops of cold water to make a thick paste. **6** Spread edge of half of each circle with paste. Fold circle into a half moon, pinching the edges together to seal. Pull corners of the dumpling close together to form a U shape. **7** In a bamboo steamer set over boiling water, steam dumplings for 10 minutes. Serve warm with soy sauce.

Gold Brand Cheddar (Extra Old)

Made by Eldorado Cheese

ZAKUSKA (CREAM CHEESE AND SALT HERRING DIP)

SERVES SIX TO EIGHT   Shari Darling — Toronto, Ontario

UKRAINIANS ARE NO STRANGERS to the custom of serving a fermented beverage with an appetizer. In Ukraine, a well-aged mead (wine made from honey) is the beverage, with the appetizers referred to as zakuska ("little bites").

1	salt herring fillet (approx ¾ lb /375 g)	1
2 tbsp	olive oil	25 mL
¼ lb	butter, softened	125 g
½ lb	cream cheese	250 g
2	hard-cooked eggs	2
	Juice of ½ lemon	
2	green onions, finely chopped	2
	Salt and pepper	
Pinch	paprika	Pinch

London Wines Honey Mead

London, Ontario

Established in 1925, London Wines was the first to revolutionize the Flor process in sherry-making. In 1965 the company made another noteworthy decision when it took over the Strawa Honey Company and began to produce Ancient Mead from fermented honey. A beverage cherished by Canada's Ukrainian community, London Wines' Honey Mead is produced from clover honey. Though the wine offers a honey-like nose with smooth honey texture, it is dry with good acidity that offsets the salty flavour of salt herring.

Other Choices:
B.C. dry Riesling

Cream cheese

Made by Evanoff Cheese

1 Soak herring fillet in cold water 1 to 2 hours to remove most of the salt and to soften the texture. Pat dry. **2** Dice fillet. In a food processor or blender combine herring, olive oil, butter, cream cheese, eggs and lemon juice; blend until creamy. Fold in onions; season to taste with salt and pepper. **3** Transfer dip to a crock; sprinkle with paprika. Chill for 2 hours before serving. Serve with thin slices of rye bread and an assortment of cold meats.

GORGONZOLA AND FLEUR D'ONTARIO PÂTÉ

SERVES FOUR TO SIX　　　　　Quality Cheese Inc. — Toronto, Ontario

QUALITY CHEESE IS OWNED by Almerigo Borgo, who has been in the cheese manufacturing business more than 40 years. Almerigo and sons Bill and Albert specialize in the production of prize-winning Italian cheeses. Their product line includes pasta filatas (mozzarella, Scamorza, bocconcini), ricotta, handmade gorgonzola and young Friulano that customers purchase in bulk to cure at home. What makes their cheeses distinctive is that all are made with microbial enzyme from plants instead of animal rennet. (Rennet comes from the stomach lining of calves, goats and sometimes pigs, and is used to coagulate milk into curds during the cheesemaking process.) Making cheese in this way has expanded the company's clientele to include a large population of vegetarians. Cheese lovers in general also buy their label. The reason is simple. The Borgo family takes a daily, hands-on approach in production in order to remain committed to their company name — "Quality." A first prize for their Scamorza in the Pasta Filata Category at the 1993 British Empire Cheese Show substantiates their commitment.

Inniskillin Wines Fleur d'Ontario

Niagara-on-the-Lake, Ontario

Fleur d'Ontario was inspired by and vinified in the tradition of Pineau des Charentes. Adding Canadian Grape Brandy arrests the fermentation process midway, resulting in a wine of 16–18 percent alcohol, balanced by the natural unfermented grape sugar. Further ageing has mellowed the brandy. Offering apricots and honey character and a long spicy finish, it is an excellent aperitif on its own or served alongside this gorgonzola-based pâté. Serve chilled.

Other Choices:
Any Canadian fortified wine

Gorgonzola

Made by Quality Cheese

1/4 cup	butter	50 mL
3/4 lb	gorgonzola cheese	375 g
1/2 lb	cream cheese	250 g
2 tbsp	Inniskillin Wines Fleur d'Ontario (aperitif wine)	25 mL
2 tsp	crushed black peppercorns	10 mL
1/2 cup	chopped walnuts, toasted	125 mL

1 In a food processor or blender combine butter, gorgonzola and cream cheese; whip until fluffy. With motor running, add wine and peppercorns. **2** Reserve 2 tbsp (25 mL) walnuts; fold remainder into pâté. **3** Pack pâté into a crock. Sprinkle with reserved walnuts. Chill. Serve with an assortment of thinly sliced rye breads.

ONION PARCELS OF SMOKED SALMON AND QUARK WITH SOUR CREAM AND CHIVES

SERVES FOUR   Chef Momir Filipovic — Saint-Sauveur, Quebec

CHEF MOMIR FILIPOVIC developed this recipe for the Dairy Bureau of Canada.

2	large white onions, peeled	2
1/4 lb	smoked salmon, boned and skinned	125 g
5	capers, drained	5
1/2 cup	Quark cheese	125 mL
2 tsp	lemon juice	10 mL
3 tbsp	whipping cream	50 mL
8	chives	8
1/4 cup	sour cream	50 mL
1/4 cup	lumpfish roe	50 mL
8	edible flowers (such as pansies)*	8

Most specialty food shops offer a selection of packaged dried edible flowers.

Vignoble Le Cep d'Argent Seyval Blanc

Magog, Quebec

A small winery producing about eight wines, Vignoble Le Cep d'Argent makes an easy-drinking Seyval Blanc that is light and crisp and does not overpower this delicate-tasting appetizer.

Other Choices:

Ontario dry Riesling or B.C. dry Riesling

LE CEP D'ARGENT

Quark

Made by Liberty

1 In a pot of boiling salted water, poach onions for 10 minutes or until soft. Drain and set aside until cool enough to handle. **2** In a food processor or blender, purée smoked salmon and capers. Add Quark cheese, lemon juice and whipping cream; blend well. Set aside. **3** Separate the onion layers and slice lengthwise into strips about 2 1/2 inches (6 cm) wide. Keep 20 of the best slices. **4** Fit a piping bag with a #12 plain tip and fill bag with smoked salmon mixture. (Or fill a small plastic bag and snip a small hole in one corner.) Pipe 1 tsp (5 mL) mixture onto each onion slice. Fold two sides of onion over the mixture. Place rolls on a plate, seam side down. Refrigerate for at least 1 hour. **5** On chilled plates, arrange five stuffed onion rolls in the shape of a flower. Use 2 chives for each stem. Fill cleaned piping bag with sour cream and pipe 1 tsp (5 mL) sour cream into the centre of each flower. Sprinkle lumpfish roe on sour cream. Arrange 2 edible flowers at the base of each stem.

BABY ASPARAGUS, BRIE AND BLUEBERRY SALAD

SERVES FOUR   Shari Darling — Toronto, Ontario

Blueberry Vinaigrette:

1/4 cup	extra virgin olive oil	50 mL
1/3 cup	blueberry vinegar*	75 mL
	Salt and freshly ground black pepper to taste	
1/4 cup	fresh blueberries	50 mL

Salad:

3	bundles pencil-thin asparagus	3
3/4 lb	Brie, diced	375 g
1	red onion, cut into thin rings	1
1 tbsp	finely chopped fresh basil	15 mL
1 tbsp	finely chopped fresh parsley	15 mL

Raspberry vinegar can be substituted.

1 To make vinaigrette, in a jar combine all vinaigrette ingredients. Shake well. Refrigerate for 1 hour. **2** Plunge asparagus into boiling salted water; cook briefly until bright green and tender-crisp. Drain and immediately rinse under cold water to preserve crispness. **3** Toss asparagus with Brie, onion rings, basil and parsley. Shake vinaigrette well and pour desired amount over salad. Refrigerate remaining vinaigrette.

Gray Monk Cellars Rotberger (Rosé)

Okanagan Centre, British Columbia

Gray Monk Cellars' wines are done in the Germanic style by winemaker and owner George Heiss Jr. Produced from a native German grape called Rotberger, this rosé has a berry-like nose and crisp acidity that matches the vinaigrette and refreshes the palate. The wine's hint of sweetness draws out the rich, creamy texture of Brie.

Other Choices:

Ontario Canadian champagne or rosé

GRAY·MONK

L'Extra Ripe Brie

Made by Agropur

BRIE BRIOCHES ON GREENS

SERVES FOUR TO SIX　　　　　Chef Charles Marin — Bromont, Quebec

A DELICIOUS RECIPE developed for Dairy Bureau of Canada.

Salad:

1	head baby romaine lettuce	1
1	head oakleaf lettuce	1
1	head radicchio	1
1	bunch watercress	1
2 tbsp	finely chopped fresh parsley	25 mL

Raspberry Vinaigrette:

1 tbsp	diced shallots	15 mL
1/4 cup	white wine	50 mL
1/4 cup	raspberry vinegar	50 mL
2/3 cup	whipping cream	150 mL
1/3 cup	butter, diced	75 mL

Brie Cheese Brioches:

1 cup	milk	250 mL
1/4 lb	sweet butter	125 g
2 tbsp	granulated sugar	25 mL
1	pkg active dry yeast	1
2 tsp	salt	10 mL
2	small beaten eggs, room temperature	2
4 cups	all-purpose flour, sifted	1 L
1 tbsp	vegetable oil	15 mL
2/3 lb	Brie, rind removed, cut into 1-inch (2.5-cm) cubes*	350 g
	Eggwash (1 egg beaten with 1 tsp/5 mL water)	
	Raspberries (for garnish)	

Use a cheese plane or vegetable peeler to remove rind on Brie cheese.

Dietrich-Jooss Vin Rosé

Iberville, Quebec

This winery offers tours and tastings and produces nine to ten wines each year. In this recipe, the raspberry vinaigrette and Brie call for a rosé, as a red wine would be too heavy for salad. The best choice is Dietrich-Jooss Vin Rosé, a lightweight wine that exhibits a berry bouquet and crisp acidity that complements the vinaigrette and Brie.

Other Choices:

Ontario or B.C. Gamay Noir

1 Tear romaine, oakleaf lettuce, radicchio and watercress into bite-sized pieces. Toss with parsley. Refrigerate until needed. **2** *To make vinaigrette*, in a small saucepan over medium heat combine shallots, white wine and raspberry vinegar; simmer, stirring occasionally, until reduced and syrupy. In another small saucepan over medium heat, reduce cream, stirring constantly, until syrupy. **3** Bring vinegar mixture to a boil. Add reduced cream, a little at a time, stirring constantly until well incorporated. Add diced butter, stirring until well blended. Set aside. **4** *To make the brioches*, in a saucepan combine milk, butter and sugar and bring to a boil. Remove pan from heat. Pour liquid into a bowl; let cool to luke warm. **5** Stir in yeast; let stand 10 minutes. Stir in salt and beaten eggs. **6** Slowly add flour, 1 cup (250 mL) at a time. **7** Knead dough for 10 minutes; form into a ball. **8** Coat ball with oil. Set in a clean bowl. Cover with a towel and let rise to triple its size, about 2 hours. **9** Transfer dough to lightly floured work surface and knead for 2 minutes. Return dough ball back to bowl, cover with towel and let rise to double its size, about 1 hour. **10** Transfer dough to a lightly floured work surface. **11** Divide the dough into twelve pieces. Flatten each piece into a circle. **12** Place a cube of Brie in the centre of each circle. Pull the dough up around the cheese, completely enclosing it. Shape dough into a ball and set into lightly greased muffin tins. Brush with eggwash. **13** Bake at 375°F (180°C) for 30 minutes or until golden. **14** On chilled plates, arrange salad greens. Garnish with raspberries. Set two brioches on each place. Open brioches and drizzle centres with raspberry vinaigrette.

Brie Cayer

Made by Fromagerie Cayer

WARM GOAT CHEESE WITH GREENS AND CREAMY HAZELNUT DRESSING

SERVES FOUR   Woolwich Dairy Inc. — Ariss, Ontario

ESTABLISHED IN 1976, Woolwich Dairy has become the largest producer of goat cheese in North America, working with 22 Ontario farmers and serving customers in Ontario, Quebec, B.C., Winnipeg, Calgary and several American states, including New York and California. Owners Tony and Olga Dutra offer a few specialty items (such as a mild Cheddar from goat's milk and a marinated goat cheese in olive oil), but their mainstays are a creamy Chevrai that uses an imported culture from France, a mild farm cheese called Gaisli and a traditional Greek feta. All Woolwich cheeses are made with microbial enzymes rather than animal rennet and contain no additives or preservatives, earning them respect from allergy sufferers, vegetarians and health-conscious consumers in general.

     This recipe was developed by talented Chef Terry Seed for Woolwich Dairy.

Mounier NV Brut,

Niagara-on-the-Lake, Ontario

A sister company sharing premises with Hillebrand Estates, Mounier makes quality sparklers in the traditional French style called méthode champenoise. Reasonably priced and well made, Mounier has a complex nose swirling with toasty, yeasty tones. Fresh pears and apples and a good balance of acidity come through in the mouth. This salad has so many flavours and textures that it is best served with a wine that simply refreshes the palate.

Other Choices:

B.C. Canadian champagne

Creamy Hazelnut Dressing:

1	egg, at room temperature	1
3 tbsp	freshly squeezed lemon juice	50 mL
Pinch	cayenne	Pinch
	Salt and white pepper to taste	
2 tbsp	honey	25 mL
1 tsp	Dijon mustard	5 mL
1 1/2 cup	olive oil	375 mL
3 tbsp	sliced, lightly toasted hazelnuts	50 mL
2 tbsp	whipping cream	25 mL

Warm Goat Cheese with Greens:

12	slices French bread 1/4 inch (5 mm) thick	12
1/4 cup	extra virgin olive oil	50 mL
	A mixture of Boston lettuce, radicchio, spinach and curly endive, torn into bite-sized pieces	
1	small red onion, julienned	1
1	medium sweet red pepper, julienned	1
1/4 lb	fresh goat cheese (Chevrai)	125 g
2 tbsp	sliced toasted hazelnuts	25 mL
	Orange segments (for garnish)	
	Freshly ground black pepper to taste	

1 To make dressing, in a blender blend well egg, lemon juice, cayenne, salt and pepper, honey and mustard. With blender running, slowly add oil. If mixture is too thick, add 1 tbsp (15 mL) warm water. Add nuts and cream; blend well. Adjust seasoning. Set aside. **2** Brush one side of bread with olive oil. Bake at 350°F (180°C) for 10 minutes or until lightly browned. Cool on a rack. **3** Arrange lettuce on four plates. Decorate with onion and peppers. Set aside. **4** Generously spread each slice of toast with goat cheese. Bake at 350°F (180°C) for 5 minutes or until goat cheese softens. Cool for 1 minute. **5** Place three cheese toasts on each salad. Drizzle with dressing. Sprinkle with hazelnuts. Garnish with orange segments and freshly ground black pepper.

Chevrai

Made by Woolwich Dairy

WARM BABY MUSTARD GREENS AND TOSSED SERRA

SERVES FOUR   Shari Darling — Toronto, Ontario

THIS ADAPTATION of a traditional Portuguese salad is a wonderful accompaniment to roast pork, chicken or turkey.

Divino Estate Winery, Trebbiano

Oliver, British Columbia

Divino is owned and operated by Joseph and Barbara Busnardo. Joseph makes wine from a few Italian grape varieties, including Trebbiano, which is usually used for blending. Divino produces a varietal Trebbiano. With vegetative aromas and flavours and a bit of spice, this dry, simple white matches the light flavour of mustard greens, allowing the rich, buttery texture of Serra to dominate the palate.

Other Choices:

Ontario Sauvignon

2 lb	baby mustard greens*	1 kg
1/4 cup	virgin olive oil	50 mL
2	large cloves garlic, minced	2
3/4 tsp	salt	4 mL
1/4 tsp	pepper	1 mL
1/2 lb	Serra cheese, diced	250 g

Mustard greens are available year-round in Asian and Portuguese markets. You can substitute beet greens.

1 Remove coarse stems and veins from greens. Wash well and pat dry. **2** In a saucepan over low heat, heat oil; sauté garlic until soft. Add greens and toss with oil, making sure all are glossy. Increase heat to high; sauté greens for 2 to 3 minutes until just wilted. Sprinkle with salt and pepper. **3** Transfer to a serving bowl and fold in cheese. Serve at once.

Serra

Made by Portuguese Cheese

FETA DANESBORG SALAD

SERVES FOUR   The Cheese Dairy — Toronto, Ontario

GETTING CHEESE LOVERS to visit The Cheese Dairy and Country Fresh cheese shops, both in downtown Toronto, is as easy as getting cows to graze. Owners and brothers Mario and Madail Dimas offer more than 300 imported and Canadian cheeses; 40 of these are low-fat versions. Exotic oils and homemade sauces and pestos stock the shelves as well, making this a regular pit stop for gourmands.

Vineland Estates St. Urban Semi-Dry Riesling

Vineland Estates is renowned for its distinctive Riesling wines possessing full body, firm acidity and forward fruit. This salad, with its vinaigrette acidity and feta tang, needs a Riesling with matching acidity but possessing a hint of sweetness for balance on the palate. Vineland's St. Urban semi-dry Riesling is an excellent choice, as it has the acidity and slight sweetness plus delicious tropical aromas and flavours and a lingering finish.

Other Choices:
B.C. off-dry Gewürztraminer

Feta

Made by Agropur

Vinaigrette:

¼ cup	white wine vinegar	50 mL
1 tbsp	lemon juice	15 mL
2 tbsp	apple juice	25 mL
2	cloves garlic, minced	2
¼ cup	olive oil	50 mL
1 tsp	finely chopped fresh oregano	5 mL
1 tsp	paprika	5 mL
	Salt and pepper to taste	

Salad:

½	head Boston lettuce	½
3	tomatoes, quartered	3
1	cucumber, sliced	1
1 cup	crumbled feta cheese	250 mL
¼ cup	finely chopped fresh chives	50 mL
¼ cup	finely chopped fresh parsley	50 mL
24	black olives	24

1 To make vinaigrette, in a bowl whisk together all vinaigrette ingredients. Chill. **2** Decoratively arrange lettuce on plates. Garnish with tomato wedges and cucumber slices. Sprinkle vegetables with feta cheese, chives and parsley. Place six olives around the edge of each plate. Drizzle vinaigrette over salad.

TAHITIAN CHICKEN SALAD IN GOAT CHEESE DRESSING

SERVES SIX | Fromagerie Ruban Bleu (Blue Ribbon) — Saint-Isidore, Quebec

BLUE RIBBON FARM has become a favourite destination of cheese-loving Quebeckers: their one-of-a-kind goat's milk cheeses can be bought only on the premises. (You may spot the odd cheese from Ruban Bleu in specialty shops, but only because the shop's owner has travelled to the farm to obtain it.) This decision to not assertively promote was a conscious one and has not hampered business in the least. Since 1986 production has consistently increased, with the farm now making close to 22,000 lb of cheese a year. Denise and Jean-Paul Rivard have 50 Toggenburg goats that are fed a special blend of soya and buttermilk. The couple believes this mixture produces a richer milk, which in turn creates a superior cheese. Many cheese lovers agree. At the moment the Rivards make three varieties — a Ruban Bleu Fromage Blanc (fresh goat cheese), Chèvre d'Or Cheddar and St-Isidore Camembert Ruban Bleu.

Cave Spring Cellars Indian Summer Riesling

Jordan, Ontario.
Available in Quebec
(La Maison des Vins)

Displaying a honeyed, apricot nose with ripe pear and apricot flavours, this Riesling is the consummate accompaniment for the chicken and its mango, banana and coconut sidekicks. With medium sweetness, the wine balances the tangy flavour of goat cheese.

Other Choices:
B.C. off-dry Riesling

Ruban Bleu Fromage Blanc

Made by Fromagerie Ruban Bleu

½ cup	raisins	125 mL
½ cup	Cave Spring Cellars Indian Summer Riesling (white wine)	125 mL
¾ cup	crumbled fresh goat cheese (Fromage Blanc)	175 mL
½ cup	salted peanuts	125 mL
1	ripe mango, diced	1
½ cup	flaked coconut	125 mL
1 lb	chicken breasts, cooked and diced	500 g
1	banana, sliced	1
	Salt and pepper	
1	head leaf lettuce	1
1	avocado, sliced (for garnish)	1
1	banana, sliced (for garnish)	1
	Juice of 1 lemon	

1 Soak raisins in white wine for 2 hours. Drain. **2** In a bowl combine raisins, goat cheese, peanuts, mango and coconut. Toss with chicken. Fold in banana. Season to taste with salt and pepper. **3** Arrange lettuce leaves on plates. Place a mound of chicken salad on top. Dip avocado and banana slices in lemon juice. Garnish each plate with slices of avocado and banana.

GRILLED DUCK AND GOAT CHEESE SALAD WITH GREEN CHILI AND LIME AIOLI

SERVES SIX TO EIGHT   Shari Darling — Toronto, Ontario

Green Chili and Lime Aioli: Makes one cup

2	green chilies, peeled, seeded, roasted and finely chopped	2
2 tbsp	finely chopped fresh kaffir lime leaves*	25 mL
1 cup	extra virgin olive oil	250 mL
	Salt and white pepper to taste	
1 tbsp	finely chopped lime rind	15 mL
	Juice of 2 limes	

Salad:

6	duck breasts, skin on	6
2	sweet yellow peppers, thickly sliced lengthwise	2
2	sweet red peppers, thickly sliced lengthwise	2
1	red onion, cut into 1/4-inch (5 mm) rings	1
1	head Bibb lettuce	1
1	bunch arugula	1
1	bunch bok choy	1
1	head radicchio	1
1	bunch fresh chives, finely chopped	1
1 cup	crumbled fresh goat cheese (Chevrai)	250 mL

*Fresh and dried kaffir lime leaves are available in Asian and Indian super-markets. If using dried leaves, use half the amount.

1 To make aioli, in a small bowl whisk together all aioli ingredients, except lime juice. Chill. **2** Set duck breasts on a greased baking sheet; grill for 4 minutes on each side until golden and cooked through. Cool. Cut into strips. **3** Place pepper slices and onion rings on baking sheet. Roast at 350°F (180°C) for 15 minutes or until vegetables are tender. **4** Tear Bibb, arugula, bok choy and radicchio leaves into bite-sized pieces. In a salad bowl toss greens with chives and crumbled goat cheese. **5** Whisk lime juice into aioli. Just moisten salad with aioli. Arrange salad on large plates; arrange duck slices and grilled vegetables on top. Serve remaining aioli on the side.

Gray Monk Cellars Gewürztraminer
(Broderson Vineyard/Off-Dry)

Okanagan Centre, British Columbia

The winery's name is a translation of the Austrian grape, Pinot Gris. Done in the Germanic style, their Gewürztraminer (Broderson Vineyard) is full bodied with grapefruit and lime aromas and flavours and a long spicy finish, making it an appropriate companion for the citrus and spicy flavours of the Green Chili and Lime Aioli. The wine's trace of sweetness balances all the tart characteristics to bring harmony to this food and wine marriage.

Other Choices:
Ontario off-dry Gewürztraminer

GRAY·MONK

Chevrai

Made by Woolwich Dairy

POTATO SALAD WITH FROMAGE FRAIS AND FRESH HERBS

SERVES SIX TO EIGHT   Liberty, Candiac — Quebec

ESTABLISHED IN 1928 as a small factory serving Montreal's Jewish and Eastern European communities, Liberty is now a large firm producing a whole array of fresh cheeses, all of which are natural and additive-free. Their old-style cream cheese is renowned in Montreal, having found its way into the city's finest cheesecake establishments, such as Franni's and La Desserte. They also make a clean, lightly acidulous cheese called Quark. Though Canadians are just discovering this cream cheese-like product, the Germans have been enjoying it for years. In fact, Quark accounts for almost half of all cheese production in Germany. Those watching their fat intake will be pleased to know that Quark is low in fat and can be made from skim milk, making it an excellent substitute in recipes for sour cream, cottage cheese, ricotta and cream cheese. Be careful when using skim-milk Quark in place of other cheeses; the Quark should be drained overnight in a coffee filter to thicken it.

Vignoble Le Cep d'Argent Seyval Blanc

Magog, Quebec

This winery offers tours and tastings. Made from Seyval grapes, this delicate white has citrus character and crispness that is a great match for the acidulous taste of Quark.

Other Choices:

Ontario Seyval or B.C. dry Müller-Thurgau

LE CEP D'ARGENT

Quark

Made by Liberty

4	large potatoes, boiled, drained and cooled	4
2	hard-cooked eggs	2
4	shallots, finely chopped	4
2	stalks celery, finely chopped	2
1/4 cup	finely chopped fresh parsley	50 mL
2 tbsp	finely chopped fresh dill	25 mL

Dressing:

1/2 cup	mayonnaise	125 mL
1/2 cup	Quark cheese	125 mL
1/2 tsp	dry mustard	2 mL
2 tsp	lemon juice	10 mL
Pinch	cayenne	Pinch
	Salt and ground pepper to taste	

1 Cut potatoes and eggs into small chunks; place in a large mixing bowl. Toss with shallots, celery, parsley and dill. **2** To make the dressing, in a bowl combine mayonnaise, Quark cheese, mustard, lemon juice, cayenne, salt and pepper. Add enough dressing to potato salad to moisten. Mix well and adjust seasonings. **3** Refrigerate for 2 hours before serving.

BRAISED DUCK BREAST WITH FOIE GRAS AND BLUE CHEESE MOUSSE, WITH MANDARIN ORANGE AND PARMESAN GLAZE

SERVES FOUR   Chef Luc Gielen — Hull, Quebec

IN HULL, FIVE MINUTES FROM the Ottawa Congress Centre, is Restaurant Le Sans-Pareil. Done in Victorian style, this cosy restaurant is owned and run by chef Luc Gielen. This recipe placed first in the Appetizer Category of the 1993 Foodservice Awards.

Brights Wines President Canadian Champagne Brut

Niagara Falls, Ontario
Available in Quebec (Société des Alcools Québec S.A.Q.)

This dish has so many competing flavours and textures that a clean, crisp sparkler, such as this one, is the best choice.

Other Choices:

Ontario Canadian champagne

½ lb	fresh foie gras (duck or goose)	250 g
	Salt and pepper to taste	
2 tbsp	white wine	25 mL
1	Muscovy duck breast (½ lb/250 g)	1

Mousse Stuffing:

¼ lb	blue cheese (Ermite), crumbled	125 g
4 tsp	finely chopped fresh parsley	20 mL
1	egg white	1
2 tsp	dried bread crumbs	10 mL
	Salt and pepper to taste	
1 cup	chicken stock	250 mL

Glaze:

3	mandarin oranges	3
¼ cup	grenadine syrup	50 mL
	Juice of ½ lime	
¼ cup	grated Parmesan cheese	50 mL
1 tsp	gelatin	5 mL
½ cup	whipping cream	125 mL

Salad:

12	Belgian endive leaves, torn	12
4	radicchio leaves, torn	4
8	chicory leaves OR leaf lettuce, torn	8

Vinaigrette:

4 tsp	virgin olive oil	20 mL
2 tsp	raspberry vinegar	10 mL
	Salt and pepper to taste	

1 Season foie gras with salt and pepper. Place it in a dish just large enough to hold it. Add wine. Cover with plastic wrap and refrigerate for at least 1 hour. **2** Pull skin away from duck breast, leaving it attached along one side. Cut away fat from the inside of the skin. Gently place skin between two sheets of waxed paper; flatten with the broad side of a cleaver. **3** *To make mousse*, in a bowl whisk together crumbled blue cheese, parsley, egg white, bread crumbs, salt and pepper. **4** Spread half of mousse over duck breast. Drain foie gras, reserving liquid. Lay foie gras on mousse. Cover foie gras with remaining mousse. **5** Stretch flattened skin over mousse; tie with kitchen string. Season skin with salt and pepper. **6** In an oven-safe saucepan over high heat sear the breast, stuffed side first for 2 minutes or until skin is light golden. Sear other side for two minutes or until light golden. Remove breast from pan and wrap carefully in cheesecloth; set aside. Drain fat from saucepan. Over high heat, deglaze saucepan with reserved fois gras liquid. Add stock; bring to a boil. **7** Place wrapped duck breast, stuffing side up, in boiling stock. Cover, and transfer to a 200°F (90°C) oven for 25 minutes. Transfer covered saucepan to refrigerator and chill for 3 hours. **8** *To make glaze*, cut mandarins in half crosswise. Extract the juice, reserving juice and keeping each half-rind whole. Reserve four empty rinds. Cut remaining two rinds into thin strips. **9** In a pot of boiling water, blanch strips of rind. Drain; return strips to the pot. Add grenadine syrup; bring to a boil. Remove from heat and let cool. Drain, reserving rind. **10** In a small saucepan blend lime juice with reserved mandarin juice; bring to a boil. Remove from heat; stir in Parmesan and gelatin. Let cool to room temperature. **11** In a bowl whip cream to soft peaks; fold into cheese-gelatin mixture. Turn mixture into empty rinds. Allow to set for 30 minutes. **12** In a bowl toss together Belgian endive, radicchio and chicory leaves. **13** In a small bowl whisk together all vinaigrette ingredients. Toss greens with vinaigrette. **14** Arrange salad on four plates. Cut each stuffed mandarin into six segments; arrange on the salad in a fan shape. Sprinkle a few strips of reserved rind in centre of each mandarin fan. **15** Remove cheesecloth and string from duck breast; cut breast into 12 slices. Arrange three slices on each plate.

Ermite

Made by L'Abbaye de Saint-Benoît-du-Lac

Tre Stelle Parmesan

Made by National Cheese

OKANAGAN APPLE, CHEDDAR AND PECAN SALAD

SERVES FOUR   Armstrong Cheese — Armstrong, British Columbia

ARMSTRONG CHEESE, a division of Dairyworld Foods, is known for its Cheddars, Monterey Jack, farmer's, Colby, mozzarella and Edam. Ivan Matte is a grand champion cheesemaker at Armstrong. Cheesemaking is not only a job for him but a family tradition. His grandfathers were cheesemakers, as was his father. Before joining Dairyworld in 1983, Ivan acquired his education and practical experience in cheesemaking at Kemptville College and Guelph University. Highly respected among cheesemakers, Ivan makes high-moisture Cheddars for mass consumption and low-moisture versions (less than 35 percent moisture) for those who love their Cheddars nippy and crumbly. "If you're going to produce a good Cheddar," says Ivan, "you have to produce a low-moisture cheese. The higher the moisture, the less keeping quality you're going to have with the cheese." At the 1992 Royal Winter Fair in Toronto, Armstrong Cheese won the Grand Championship, Reserve Grand Championship, High Aggregate Award (highest total score in all categories) and six first-place awards for their Cheddar. The following year proved just as successful: Armstrong won the Grand Championship at the Pacific National Exhibition in Vancouver, the Grand Championship at the Mammoth Cheese Competition in Ottawa and the High Aggregate Award at the Royal Winter Fair and the British Empire Cheese Show in Belleville.

Quails' Gate Vineyards Estate Winery Chasselas

Owned by Ben and Ruth Stewart, Quails' Gate is situated in a pioneer log cabin. Their Chasselas is full bodied and easy drinking, with apple and black pepper aromas and citrus flavours that complement the apple and Cheddar chunks in this salad.

Other Choices:
Ontario Chardonnay

Medium Cheddar

Made by Armstrong Cheese

Dressing:

1/3 cup	virgin olive oil	75 mL
	Juice of 1 lemon	
	Freshly ground pepper to taste	

Salad:

1	head leaf lettuce, torn into bite-sized pieces	1
1/4 lb	medium Cheddar cheese, shredded	125 g
2	apples, diced	2
1 cup	pecan halves	250 mL

1 In a small bowl whisk together dressing ingredients; set aside. **2** Arrange lettuce on four plates. In a bowl toss together Cheddar, apples and pecans; spoon onto lettuce. Pour dressing over salad.

MEDLEY OF SEAFOOD ON BIBB LETTUCE WITH ERMITE BLUE VINAIGRETTE

SERVES FOUR TO SIX   Executive Chef Zdravko Kalabric — Toronto, Ontario

CREATED FOR THE DAIRY BUREAU of Canada by Executive Chef Zdravko Kalabric of The York Downs Golf and Country Club.

24	mussels, scrubbed and debearded	24
24	clams	24
¼ lb	sea scallops	125 g
¼ lb	medium shrimp, shelled and deveined	125 g

Ermite Blue Vinaigrette:

2 tsp	lemon juice	10 mL
⅓ cup	crumbled blue cheese (Ermite)	75 mL
1 tbsp	finely chopped fresh rosemary	15 mL
	Salt and pepper to taste	
¼ cup	extra virgin olive oil	50 mL

1	head Bibb lettuce	1

1 In a steamer set over boiling water, steam mussels and clams for 2 minutes. Add scallops and shrimp; steam for another 4 minutes, until mussels and clams open, scallops are tender and shrimp are pink. Discard unopened mussels or clams. Let seafood cool about 10 minutes. **2** To make vinaigrette, in a food processor combine lemon juice, blue cheese, rosemary, salt and pepper. With motor running, slowly add oil to form a vinaigrette consistency. **3** Line plates with lettuce leaves. Arrange seafood on plates. Serve vinaigrette on the side.

Magnotta Wines Chardonnay

Vaughan, Ontario

Magnotta Wines produces a wide range of Ontario wines that meet VQA standards, as well as reasonably priced blends. Made from 100 percent Niagara grapes, this Chardonnay is light to medium bodied and dry, with delicate apple aromas and flavours. A good match for the variety of seafood.

Other Choices:
B.C. Pinot Blanc

Ermite

Made by L'Abbaye de Saint-Benoît-du-Lac

VELOUTÉ OF FIDDLEHEADS AND OKA

SERVES FOUR — Chef Gaetane Palardy — Vancouver, British Columbia

CREATED FOR the Dairy Bureau of Canada.

2 tsp	butter	10 mL
½	medium onion, diced	½
1¼ cups	fresh fiddleheads, washed and trimmed	300 mL
2 tsp	all-purpose flour	10 mL
2 cups	chicken stock	500 mL
	Salt and white pepper to taste	
¼ lb	Oka cheese, diced	125 g
1	lemon, quartered (for garnish)	1

1 In a large saucepan over low heat, melt butter; sweat onion for 2 to 3 minutes or until soft. **2** Add fiddleheads and sprinkle with flour. Cook for 4 to 5 minutes, stirring constantly to avoid burning. **3** Add 1 1/2 cups chicken stock; season with salt and pepper. Simmer gently, stirring occasionally, for 20 minutes to combine flavours. Add additional stock if mixture becomes too thick. **4** Strain velouté through a sieve; return velouté to saucepan. **5** In a food processor or blender purée fiddleheads and onion; stir into velouté. **6** Bring velouté to a gentle boil. Gradually add Oka stirring until velouté is thickened. **7** Pour velouté into heated soup bowls and garnish with lemon wedges.

Vignoble La Bauge Seyval

Brigham, Quebec

Owner and winemaker Alcide Naud's Seyval Blanc is dry and light and refreshes the palate. Yet it is still subtle enough to allow the delicate flavours of fiddleheads and Oka to come through on the palate.

Other Choices:

Ontario Seyval or B.C. dry Müller-Thurgau

Oka

Made by Agropur

BELFAIR BRUSSELS SPROUT AND CHESTNUT SOUP WITH APPLE CREAM

SERVES FOUR   Mariposa Dairy — Oakwood, Ontario

IT'S NOT SURPRISING THAT CHEESE LOVERS, including vegetarians, throughout Ontario praise Mariposa Dairy for their feta and a Gouda-style cheese called Belfair. Both varieties are free of preservatives, additives and rennet. According to Mariposa's customers, the cheeses have a distinctive flavour, having been produced on the farm from four goat breeds (Alpine, Nubian, Saanen and Toggenburg). What makes this dairy particularly special is that owners Bruce and Sharon Vanden Berg will make the feta to order. If you prefer the piquant flavour of an aged Greek-style feta instead of the milder version, the Vanden Bergs will meet your needs.

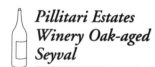

Pillitari Estates Winery Oak-aged Seyval

Niagara-on-the-Lake, Ontario

Family-run Pillitari Estates is one of the newest wineries in Niagara. Owner Gary began as a prize-winning amateur winemaker, though now he operates the business and leaves the winemaking to the skills of Joseph Will. Produced from Seyval grapes, this white was aged in oak. Delicate enough for soup but showing overtones of oak and vanilla, this soup draws attention to the chestnut flavours while complementing the apple cream.

Other Choices:

B.C. barrel-aged Chardonnay

1 lb	brussels sprouts	500 g
¾ cup	sour cream	175 mL
½	apple, peeled and grated	½
1½ cups	fresh chestnuts	375 mL
5 tbsp	butter	75 mL
5 cups	vegetable stock	1.25 L
1	bay leaf	1
¼ cup	all-purpose flour	50 mL
	Salt and pepper to taste	
¼ lb	Gouda cheese (Belfair), grated	125 g
	Croutons (for garnish)	

1 Soak brussels sprouts in water for 20 minutes. **2** In a bowl combine sour cream with apple. Chill. **3** Cut a deep **X** in the flat side of each chestnut, piercing the tough outer skin. Arrange on a baking sheet, sprinkle with water and bake at 400°F (200°C) for 5 minutes. Turn chestnuts and bake another 5 minutes. Using a sharp knife, peel chestnuts while still hot. If chestnuts cool while you're peeling, reheat in oven for 2 minutes. **4** In a large saucepan over medium heat, melt 3 tbsp (50 mL) butter. Add drained sprouts and chestnuts; cook, stirring constantly, for 3 minutes. Add stock and bay leaf. Reduce heat and simmer, covered, for 40 minutes. Discard bay leaf. **5** In a food processor or blender purée soup in batches. Set aside. **6** In the cleaned saucepan melt remaining 2 tbsp (25 mL) butter. Add flour; cook for 3 minutes, stirring constantly, without browning. Remove pan from heat and gradually stir in puréed soup. Return to low heat and cook for 10 minutes. Season with salt and pepper. Remove from heat. **7** Add Gouda, stirring constantly until cheese is melted and soup is thickened. Pour into soup bowls. Garnish with a dollop of apple cream and croutons.

Belfair (Gouda-Style)

Made by Westhill Dairy

COLD MELON AND ICEWINE SOUP WITH CREAM CHEESE

SERVES SIX — Chef Jean-Claude Belmont — Quebec

THE ORIGINAL VERSION OF THIS RECIPE called for the rich dessert wine Monbazillac. I have revised the recipe to use a Canadian Icewine, which adds as much flavour and is wonderfully festive. Serving this soup with a small glass of Icewine as a starter dish during the summer is an interesting and unconventional way to bring the palate to life.

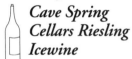

Cave Spring Cellars Riesling Icewine

Jordan, Ontario
Available in Quebec (La Maison des Vins)

On The Twenty is a new restaurant on the same premises as the winery. Here you can get a wide range of Cave Spring wines and reasonably priced gourmet fare. Honey and mandarin aromas prepare the palate for similar flavours, with good Riesling acidity to balance the sweetness. These qualities enhance the fresh grapefruit and melon purée in this soup.

Other Choices:
B.C. Icewine

Cream Cheese

Made by Westhill Dairy

1/2	honeydew melon	1/2
1/2	cantaloupe	1/2
	Juice of 1 1/2 pink grapefruits	
	Juice of 1/2 lemon	
1/2	bottle Cave Spring Cellars Icewine	1/2
3 oz	cream cheese	75 g
1 tbsp	melon liqueur	15 mL
1 tbsp	whipping cream	15 mL
	Mint leaves (for garnish)	

1 Peel and dice melon and cantaloupe. In a food processor or blender, purée fruit. Add grapefruit juice, lemon juice and Icewine. Purée until well blended. Refrigerate. **2** In a small bowl, blend cream cheese, melon liqueur and cream. Refrigerate. **3** Ladle soup into cold soup plates. Spoon some cheese mixture onto soup and, with the blade of a knife, make a pattern. Garnish with mint leaves.

ERMITE BLUE AND WALNUT SOUP

SERVES FOUR   Forster's Fine Cheese — Vancouver, British Columbia

THERE IS NOTHING STEPHEN AND ELIZABETH FORSTER enjoy more than rummaging through old bookstores in search of rare books on exotic cheeses. Well...maybe travelling around the world in search of the rarest and most exotic cheeses. But there's definitely nothing Vancouver's cheese lovers like more than stocking up on the Forsters' findings. Though quality is their focus, this couple believes in offering variety, which is why they always have more than 230 different cheeses in the shop at any one time. Some of these are Canada's finest varieties.

CedarCreek Estate Winery Chancellor

Kelowna, British Columbia

This rich, creamy soup with its nippy blue cheese and walnut flavour deserves nothing less than a full-bodied red. Chancellor's velvety texture is a good match for the soup's creaminess, while its jammy raspberry aromas and flavours and hint of spice are a natural complement to the taste of blue cheese and walnuts.

Other Choices:
Ontario Merlot

CEDARCREEK
Estate Winery

2 tbsp	butter	25 mL
1	onion, finely chopped	1
5	stalks celery, finely chopped	5
2 tbsp	all-purpose flour	25 mL
2½ cups	chicken stock	625 mL
½ cup	coarsely chopped walnuts	125 mL
⅔ cup	milk	150 mL
¼ lb	blue cheese (Ermite), crumbled	125 g
3 oz	double-cream Brie, diced	75 g
	Salt and pepper to taste	

1 In a large saucepan over medium heat, melt butter; sauté onion and celery for 5 minutes or until tender. **2** Stir in flour and cook another 2 minutes, stirring constantly. Remove from heat. **3** Stir in stock. Over high heat bring soup to a boil, stirring constantly until thickened. Lower heat and simmer, stirring occasionally, for 30 minutes. **4** Transfer soup in batches to a blender or food processor. Add walnuts. Purée until smooth. **5** Press soup through a sieve into the cleaned saucepan. Stir in milk and heat over low heat. Slowly stir in blue cheese and double-cream Brie, stirring constantly until well blended. **6** Season with salt and pepper. Serve in heated bowls.

Ermite

Made by L'Abbaye de Saint-Benoît-du-Lac

Double-cream Brie

Made by Fromagerie Clement

CHEDDAR AND GREEN CHILI CHOWDER

SERVES FOUR   Country Gourmet — Aurora, Ontario

AURORA'S LOCALS NEED NOT TRAVEL far to experience the world's finest cheeses. A quick jaunt to Betty Jarvis's Country Gourmet and visitors are sure to be tempted. French Brie, German Cambozola, English Stilton and Canadian Cheddars are but a few of the dairy delights offered here. This general store also brims with European chocolates, homemade preserves and gifts.

1 tbsp	vegetable oil	15 mL
1	clove garlic, minced	1
2	green chilies, seeded and finely chopped	2
1/4 cup	chopped onion	50 mL
1/4 cup	diced black olives	50 mL
1/3 cup	all-purpose flour	75 mL
4 cups	milk	1 L
4 cups	shredded extra-old white Cheddar cheese	1 L
1/2 tsp	dry mustard	2 mL
1/2 tsp	chili powder	2 mL
Pinch	cayenne	Pinch
	Salt and white pepper to taste	
	Black olives (for garnish)	
	Croutons (for garnish)	

Marynissen Estates Lot 31A Cabernet Sauvignon

Owner and winemaker John Marynissen has some of the oldest Cabernet Sauvignon vines in Ontario. Aged in American oak, this full-bodied Cabernet Sauvignon stands up to this hearty soup, while its ripe raspberry fruit enhances Cheddar and its spicy oak tones match the chilies and cayenne.

Other Choices:

B.C. Cabernet Sauvignon (International Blend)

Extra-Old White Cheddar

Made by Pine River Cheese

1 In a large saucepan over medium heat, heat oil; sauté garlic, chilies, onion and black olives for 2 to 3 minutes or until onion is tender. **2** Gradually stir in flour until mixture begins to thicken. Add milk, a little at a time, stirring until mixture is smooth. **3** Add Cheddar cheese, 1 cup (250 mL) at a time, stirring constantly until cheese is melted. **4** Ladle 1 cup (250 mL) soup into a small bowl. Blend in dry mustard, chili powder, cayenne, salt and white pepper. Stir mixture into soup. **5** Simmer soup for 10 minutes, stirring frequently. **6** Pour soup into bowls. Garnish with black olives and croutons.

VELOUTÉ OF SPINACH AND FETA

SERVES FOUR   Evanoff Cheese — Caledon, Ontario

EVANOFF CHEESE IS SMALL IN THE REALM of Canada's corporate dairy industry, but its production of 6,000 lb of feta and cream cheese each year is enough to keep Stephanie Evanoff extremely busy. During the week you'll find Stephanie at the factory; on Saturdays, at Toronto's St. Lawrence Market. Her late husband, Nemo, created Evanoff Cheese in 1953, when quality feta and cream cheese were hard to find in Southern Ontario. Though both cheeses are made in abundance today, Stephanie has kept many of their original customers by using quality ingredients and sticking to the traditional recipe. Her cream cheese, for example, is still made with fresh 35% cream, giving it a thick, creamy texture and deliciously rich flavour.

Inniskillin Wines Melon

Niagara-on-the-Lake, Ontario

Inniskillin's Melon is made from 100 percent Niagara grapes. Medium-bodied and dry, this white equals the weight of the soup while its crisp acidity enhances the tangy flavour of feta. Its light pear aromas and tangerine and herbal flavours go well with the soup's spinach base.

Other Choices:

B.C. dry Müller-Thurgau

Feta cheese

Made by Evanoff Cheese

1	bunch fresh spinach, stems removed, steamed	1
¼ cup	chicken stock	50 mL
½ tsp	sugar	2 mL
1 cup	milk	250 mL
1 cup	half-and-half cream	250 mL
¼ cup	Inniskillin Wines Melon (white wine)	50 mL
1 tsp	lemon rind	5 mL
	Salt and pepper to taste	
½ cup	crumbled feta cheese	125 mL

1 In a food processor or blender, combine steamed spinach with chicken stock. Purée until smooth. Pass mixture through a sieve. **2** In a medium saucepan over low heat, combine puréed mixture, sugar, milk, cream, wine and lemon rind. Season with salt and pepper. Simmer for 15 minutes or until flavours are well blended. **3** Pass through sieve again. Texture should be velvety. **4** Pour soup into soup bowls. Sprinkle with feta cheese.

FRENCH ONION SOUP WITH MIRANDA CHEESE AND PINOT NOIR

SERVES SIX   Shari Darling — Toronto, Ontario

¼ cup	butter	50 mL
2 lb	yellow onions, thinly sliced	1 kg
6 cups	brown stock OR beef stock	1.5 L
	Salt and pepper to taste	
18	slices French bread	18
2 tbsp	Château des Charmes Pinot Noir (red wine)	30 mL
¾ cup	shredded Gruyère-type cheese (Miranda)	175 mL

1 In a large saucepan over medium heat melt butter; sauté onions until golden, about 15 minutes. Add stock; season with salt and pepper. Simmer another 10 minutes. **2** Arrange bread slices on baking sheet and bake at 350°F (180°C) until lightly golden. Place three slices in each soup bowl. Drizzle with 1 tsp (5 mL) wine over each bowl. **3** Bring soup to a boil. Pour over bread. Garnish each bowl with shredded cheese.

Pelee Island Pinot Noir

Kingsville, Ontario

Pinot Noir embodies medium weight and cherry fruit that support the soup's weight and marry well with the delicate almond quality found in this French-style cheese.

Other Choices:

B.C. Pinot Noir

PELEE ISLAND WINERY

Miranda

Made by Fromagerie Fritz Kaiser

LIMBURGER AND WILD MUSHROOM SOUP

SERVES FOUR TO SIX   Shari Darling — Toronto, Ontario

OF BELGIAN ORIGIN, Limburger is a surface-ripened cheese. During the ripening process the exterior is washed with a coryne bacteria that begins the development of an orange or brownish mould. Though the cheese is well known for its powerful, pungent odour, its creamy interior is delicate and zesty.

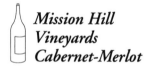

Mission Hill Vineyards Cabernet-Merlot

Westbank, British Columbia

Though soup and wine don't always work together, this particular recipe is extremely flavourful, thus deserving of wine. Limburger cheese and wild mushrooms both require a robust red like this blend. The wine's smoky character draws out the woody taste of the wild mushrooms, while hidden blackberry fruit complements Limburger. With medium body, the wine matches the soup's weight.

Rocky Mountain Limburger

Made by Neapolis Dairy Products

Tre Stelle Parmesan

Made by National Cheese

1 oz	dried porcini mushrooms	25 g
1/2 cup	water	125 mL
1 tbsp	butter	15 mL
1/2 cup	sliced fresh shiitake mushrooms	125 mL
1/4 cup	pearl barley	50 mL
4 cups	water	1 L
	Bouquet garni (made with 2 bay leaves and 4 black peppercorns)	
2 tbsp	whipping cream	25 mL
1/4 lb	Limburger cheese, diced	125 g
1	egg yolk, beaten (if needed)	1
	Salt and pepper to taste	
1 1/4 cups	Parmesan cheese, grated (for garnish)	300 mL
	Finely chopped fresh parsley (for garnish)	

1 Soak porcini mushrooms in 1/2 cup (125 mL) water for 1 hour. Drain, reserving liquid. Dice porcini mushrooms; set aside. **2** In a large saucepan over medium heat, melt butter; sauté shiitake mushrooms until tender, about 5 minutes. **3** Add barley, porcini mushrooms and reserved liquid, and 4 cups (1 L) water. Over high heat bring mixture to a boil. Reduce heat to low. Add bouquet garni. Simmer for 25 minutes or until barley is tender. Remove bouquet garni. **4** Add cream and Limburger cheese; simmer, stirring constantly, until cheese is melted, about 5 minutes. Remove from heat. If needed, blend in egg yolk to bind soup. Season to taste with salt and pepper. **5** Pour soup into heated bowls. Garnish with Parmesan cheese and chopped parsley.

SOUP OF MUSSELS AND BRIE

SERVES FOUR   Chef Gordon Landy — Toronto, Ontario

A MASTERPIECE created for the Dairy Bureau of Canada.

4 tsp	whey butter	20 mL
1/3 cup	diced leeks	75 mL
2 cups	fish stock	500 mL
2/3 cups	whipping cream	150 mL
1 tsp	finely chopped shallots	5 mL
1	clove garlic	1
4 tsp	vermouth	20 mL
4 tsp	white wine	20 mL
12	mussels, scrubbed and debearded	12
3/4 cup	diced Brie	175 mL
1 tbsp	crumbled blue cheese (Ermite)	15 mL
	Salt and pepper to taste	
4	sprigs fresh chervil	4

1 In a large saucepan over medium heat, melt butter; sweat leeks until soft. Add fish stock and simmer gently for 15 minutes. Strain stock; reserve leeks. Return stock to the saucepan and bring to a simmer. Gradually stir in cream. Remove from heat. **2** In another saucepan over medium-high heat, combine shallots, garlic, vermouth and wine; bring to a boil. Add mussels. Cover and steam for 3 to 5 minutes or until mussels have opened. Remove mussels with a slotted spoon. Discard unopened mussels. Shell mussels and keep warm. **3** Strain mussel stock. Stir into creamy stock and bring to a boil. **4** Whisk in Brie and blue cheese. Season with salt and pepper. Strain soup. **5** Place three mussels in each heated bowl. Divide leeks evenly among bowls. Pour soup over mussels and leeks. Garnish each bowl with a chervil sprig.

Pelee Island Winery Pinot Noir

Kingsville, Ontario

Winemaker Walter Schmoranz makes one of the most consistently good Pinot Noirs in Ontario year to year. A medium-bodied, well-balanced Pinot Noir with cherry character and softness that parallels Brie's rich, creamy texture without overpowering mussels.

Other Choices:
B.C. Gamay Noir

PELEE ISLAND WINERY

Damafro Brie

Made by Fromagerie Clement

Ermite

Made by L'Abbaye de Saint-Benoît-du-Lac

RED CABBAGE SOUP WITH FOUR CHEESES

SERVES FOUR   Chef Christopher English — Petit-Saguenay, Quebec

A TASTY SOUP created for the Dairy Bureau of Canada.

Stoney Ridge Cellars Chardonnay

(Barrel-Fermented and -Aged)
Winona, Ontario

A gorgeous farm winery by the Niagara Escarpment, Stoney Ridge makes a wide range of wines, all meeting VQA standards each year. This barrel-fermented Chardonnay, displaying a smoky bouquet and caramel and melon flavours with a long spicy finish is a perfect partner for this soup. The wine's buttery texture matches the weight of the soup's cream base, while having enough character to stand up to the combination of cheese and hearty ingredients.

Other Choices:

B.C. barrel-fermented and/or -aged Chardonnay

Kawartha brand Feta

Made by Kawartha Goat Cheese

Ricotta

Made by Mannina Cheese

Tre Stelle Parmesan

Made by National Cheese

Romano

Made by Saputo Cheeses

¾ cup	shredded red cabbage	175 mL
⅓ cup	sliced onions	75 mL
⅔ cup	diced potatoes	150 mL
4 cups	chicken stock	1 L
4 tsp	butter	20 mL
¼ cup	julienned leeks	50 mL
¾ cup	half-and-half cream	175 mL
⅔ cup	whipping cream	150 mL
⅓ cup	crumbled feta cheese	75 mL
¼ cup	ricotta cheese	50 mL
¼ cup	grated Parmesan cheese	50 mL
¼ cup	grated Romano cheese	50 mL
	Whipping cream (for garnish)	
	Edible flower petals (for garnish)*	

Most specialty food shops sell packaged dried edible flowers.

1 In a stock pot over medium heat, combine cabbage, onions, potatoes and stock. Simmer for 25 minutes or until vegetables are tender. **2** Meanwhile, in a saucepan over medium heat, melt butter; sauté leeks until tender. **3** Transfer leeks to the stock. Bring stock to a boil. Stir in half-and-half cream and 2/3 cup (150 mL) whipping cream. Return to a boil. **4** Add feta, ricotta, Parmesan and Romano cheeses. Stir until cheeses are completely melted. **5** In a food processor or blender, purée soup in batches. **6** Pour soup into heated bowls. Garnish with a dollop of whipping cream and flower petals.

CURRIED VELOUTÉ WITH APPLE AND NEUFCHATEL

SERVES FOUR   Chef Zdravko Kalabric — Toronto, Ontario

CREATED BY EXECUTIVE CHEF Zdravko Kalabric, of The York Downs Golf and Country Club, for the Dairy Bureau of Canada, this recipe can be served cold or hot.

2 tsp	butter	10 mL
2	slices bacon	2
½	onion, sliced	½
1	apple, peeled and diced	1
1 tsp	curry powder	5 mL
1 cup	chicken stock	250 mL
¼ cup	whipping cream	50 mL
⅓ cup	Neufchatel cheese	75 mL
1	egg yolk, lightly beaten	1
	Salt and pepper to taste	
	Croutons (for garnish)	

1 In a saucepan over medium heat, melt butter; cook bacon and onion until bacon is browned and onion is soft. Drain fat from saucepan. **2** Stir in apple and curry powder. Add stock; cook for 5 minutes. **3** Stir in cream; simmer for 2 minutes. **4** Add Neufchatel cheese, stirring constantly until cheese is melted. Remove saucepan from heat. **5** Blend in egg yolk. Season to taste with salt and pepper. Serve hot or cold garnished with croutons.

Sumac Ridge Estate Winery Chardonnay

Summerland, British Columbia

Harry McWatters is a leading force behind the B.C. wine industry. His winery was the first in B.C. to produce méthode champenoise champagnes. Fresh green apples govern the bouquet and mouth of this white. Its crisp acidity offsets the soup's rich cream base, refreshing the palate.

Other Choices:

Ontario Chardonnay

S U M A C
R I D G E
E S T A T E   W I N E R Y

Baron Roula Neufchatel

Made by Fromagerie Cayer

POTATO, CHEDDAR AND BACON SOUP

SERVES FOUR   Tavistock Cheese Co. Ltd. — Tavistock, Ontario

ANTIQUE EMPORIUMS AND SPECIALTY SHOPS are not the only attractions in Tavistock, Ontario. Located on Hope Street West is Tavistock Cheese. Here, you'll find a wide selection of cheeses, all made on the premises — Cheddars, Colby, brick, Monterey Jack and a wide range of seasoned farmer's cheeses. A division of McCain Refrigerated Foods, Tavistock has roots extending to the 1800s, when two cheese companies amalgamated. One was called the German Union Cheese Manufacturing Company, founded in 1879; the other, Tavistock Cheese and Butter Company, founded in 1884. Drawing on more than a century of experience acquired at these companies, Tavistock Cheese can now produce more than 8.8 million lb of Canadian cheese each year.

Henry of Pelham Estate Winery Merlot

St. Catharines, Ontario

Bacon, Cheddar and Parmesan all demand red wine. Merlot is appropriate for this soup, as it offers enough character to complement these ingredients but with medium body so as not to overpower this heavy soup. Blackberries and spice command the bouquet and flavours, and a peppery finish tastes absolutely wonderful with Cheddar.

Other Choices:

B.C. Merlot

Old Cheddar

Made by Tavistock Cheese

Parmesan

Made by Harrowsmith Cheese Factory

6	slices bacon	6
2	medium potatoes, finely chopped	2
1	yellow onion, finely chopped	1
½ cup	chicken stock	125 mL
¼ cup	finely chopped fresh dill	50 mL
1½ cups	shredded old Cheddar cheese	375 mL
1 cup	milk	250 mL
1 cup	grated Parmesan cheese	250 mL
	Croutons (optional)	
	Pepper to taste	

1 In a large saucepan over medium heat, fry bacon until crispy; drain on paper towels. **2** Drain fat from saucepan. In the saucepan combine potatoes, onion, chicken stock and dill. Bring to a boil; simmer, partly covered, for 20 minutes, stirring occasionally. Remove from heat. **3** Add Cheddar cheese in batches and milk, stirring until melted. **4** In a food processor or blender purée soup. Return soup to saucepan and reheat. Do not boil. **5** Pour soup into heated bowls. Garnish with crumbled bacon, Parmesan, croutons (if using) and pepper.

CHEDDAR LOAF

SERVES FOUR TO SIX   Fitz-Henri Catering Kitchen — North York, Ontario

SIMPLE YET UTTERLY DELICIOUS, this recipe was created by Judith Fitzhenri, owner of Fitz-Henri Fine Foods.

¼ cup	butter, softened	50 mL
2 tbsp	sugar	25 mL
2	eggs	2
1 cup	buttermilk	250 mL
½ tsp	hot pepper sauce	2 mL
2 cups	sifted all-purpose flour	500 mL
1 tsp	salt	5 mL
1 tsp	baking powder	5 mL
1 tsp	baking soda	5 mL
¾ cup	shredded old Cheddar cheese	175 mL
¼ cup	grated Parmesan cheese	50 mL

1 In a large bowl cream butter and sugar. Beat in eggs, buttermilk and hot pepper sauce. **2** In another large bowl combine flour, salt, baking powder, baking soda, Cheddar and Parmesan. **3** Gradually add dry mixture to wet mixture, stirring until all flour is moistened. Divide dough into two well-greased and lightly floured 8- by 4-inch (1.5 L) loaf pans. **4** Bake at 350°F (180°C) for 40 to 45 minutes or until skewer inserted in centre comes out clean.

4-year-old Cheddar

Made by Maple Dale Cheese

Tre Stelle Parmesan

Made by National Cheese

CAULIFLOWER, MUSHROOM AND CHEDDAR CASSEROLE

SERVES FOUR   Great Canadian Food Products Co. — Toronto, Ontario

THE GREAT CANADIAN FOOD PRODUCTS store is renowned in Toronto for its line of kosher cheeses and prepared cuisine. Entrees include lasagna, pizza crusts, ready-made pizzas, manicotti, tortellini and cheese noodle kugel. Desserts, made by baker Rhonda Litwack, include Berry Strata Cheesecake, Chocolate Cointreau Layer Cake, White Chocolate Cheese Cake and Tiramisù. Owners Marci and Harold Rapp also make their own kosher hard cheeses (Cheddar, mozzarella), ricotta, Brie and Camembert.

Kittling Ridge Sauvignon Blanc
Grimsby, Ontario

Owned by Rieder Distillery, Kittling Ridge is one of Ontario's newest wineries. Normally, Cheddar works best with red wine. In this case, a red would overpower all the vegetables, making a white wine more suitable. Kittling Ridge's Sauvignon Blanc is simple, crisp and clean, making it a good match for this casserole. (Not kosher.)

Other Choices:
B.C. Müller-Thurgau

Cheddar
Made by Great Canadian Food Products

1	head cauliflower (approx 2/3 lb/350 g)	1
2 tbsp	butter	25 mL
1 cup	sliced button mushrooms	250 mL
1	medium onion, thinly sliced	1
2 tbsp	all-purpose flour	25 mL
1 cup	half-and-half cream	250 mL
¼ lb	Cheddar cheese, shredded	125 g
	Salt and pepper to taste	
½ cup	crushed corn flakes	125 mL
1 tbsp	butter	15 mL

1 Break cauliflower into florets. Steam cauliflower; drain. **2** In a medium saucepan over medium heat, melt 2 tbsp (25 mL) butter; sauté mushrooms and onions until tender. Stir in flour. **3** Reduce heat to low. Blend in cream; simmer until sauce thickens slightly, about 3 to 4 minutes. **4** Arrange cauliflower in a 9-inch (2.5 L) square baking dish. Pour sauce over cauliflower. Sprinkle with Cheddar cheese. Season with salt and pepper. Sprinkle with corn flake crumbs. Dot with 1 tbsp (15 mL) butter. **5** Bake at 350°F (180°C) for 20 minutes or until cauliflower is tender. Serve hot.

MOROCCAN WALNUT COUSCOUS SALAD WITH FETA CHEESE

SERVES FOUR   Michelle Ramsay — Toronto, Ontario

THIS SIMPLE, DELICIOUS RECIPE was created by Michelle Ramsay, a food writer and my co-author of *Canada's Wine Country Cookbook*.

1 1/2 cups	water	375 mL
2 tbsp	vegetable oil	25 mL
1/2 tsp	salt	2 mL
1 cup	instant medium couscous	250 mL
1/3 cup	chopped green onion	75 mL
2	medium tomatoes, diced	2
1/4 lb	feta cheese, crumbled	125 g
1/4 lb	California walnut pieces	125 g
2 tbsp	finely chopped fresh mint	25 mL
2 tbsp	finely chopped fresh oregano	25 mL
1/4 cup	fresh lemon juice	50 mL
1/3 cup	extra virgin olive oil	75 mL
	Freshly ground pepper to taste	

Vignoble Les Blancs Coteaux La Taste Seyval

Dunham, Quebec

Translating as "the White Hills," Les Blancs Coteaux is operated by Marie-Claude Lizotta and Pierre Genesse. This dry, light white does not overpower the delicate nature of couscous, while its crisp acidity complements the tangy flavour of feta.

Other Choices:

Ontario Seyval or B.C. dry Kerner

> *Les Blancs Coteaux*

Feta

Made by Fromagerie Cayer

1 In a medium saucepan, bring water, 1 tbsp (15 mL) vegetable oil and salt to a boil. Stir in couscous, stir. Cover and remove from heat; let stand for 4 minutes. Add remaining vegetable oil and stir with fork to separate grains. Let cool to room temperature. **2** In a large bowl, combine couscous, green onions, tomatoes, feta cheese, walnut pieces, mint and oregano. In a small bowl whisk together lemon juice and olive oil; pour over salad, combining well. Season with freshly ground pepper.

SCALLOPED BABY EGGPLANT WITH CHEDDAR

SERVES FOUR   Shari Darling — Toronto, Ontario

4 tbsp	butter	50 mL
1 cup	thinly sliced onion	250 mL
2 tbsp	all-purpose flour	25 mL
1¾ cups	scalded milk	425 mL
	Salt and pepper to taste	
5	baby eggplants	5
1 cup	shredded old Cheddar cheese	250 mL
2 tbsp	dry bread crumbs	25 mL
1 tbsp	butter	15 mL

1 In a large skillet over medium heat melt 2 tbsp (25 mL) butter; cook onions until soft. Remove onions. **2** Melt remaining 2 tbsp (25 mL) butter. Whisk in flour. Cook, stirring constantly, for 3 minutes. Increase heat to high. Add scalded milk and bring mixture to a boil, stirring constantly. Reduce heat to low; simmer for 1 minute. Remove from heat and season with salt and pepper. **3** Peel eggplants and slice 1/8 inch (3 mm) thick. **4** Spread half of sauce in a well-buttered 13- by 9-inch (3.5 L) baking dish. Cover sauce with half the eggplant slices, overlapping the slices slightly. Spread onions over eggplant; spread half of Cheddar over onions. Top with another layer of sauce, eggplant and Cheddar. Sprinkle with bread crumbs; dot with 1 tbsp (15 mL) butter. Cover with foil. **5** Bake at 375°F (180°C) for 30 minutes. Remove foil and bake for another 30 minutes or until the top is golden and eggplant is tender.

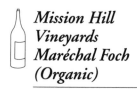

Mission Hill Vineyards Maréchal Foch (Organic)

Westbank, British Columbia

Mission Hill purchases grapes from more than 200 vineyards across B.C. Full-bodied with soft tannin, this red does not overshadow eggplant, while its blackberry bouquet and flavours complement the tangy Cheddar taste.

Other Choices:
Ontario Maréchal Foch

Old Cheddar

Made by Armstrong Cheese

ONIONS STUFFED WITH CHICKEN, LE MOINE AND CRANBERRY SAUCE

SERVES FOUR   Shari Darling — Toronto, Ontario

Vignoble Morou Red Reserve

Napierville, Quebec

Established in 1987, Vignoble Morou is owned and operated by Etienne Heroux and Monique Morin. The winery is quickly gaining recognition, having won two silver medals in the White Varietal Category at the 1993 Atlanta, Georgia, Wine Summit for the White Reserve (made from mostly Seyval grapes) and Clos Napierois (made from mostly Geisenheim grapes). The Red Reserve is produced from de Chaunac, Maréchal Foch and Chancellor grapes. It is light bodied with soft tannin, berry aromas and flavour and a hint of spice; it tastes great alongside the Le Moine cheese and cranberry sauce.

Other Choices:
Ontario Pinot Noir or B.C. Gamay Noir

Le Moine

Made by L'Abbaye de Saint-Benoît-du-Lac

4	Spanish onions (¾ lb/375 g)	4
¼ cup	chicken broth	50 mL
2 tbsp	cup whipping cream	25 mL
2 tbsp	Vignoble Morou Red Reserve (red wine)	25 mL
	Salt and pepper to taste	
2 cups	shredded cooked chicken	500 mL
½ lb	Gruyère-style cheese (Le Moine), shredded	250 g
½ cup	cranberry sauce	125 mL
1 cup	mashed potatoes	250 mL

1 Cut the top 1/2 inch (1 cm) from each onion. Peel onions. With a melon-baller scoop out the centres, leaving two layers of onion on the sides and 1/2 inch (1 cm) on the bottom. **2** Dice onion centres. Put diced onion in a 9-inch (2.5 L) square baking dish. Pour in chicken broth. Cover with aluminum foil. **3** Bake at 425°F (220°C) for 30 minutes or until onion is tender. Stir in cream and wine. Season with salt and pepper. Bake, uncovered, at 425°F (220°C) for 15 minutes, stirring occasionally. **4** Meanwhile, stuff each onion shell with one-quarter of chicken, cheese and cranberry sauce; top with one-quarter of mashed potatoes. **5** Set stuffed onions on top of onion pieces in baking dish. Bake at 425°F (220°C) for 35 minutes or until onions are tender and potatoes are golden. **6** Set stuffed onions on serving plates. Top with some of the diced onion mixture.

ARTICHOKE BOTTOMS STUFFED WITH SNOW GOAT CHEESE AND SUN-DRIED TOMATOES

MAKES SIX   Cheese Boutique & Deli Ltd. — Toronto, Ontario

THE SAVOURY SMELL of fresh bread permeates the Cheese Boutique & Deli. But it's the vast assortment of creamy Camemberts and nippy Cheddars that will make you salivate. And these are just two of the many imported and domestic varieties on display in this cheese lover's haven. The shop's continued success and panache can be attributed to owner Fatin Pristine. An Albanian native, Fatin has an eclectic background, having spent a good part of his youth travelling through remote villages and towns in Belgium, France and Turkey. It is in these countries that he discovered some of the world's rarest cheeses. In 1972 he decided to put this knowledge and experience to good use and opened the Cheese Boutique & Deli in Toronto's Bloor West Village.

Vinoteca Wines Pinot Noir

Woodbridge, Ontario

Winemaker Giovanni Follegot opened the winery in 1989. He produces a number of varietals, among them different-styled Chardonnays, two Pinot Noirs (one oak aged), Cabernet Sauvignon and Vidal Icewine. The Pinot Noir is light bodied and soft with cherry character, making it a perfect wine for sun-dried tomatoes and the tangy flavour and creamy texture of goat cheese.

Other Choices:

B.C. Pinot Noir

Vinoteca

6	large artichokes, 4½ inches (10 cm) wide	6
	Juice of 2 lemons	
4 cups	cold water	1 L
¼ cup	all-purpose flour	50 mL
1 tsp	salt	5 mL

Stuffing:

2 tbsp	butter	25 mL
2 tbsp	minced shallots	25 mL
¼ cup	coarsely chopped sun-dried tomatoes (packed in oil)	50 mL
⅓ cup	white wine	75 mL
1 tbsp	finely chopped fresh chives	15 mL
1 tbsp	finely chopped fresh parsley	15 mL
1	egg yolk	1
⅔ cup	crumbled fresh goat cheese (Chèvre des Neiges)	150 mL

1 *To prepare artichokes,* remove bottom leaves until you come to the cone of leaves folding inward like a rose bud. Cut off this cone close to the top of the artichoke. Immediately rub the cut area with lemon juice to prevent discolouring. Trim the tips of the leaves, removing all bits of green to show the white surface. (The artichoke will have the shape of a hockey puck.) Rub all cut areas with lemon juice again. Set artichokes in a large bowl of cold water. Add 1 tbsp (15 mL) lemon juice.

2 In a large saucepan whisk 2 tbsp (25 mL) cold water with flour to make a smooth paste, adding more water if necessary. Whisk in remaining water, 2 tbsp (25 mL) lemon juice and salt. Over high heat bring mixture to a boil. **3** Add artichokes. Add more water if necessary to completely cover artichokes. Over high heat bring mixture to a boil again; lower heat and simmer for 40 minutes or until artichokes are tender when pierced. **4** Let artichokes cool in their liquid; drain. Carefully scoop out the choke with a spoon. Discard choke, reserving artichoke bottoms. **5** *To make stuffing*, in a medium saucepan over medium heat, melt butter; sauté shallots until tender. Add sun-dried tomatoes; simmer until tender, about 3 minutes. Pour in wine. Increase heat and boil until wine is almost evaporated. **6** Stir in chives and parsley. Simmer for 1 minute. Let cool. **7** In a medium bowl beat egg yolk with goat cheese. Fold shallot and tomato mixture into cheese. **8** Put artichoke bottoms in a 9-inch square (2.5 L) baking dish. Fill each artichoke with goat cheese mixture. **9** Bake at 375°F (190°C) in upper third of oven until warmed through and cheese has browned lightly, about 10 to 15 minutes. Serve warm.

Chèvre des Neiges
(Snow Goat Cheese)

Made by Fromagerie Cayer

YORKSHIRE PUDDING WITH CANADIAN BLUE

SERVES FOUR L'Abbaye de Saint-Benoît-du-Lac — Saint-Benoît-du-Lac, Quebec

ESTABLISHED IN 1912, L'Abbaye de Saint-Benoît-du-Lac has produced Canada's famous Ermite blue cheese since 1943. The factory has been under the direction of Father Dominique Minier since 1964. Ermite is similar to gorgonzola cheese but is slightly drier in texture. Its interior is mottled with green veins, like gorgonzola, caused by a mould powder. Just before the ripening process, the cheese is punctured with wire pins to permit air flow; the mould grows inside these small tubes. In the first month of ripening, the surface is rubbed and scraped to keep it free of this mould. It is then left to ripen for two months to obtain flavour. This factory also makes two Gruyère-style cheeses, called Mont Saint-Benoît (aged for one month) and Le Moine (aged for two months).

This dish, created by chef Martin Boucher, is a perfect accompaniment to Veal Saddle Gratin with Asiago Cheese (recipe on page 158).

1 tbsp	butter	15 mL
1 tbsp	finely chopped shallots	15 mL
6	eggs	6
½ cup	milk	125 mL
½ cup	all-purpose flour	125 mL
3 oz	blue cheese (Ermite), crumbled	75 g
2 tbsp	diced sun-dried tomatoes (packed in oil)	25 mL
	Vegetable oil as needed	

1 In a small saucepan over medium heat, melt butter; sweat shallots for about 2 minutes. **2** In a large bowl beat together eggs, milk and flour. **3** Fold in shallots, cheese and tomatoes. Let rest for 5 minutes. **4** Pour 1 tbsp (15 mL) vegetable oil in each of 12 cups of a muffin tin. Heat tin in a 400°F (200°C) oven for 3 to 4 minutes or until oil is smoking. **5** Fill cups with batter about three-quarters full. Bake 10 minutes. Reduce heat to 350°F (180°C) and bake another 10 minutes or until golden. Serve warm.

Ermite

Made by L'Abbaye de Saint-Benoît-du-Lac

CURD SCONES

MAKES TWELVE Pine River Cheese & Butter Co-operative — Ripley, Ontario

ONE OF ONTARIO'S OLDEST cheese factories, founded in 1885, Pine River has been owned and operated by the dairy farmers of Huron Township for five generations. Cheddars are their specialty, although they do produce mozzarella, Colby, brick and farmer's cheese as well.

Unlike shredded Cheddar, curds do not melt into the dough, but remain whole, hot and stringy, adding a delectable texture to these scones.

2¼ cups	bleached all-purpose flour	550 mL
4 tsp	baking powder	20 mL
½ tsp	salt	2 mL
¼ cup	butter	50 mL
⅔ cup	vegetable shortening	150 mL
1 cup	cheese curds, cut into ½-inch (1 cm) pieces	250 mL
⅓ cup	sultana raisins	75 mL
1 cup	milk	250 mL

1 In a large bowl, mix together flour, baking powder and salt. Cut in butter and shortening until mixture is pebbly. Stir in curds and raisins. Gradually pour in milk, stirring with a fork to make a fairly wet dough. **2** On a lightly floured work surface, knead dough, turning about 10 times. Press into a square about 1 3/4 inches (4.5 cm) thick. Using a cookie cutter, cut into 12 scones. Transfer to well greased baking sheet, leaving about 1 inch (2.5 cm) between scones. **3** Bake at 450°F (230°C) for 12 to 15 minutes or until scones are golden. Serve immediately.

Cheese Curds

Made by Pine River Cheese & Butter Co-op

SAINT PAULIN CORN BREAD

SERVES FOUR   Shari Darling — Toronto, Ontario

A SEMI-SOFT CHEESE made from pasteurized cow's milk, Saint Paulin is a pressed, uncooked cheese that is white or pale yellow with a creamy texture and mild, buttery flavour.

1 tbsp	vegetable oil	15 mL
½ cup	finely chopped onion	125 mL
¾ cup	fresh corn kernels	175 mL
¾ cup	yellow cornmeal	175 mL
¾ cup	cottage cheese	175 mL
⅓ lb	Saint Paulin cheese, shredded	175 g
½ cup	buttermilk	125 mL
½ tsp	salt	2 mL
3	eggs, separated	3

1 In a skillet over medium heat, heat oil; sauté onion until soft. **2** In a food processor or blender purée corn kernels. Transfer corn to a large bowl. Add onion, cornmeal, cottage cheese, Saint Paulin cheese, buttermilk and salt. Mix well. **3** Beat egg yolks until thick. In another bowl beat egg whites until soft peaks form. Fold yolks carefully into whites. Add one-third of egg mixture to batter, combining well. Fold in remaining eggs. **4** Butter an 8- by 4-inch (1.5 L) loaf pan. Pour in batter. Bake at 400°F (200°C) for 30 minutes or until bread is brown. Serve warm and buttered.

Saint Paulin

Made by Fromagerie Fritz Kaiser

PEPPERS STUFFED WITH OLD BRA CHEESE AND ITALIAN SAUSAGE

SERVES SIX   Shari Darling — Toronto, Ontario

6	large sweet green peppers	6
2 tbsp	olive oil	25 mL
1	clove garlic, minced	1
2 cups	finely chopped onions	500 mL
1 lb	Italian sausage, removed from casings	500 g
1 lb	button mushrooms, chopped	500 g
2 cups	fresh bread crumbs	500 mL
2	eggs, beaten	2
	Salt and pepper to taste	
¾ cup	tomato sauce	175 mL
1 cup	grated Old Bra (or Romano) cheese	250 mL

1 Cut peppers in half lengthwise; discard seeds and veins. **2** In a large skillet over medium heat, heat oil; sauté garlic and onions until tender. Add sausage meat and mushrooms; cook 3 to 5 minutes or until mushrooms are soft. Remove from heat. **3** Mix in bread crumbs, eggs, salt and pepper; combine well. **4** Divide stuffing into 12 equal portions and stuff pepper halves. **5** Arrange peppers on a well-greased baking sheet. Spoon 1 tbsp (15 mL) tomato sauce over each pepper; sprinkle generously with Old Bra cheese. **6** Bake at 425°F (220°C) for 40 to 45 minutes or until peppers are tender.

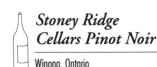

Stoney Ridge Cellars Pinot Noir

Winona, Ontario

A light-bodied Pinot Noir with sour cherry character and good acidity, this wine is delicate enough for the peppers, but still works well with Italian sausage and Old Bra.

Other Choices:
B.C. Gamay Noir or Pinot Noir

Old Bra

Made by Oak Grove Cheese Factory

POTATO AND HAVARTI PUDDING

SERVES FOUR   Gay Lea Foods — Baden, Ontario

GAY LEA HAS BEEN MAKING cheese since 1982 at their Baden plant. With English-born cheese-maker John Forster in charge of production, the company makes a wide variety of cheeses under the Oxford Farms label, including Gouda, Edam, mozzarella and Havarti. This side dish is part of chef Harald Bonkowski's award-winning recipe Bison or Beef Variety on a Roasted Garlic and Brie Sauce (recipe on page 180).

½ cup	peeled, diced potatoes	125 mL
3 oz	Havarti cheese, diced	75 g
⅓ cup	half-and-half cream	75 mL
2	eggs	2
Pinch	nutmeg	Pinch
	Salt and pepper to taste	

1 In a pot of boiling salted water cook potatoes for 5 to 6 minutes or until al dente. Drain and cool. Place in four greased 2-inch (5 cm) high custard cups. Top with Havarti cheese. **2** Whisk cream with eggs; season with nutmeg, salt and pepper. Divide equally among moulds. **3** Set moulds in a pan of hot water. Bake at 350°F (180°C) for 30 minutes or until a knife inserted in centre comes out clean. **4** Using a small sharp knife, loosen puddings from sides of moulds. Leave moulds in pan of water until serving time. **5** Just before serving, unmould puddings onto four plates.

Oxford Farms Havarti

Made by Gay Lea

SAUTÉED CABBAGE AND FETA CHEESE

SERVES SIX — Shari Darling — Toronto, Ontario

CURED AND PACKED in its own salty whey, feta is often called a pickled cheese. Canadian feta is made in one of three ways: from pasteurized cow's milk or from pasteurized or unpasteurized goat's milk. Feta made from pasteurized cow's milk is usually white and soft with a mild tangy flavour. That made from goat's milk has an intense piquant taste, especially if aged. This recipe can be served as a side dish or as a light meal.

1		head green cabbage (2 lb/1 kg), cored and thinly sliced	1
3 tbsp		butter	50 mL
1/4 cup		sour cream	50 mL
2		large eggs	2
1/4 cup		finely chopped fresh parsley	50 mL
		Salt and pepper to taste	
1 1/4 cup		crumbled feta cheese	300 mL
1/2 cup		dried bread crumbs	125 mL

1 In a large pot of boiling salted water, blanch cabbage for 2 minutes. Drain and dry. **2** In a large skillet over medium heat, melt butter; sauté cabbage, stirring constantly, for 15 to 20 minutes, until golden. **3** In a large bowl mix together sour cream, eggs and parsley. Fold in cabbage. Season with salt and pepper. Turn mixture into a 9-inch (2.5 L) baking dish. **4** In the rinsed bowl mix together feta cheese and bread crumbs. Sprinkle mixture over cabbage. **5** Bake at 350°F (180°C) for 15 minutes or until eggs are set.

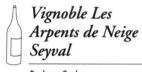

Vignoble Les Arpents de Neige Seyval

Dunham, Quebec

Trained in Alsace, winemaker Alain Belanger produces approximately 2,000 cases of wine each year. This Seyval is light and dry with vegetative qualities that complement cabbage and tangy feta.

Other Choices:
Ontario Sauvignon or B.C. Müller-Thurgau

Capriati Feta

Made by Fromagerie Tournevent

SPRING VEGETABLE AND HAVARTI TUREEN

SERVES SIX   Amalgamated Dairies Ltd. — Summerside, P.E.I.

IN 1953 SIX COMPANIES — Tyne Valley, Grand River, Abrams Village, Tryon, Dunk River and Kensington — joined forces to form Amalgamated Dairies Ltd. Since this time Amalgamated Dairies has expanded in size and in its product line. The five plants make butter, ice cream, condensed milk, fluid milk and cheeses such as brick, Colby, mozzarella, feta and Havarti.

1 lb	broccoli	500 g
4 cups	water	1 L
½ tsp	salt	2 mL
1 lb	carrots, julienned	500 g
6	eggs	6
⅔ cup	half-and-half cream	150 mL
⅓ lb	Havarti cheese, shredded	175 g
2 tsp	grated onion	10 mL
	Salt and pepper to taste	

1 Break broccoli into small florets. In a pot of boiling salted water, cook broccoli until tender, about 3 minutes; remove with a slotted spoon and set aside. **2** Cook carrots in same water until tender, about 8 minutes; drain and set aside. **3** In a bowl beat eggs with cream. Stir in Havarti cheese and onion. Season with salt and pepper. **4** Lay half the broccoli in a buttered 8-inch (2 L) square baking dish with heads all pointing the same way. Pour one-third of egg mixture over broccoli. Lay carrots in an even layer on top. Briefly beat egg mixture again; pour another one-third of egg mixture over carrots. Top with remaining broccoli with heads pointing in opposite direction. Briefly beat egg mixture again; pour over broccoli. **5** Cover with foil and bake at 350°F (180°C) for 1 hour or until eggs are set.

L'Ambiance

Available in P.E.I. (Liquor Control Commission)

A blend of Seyval and Vidal grapes, pale straw in colour, this white is clean, crisp and easy drinking, with a pear-like nose and delicate fruit palate. Does not overpower vegetables or the mild flavour of Havarti in this casserole.

Other Choices:
Ontario Chardonnay

A.D.L. brand Havarti

Made by Amalgamated Dairies

CAPPELLETTI WITH GOAT CHEESE AND SUN-DRIED TOMATOES

SERVES FOUR   Tony Loschiavo — Toronto, Ontario

Hillside Cellars
Gamay Beaujolais

Penticton, British Columbia

From grapes grown on the 5.6-acre vineyard, winemaker Vera Klockocka makes a few wines, including Johannisberg Riesling, Muscat and Gamay Beaujolais. Made from 100 percent Gamay Noir grapes, the Gamay Beaujolais is a simple red with a light ruby colour, strawberry aromas and flavours and a hint of spice on the finish. Always a perfect partner for goat cheese.

Other Choices:
Ontario Pinot Noir

Chevrai

Made by Woolwich Dairy
Parmesan

Made by National Cheese

½ lb	cappelletti	250 g
2 tbsp	extra virgin olive oil	25 mL
1	clove garlic, minced	1
1 cup	sun-dried tomatoes (packed in oil), thinly sliced	250 mL
Pinch	salt	Pinch
½ tsp	pepper	2 mL
2 cups	chicken stock	500 mL
	Juice of 1 lemon	
1 cup	grated Parmesan cheese	250 mL
½ lb	fresh goat cheese	250 g
4	sprigs fresh rosemary (for garnish)	4

1 In a large pot of boiling salted water, cook cappelletti until al dente; drain and keep warm. **2** In a large saucepan over medium heat, heat olive oil; sauté garlic until golden. Add sun-dried tomatoes, salt and pepper. Cook 1 minute. **3** Add chicken stock. Increase heat to high and bring stock to a boil. Add lemon juice, stirring well. **4** Gently stir in cappelletti and parmesan cheese. **5** Spoon mixture into serving bowls. Top each serving with a generous dollop of goat cheese. Garnish with a rosemary sprig. Serve hot.

VEAL AND PRAWN PAUPIETTES WITH OKA SAUCE AND RICOTTA AND PECAN RAVIOLI

SERVES FOUR   Chef Harald Bonkowski — Vancouver, British Columbia

HARALD BONKOWSKI has held the prestigious position of souschef at the Four Seasons Hotel and the Avantis Restaurant in Vancouver and the Creek House Restaurant in Whistler. He is now a chef instructor at Vancouver Community College. Gold, silver and bronze medals from such competitions as the Vancouver Culinary Show, the Annual Foodservice Awards and Le Grand Salon Culinaire in Montreal are proof that Harald is a culinary master. A version of this dish was the overall Grand Prize Winner in the 1992 Annual Foodservice Awards held in Jasper.

Mission Hill Vineyards Grand Reserve Barrel Select Chardonnay

Westbank, British Columbia

This is a heavy-textured dish with competing flavours and a predominant Oka sauce, thus deserving a flavourful white with good weight. Mission Hill's Barrel Select Chardonnay is most suitable, as it has spicy oak character with a buttery texture that complements the creamy texture, weight and flavour of the Oka sauce.

Other Choices:

Ontario barrel-fermented and/or -aged Chardonnay

4	lean veal loins (3 oz/75 g each)	4

Prawn Mousseline:

½ lb	prawns, deveined, peeled and shells reserved	250 g
1	egg white	1
½ cup	whipping cream	125 mL
1 tsp	lemon juice	5 mL
	Salt and pepper to taste	
2 tbsp	finely chopped spinach, blanched	25 mL
⅓ cup	diced prawns	75 mL

Oka Sauce:

2 tsp	butter	10 mL
2 tbsp	finely chopped onion	25 mL
1 oz	prawn shells	25 g
3 tbsp	Mission Hill Grand Reserve Barrel-Select Chardonnay (white wine)	50 mL
⅓ cup	whipping cream	75 mL
¼ cup	veal OR chicken stock	50 mL
3 oz	Oka cheese, diced	75 g
	Salt and pepper to taste	

Ravioli Filling:

⅓ cup	ricotta cheese, drained	75 mL
½ tsp	lemon juice	2 mL
	Salt and pepper to taste	

Pecan and Ricotta Ravioli:

½ cup	semolina flour	125 mL
½ cup	all-purpose flour	125 mL
4 tsp	finely chopped roasted pecans	20 mL
1 tsp	water	5 mL
¼ tsp	vegetable oil	1 mL
1	egg, beaten	1
	Eggwash (1 egg beaten with 1 tsp/5 mL water)	
1 tsp	vegetable oil	5 mL

1 Place veal loins between two sheets of plastic wrap; pound with mallet until paper-thin. Set aside. **2** *To make prawn mousse-line*, in a food processor or blender blend prawns and egg white, slowly adding cream and lemon juice. Season with salt and pepper. **3** Pour mixture into a bowl; fold in spinach and diced prawns. **4** *To make paupiettes*, place one-quarter of prawn mousseline along one edge of each loin. Roll up loin in jelly-roll fashion. Wrap each paupiette in plastic wrap, then in aluminum foil. **5** In a large pot of boiling water, poach paupiettes 8 minutes for rare, 15 minutes for well done. Drain. Remove wrapping and dry loins on paper towel. Cut into 4 slices; keep warm. **6** *To make Oka sauce*, in a medium saucepan over medium heat melt butter; sweat onions for 2 minutes. Add prawn shells; sauté until shells turn red. Pour in wine. **7** Increase heat to high and boil liquid until reduced by half. Reduce heat. Stir in cream; simmer for 5 minutes. Stir in stock; simmer for 5 minutes. **8** Strain sauce through a fine sieve; discard shells. Return sauce to saucepan; over low heat. **9** Add Oka cheese, stirring constantly until cheese is melted and well blended. Season with salt and pepper; keep warm. **10** *To make ravioli filling*, combine ricotta cheese, lemon juice, salt and pepper; set aside. **11** *To make ravioli*, in a large bowl combine both flours, pecans, water, oil. Mix until dough is stiff. Add more flour if needed. Refrigerate for 30 minutes. **12** On a lightly floured work surface, roll out dough to paper-thin, less than 1/8 inch (3 mm) thick. Using a 4-inch (10 cm) cookie cutter, cut out 16 rounds. **13** Spoon 1/2 tsp (2 mL) ricotta filling onto 8 rounds. Brush edges of each round with eggwash; place another round on top, pressing edges gently together to seal. **14** Bring a large pot of salted water to a boil. Add 1 tsp (5 mL) oil. Cook ravioli until al dente, about 4 minutes. Drain. **15** Spoon a pool of Oka sauce on each plate. Arrange veal and prawn paupiettes and ravioli on sauce.

Oka

Made by Agropur

Ricotta

Made by Saputo Cheeses

RICOTTA GNOCCHI WITH PARMESAN

SERVES FOUR   Saputo Cheeses Limited — Montreal, Quebec

WHEN WE THINK OF SAPUTO CHEESE today, we think gigantic — a national corporation based in Montreal, operating eight plants, employing 700 people and distributing more than 30 Italian-style cheeses nationally. It wasn't always this way. In 1954 Sicilian cheesemaker Giuseppe Saputo and his wife, Maria, started a small cheese factory to produce ricotta and mozzarella for Montreal's Italian community. When Canadians developed an insatiable appetite for pizza in the 1960s, Giuseppe's truck engines were revved up and ready. Within a few years pizzerias and restaurants across the country were smothering their pizzas with Saputo's mozzarella. The company's aggressive expansion has not deterred quality. Every year Saputo's ricotta and mozzarella win at least one medal, usually first or second place in Quebec's famed Le Concours Lys d'Or (the Golden Lily Competition).

Château des Charmes Paul Bosc Estate Cabernet Sauvignon

Niagara-on-the-Lake, Ontario
Available in Quebec (La Maison des Vins)
Available in Ottawa (Château des Charmes Wine Boutique, Minto Place, Laurier Ave., 613-782-2410).

Aged in Nevers oak, this full-bodied red has tobacco, green peppers and berry fruit in the bouquet with a palate of tobacco, blackberries and a touch of chocolate. Has enough complexity to marry to the heavy texture of the gnocchi and the piquant taste of Parmesan.

Other Choices:
B.C. Cabernet Sauvignon
(International Blend)

3 large	eggs	3
2 cups	ricotta cheese	500 mL
1½ cups	semolina flour	375 mL
Pinch	salt	Pinch
¼ cup	butter, melted	50 mL
2 cups	grated Parmesan cheese	500 mL

1 In a large bowl beat eggs. Blend in ricotta cheese, flour and salt. Chill for 30 minutes. **2** On a lightly floured work surface, roll out one-third of dough into a long roll about 1 inch (2.5 cm) thick. With a sharp knife, cut into 1-inch (2.5 cm) pieces. Repeat with remaining dough. **3** In a large pot of boiling salted water cook gnocchi until al dente, about 3 minutes. Drain. **4** In a warm serving bowl, toss gnocchi with melted butter. Sprinkle with Parmesan. Serve immediately.

Ricotta and Parmesan

Made by Saputo Cheeses

CANADIAN WILD RICE MAMIROLLE

SERVES FOUR | Fromagerie de Plaisance Inc. — Plaisance, Quebec

FROMAGERIE DE PLAISANCE produces Cheddar, Colby, Monterey Jack, farmer's and brick. Recently, the company acquired the only North American licence to use the trade name Le Mamirolle for their Oka-style cheese. Originating in France, traditional Mamirolle is a Limburger-like cheese, developed at the French dairy school at Mamirolle. Our Canadian version, made by Fromagerie de Plaisance, has a light, fruity taste when young and a more buttery, nutty flavour when aged, much like Oka. Store Mamirolle in its original aluminum wrapper, which allows the cheese to breathe. Plastic wrap will age the cheese too quickly and make it sticky and smelly.

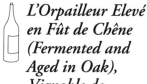

L'Orpailleur Elevé en Fût de Chêne (Fermented and Aged in Oak), Vignoble de L'Orpailleur

Dunham, Quebec

Using 100 percent Quebec grapes, Vignoble de L'Orpailleur produces more than 6,500 cases of wine each year and offers tours, tastings and dining. Produced from 100 percent Seyval and fermented and aged in oak, this dry white has a vanilla bouquet with lean fruit overlaid by vanilla and spice, making it an ideal match in weight to the cheese sauce.

Other Choices:
Ontario or B.C. barrel-fermented and/or -aged Chardonnay

Le Mamirolle (Oka-style)

Made by Fromagerie de Plaisance

1 cup	wild rice	250 mL
3 cups	vegetable stock	750 mL
Pinch	each salt and pepper	Pinch
¼ cup	butter	50 mL
2	shallots, finely chopped	2
1 cup	sliced button mushrooms	250 mL
1 cup	shredded carrots	250 mL
½ cup	half-and-half cream	125 mL
1	egg, lightly beaten	1
2 tbsp	brandy	25 mL
¼ cup	finely chopped fresh parsley	50 mL
1 tsp	finely chopped fresh thyme	5 mL
¾ lb	Oka-style cheese (Mamirolle), shredded	375 g

1 Wash rice under cold water. Drain. **2** In a large skillet over high heat, bring vegetable stock to a boil. Lower heat to medium and stir in rice; simmer 15 minutes. Add remaining ingredients except Mamirolle; cook another 15 minutes, stirring occasionally, until all liquid is absorbed. **3** Fold Mamirolle into hot rice. Serve immediately.

LINGUINE IN A CREAMY QUARK AND CLAM SAUCE

SERVES FOUR Neapolis Dairy Products Ltd. — Didsbury, Alberta

NEAPOLIS DAIRY'S AWARD-WINNING Rocky Mountain line consists of creamy, buttery Brie and Camembert, zesty Limburger and a fresh, salt-free Quark. Their Jersey Supreme Cheddars are made from none other than Jersey milk, which is higher in butterfat and protein than Holstein milk, giving the Cheddars a creamy consistency. The Jersey milk comes from specific farms in and around Didsbury. Neapolis Dairy also makes Parisee Cream Cheese with no additives or preservatives. They are the only commercial manufacturer of Camembert and Brie in western Canada.

Gray Monk Cellars Pinot Blanc

Okanagan Centre, British Columbia
Available in Alberta (Vintage
Consultants Ltd., 403-244-0324)

Displaying fresh apple character on the nose and palate with medium body, this white is heavy enough for pasta while not overpowering the clams. A hint of sweetness offsets the tangy flavour of the Quark sauce.

Other Choices:
Ontario Chardonnay

Rocky Mountain Quark

Made by Neapolis Dairy Products
Parmesan

Made by National Cheese

42	clams	42
1	medium onion, finely chopped	1
2	cloves garlic, minced	2
1/4 tsp	finely chopped fresh thyme	1 mL
2½ cups	zucchini, cubed	625 mL
1	large sweet red pepper, diced	1
1/4 lb	Quark cheese	125 g
Pinch	each salt and freshly ground pepper	Pinch
3/4 lb	linguine	375 g
1/4 cup	freshly grated Parmesan cheese	50 mL
2 tbsp	finely chopped fresh parsley	25 mL

1 Shuck clams. Corsely chop clams, reserving liquor. **2** In large saucepan over medium heat cook onion, garlic and thyme in 1/3 cup (75 mL) clam liquor, stirring occasionally, for about 5 minutes or until onions are translucent. (If you do not have enough liquor, add bottled clam juice.) **3** Add zucchini and red pepper; cook for 3 minutes or until pepper is tender. **4** Add remaining clam liquor; increase heat to medium-high and bring to a simmer. **5** Stir in Quark cheese; cook, stirring, until slightly thickened. Add reserved clams, salt and pepper. Stir until clams are heated through. **6** Meanwhile, in a large pot of boiling salted water, cook linguine until al dente, about 8 minutes. Drain well. **7** Toss with clam sauce, Parmesan cheese and parsley. Serve immediately.

FARFALLE WITH PORCINI, HICKORY-SMOKED BACON AND PARMESAN CHEESE

SERVES FOUR   Schwab's Meat Producers Ltd. — Windsor, Ontario

WITH 10 LOCATIONS in Essex and Kent counties in southwestern Ontario, Schwab's produces 81 meat products, all free of chemicals, cereal fillers, milk powders and MSG. The sausages, hams and bacons are all cured with natural hickory smoke, a time-honoured method that has pleased Essex and Kent's European communities for more than 38 years. Though meat is their forte, Schwab's offers more than 30 varieties of imported and domestic cheeses, including six Canadian Cheddars.

Magnotta Wines Cabernet Sauvignon Special Reserve

The 1990 version won several awards, including a silver in the 1993 VinItaly Competition. Full-bodied and loaded with black cherry character and austere tannins, this Cabernet Sauvignon has enough character to stand up to the piquant taste of the Parmesan and smoky flavour that dominates the sauce.

Other Choices:
B.C. Cabernet Sauvignon (International Blend)

Black Parmesan
Made by Paron Dairy

1/2 oz	dried porcini mushrooms	15 g
1/2 cup	Magnotta Wines Cabernet Sauvignon Special Reserve (red wine)	125 mL
1/4 cup	extra virgin olive oil	50 mL
2	cloves garlic, minced	2
2	shallots, thinly sliced	2
2 tbsp	finely chopped fresh basil	25 mL
3/4 cup	finely chopped Schwab's Heavy Smoke Bacon	175 mL
1 cup	chicken stock	250 mL
3/4 lb	farfalle (bow-tie pasta)	375 g
	Salt and pepper to taste	
1/2 cup	grated Parmesan cheese	125 mL

1 Soak porcini mushrooms in white wine for 45 minutes. Drain, reserving liquid. **2** In a medium saucepan over medium heat, heat oil; sauté porcini mushrooms, garlic, shallots, basil and bacon until shallots are soft. Add reserved wine. Reduce heat to low; simmer for 5 minutes or until wine is syrupy. **3** Add chicken stock; simmer for 20 minutes. **4** Meanwhile, in a pot of boiling salted water cook pasta until al dente. Drain. **5** Toss pasta with sauce. Season with salt and pepper. Divide between four plates and sprinkle with Parmesan cheese.

MANICOTTI STUFFED WITH VEAL, RICOTTA AND SMOKED MOZZARELLA

SERVES FOUR   World of Cheese Ltd. — Toronto, Ontario

WORLD OF CHEESE has been catering to Toronto's Greek and Italian communities for more than 15 years. Nestled among the homemade sausages and cured meats is a fantastic assortment of imported and Canadian cheeses, many of them local. The Di Somma family offers four domestic ricottas. One of these is Silani's Ricotta, made from the whey of mozzarella, whole milk and cream, creating a cheese that is ideal for cooking. Customers seem to prefer Ferrante's light, unsalted Ricotta (6 to 10% fat) as a spread and an accompaniment to fresh fruit.

Inniskillin Wines Maréchal Foch

Niagara-on-the-Lake, Ontario

Inniskillin's president, Donald Ziraldo, is the leading force behind the creation and implementation of the VQA in Ontario, a move that has helped put Canada on the wine world map. Donald's partner, Karl Kaiser, is winemaker. He produces a wide range of varietal wines, one being Maréchal Foch. Exhibiting berry aromas with smoky, berry flavours, this red complements the smoky mozzarella taste, while offering enough body to compete with the heavy pasta. Offers enough tannin to balance the tomato sauce as well.

Other Choices:
B.C. Chancellor

Tomato Sauce: (Makes approx 4 cups/1 L)

5 lb	ripe plum tomatoes, skinned and seeded	2.2 kg
1	can (6 oz/170 g) tomato paste	1
2 tbsp	finely chopped fresh basil	25 mL
2 tbsp	finely chopped fresh oregano	25 mL
2	cloves garlic, minced	2
4 cups	water	1 L
	Salt and freshly ground black pepper to taste	
1/2 cup	finely chopped fresh parsley	125 mL

Manicotti:

14	manicotti shells	14
2 tbsp	extra virgin olive oil	25 mL
1	clove garlic, minced	1
1 cup	sliced mushrooms	250 mL
2	shallots, finely chopped	2
1 cup	Inniskillin Wines Maréchal Foch (red wine)	250 mL
1 1/2 lb	ground veal	750 mg
1 cup	ricotta cheese	250 mL
1/4 lb	smoked mozzarella cheese, shredded	125 g
	Salt and pepper to taste	
1 cup	freshly grated Parmesan cheese	250 mL

1 To make tomato sauce, in a large saucepan over medium heat combine tomatoes, tomato paste, basil, oregano and garlic. Simmer for 10 to 12 minutes or until tomatoes are tender. **2** Add water. Season with salt and pepper. Reduce heat to low and simmer, uncovered for 3 hours. Stir in parsley and simmer another 4 minutes. **3** In a large pot of boiling salted water, cook manicotti until al dente, about 6 to 8 minutes. Drain. Lay manicotti side by side so they do not stick together. **4** In a large saucepan over medium heat, heat oil; sauté garlic, mushrooms and shallots until tender, about 5 minutes. Add wine. Bring to a boil and reduce wine by half. Stir in veal. Simmer for 10 minutes or until veal is cooked through. **5** In a large bowl combine ricotta with smoked mozzarella. Add cooked veal mixture and mix well. Season with salt and pepper. **6** Stuff manicotti shells with mixture; arrange side by side in a 13- by 9-inch (3.5 L) baking dish. **7** Pour tomato sauce over manicotti, spreading well. Sprinkle with Parmesan cheese. **8** Bake at 350°F (180°C) for 30 minutes or until sauce is bubbling and Parmesan is golden. Serve hot.

Ricotta

Made by Silani Sweet Cheese

Smoked Mozzarella

Made by Mannina Cheese

Tre Stelle Parmesan

Made by National Cheese

VERMICELLI WITH ANCHOVIES, BLACK OLIVES AND ROMANO CHEESE

SERVES FOUR   Shari Darling — Toronto, Ontario

8	anchovy fillets in oil, drained	8
¼ cup	milk	50 mL
⅓ cup	extra virgin olive oil	75 mL
1	clove garlic, minced	1
1 lb	tomatoes, peeled and chopped	500 g
1 tbsp	tomato paste	15 mL
2 tbsp	capers	25 mL
¾ lb	vermicelli noodles	375 g
1 cup	pitted black olives	250 mL
	Salt and pepper to taste	
½ cup	grated Romano cheese	125 mL

Gray Monk Cellars Gewürztraminer (Broderson Vineyard)

Okanagan Centre, British Columbia

Being full-bodied, this white can stand up to this oil and garlic pasta. Displaying grapefruit-like character on the nose and mouth with good acidity, the wine can compete with the saltiness of anchovies and Romano.

Other Choices:
Ontario dry Gewürztraminer

GRAY·MONK

Romano

Made by Saputo Cheeses

1 In a small bowl combine anchovies and milk. Soak for 10 minutes. **2** In a saucepan over medium heat, heat olive oil; sauté garlic for 2 minutes. **3** Drain anchovies and discard milk. Finely chop anchovies and add to garlic. Sauté for 3 minutes. **4** Stir in tomatoes, tomato paste and capers. Bring to a boil and simmer, covered, for 15 minutes. **5** Meanwhile, in a large pot of boiling salted water, cook vermicelli noodles until al dente. Drain. **6** Toss noodles with tomato sauce and black olives until noodles are well coated. Season with salt and pepper. Spoon onto serving plates and sprinkle with Romano cheese.

PENNE CHEDDAR CASSEROLE

SERVES FOUR   Balderson Cheese Company — Balderson, Ontario

THE ENGLISH VILLAGE OF CHEDDAR may be known as the hometown of the world's favourite cheese, but the village of Balderson is famous for being the hometown of a world-class Cheddar. Balderson Cheese, established in 1881 by a group of local dairy producers, has won many international awards for their Cheddar, including the Grand Championship at the 1986 World's Natural Cheese Making Competition in Wisconsin. They offer six Cheddars, all of which are additive free and aged for various lengths of time. The oldest, called Heritage Cheddar, is aged from three to five years. This extensive curing allows the cheese to be smooth in texture and crumbly while concentrating its salts and acids to give it the characteristic Balderson bite. The factory itself has become a tourist destination because of the on-site gourmet shop featuring a wine cellar, art gallery and mini-museum. The shop highlights Balderson cheese, but offers as well a wide selection of imported cheeses, honey, maple syrup, jams and preserves, teas, chocolates, gifts and cookbooks.

Jackson-Triggs Cabernet Sauvignon (International Blend), Cartier Wines

Niagara Falls, Ontario

Combining Cabernet from Chile and Ontario, this red blend has ripe plums on the nose and mouth, hints of pepper on the finish and enough weight to stand up to the Cheddar sauce.

Other Choices:
B.C. Cabernet Sauvignon (International Blend)

JACKSON-TRIGGS

Heritage Cheddar

Made by Balderson Cheese

3 tbsp	butter	50 mL
3 tbsp	all-purpose flour	50 mL
1 1/2 cups	hot milk	375 mL
1 tsp	salt	5 mL
1/2 tsp	dry mustard	2 mL
Dash	hot pepper sauce	Dash
1/2 lb	penne	250 g
3/4 lb	extra-old Cheddar cheese, shredded	375 g
1/2 cup	buttered bread crumbs	125 mL

1 To make sauce, in a medium saucepan over medium heat, melt butter. Simmer for 1 minute. Stir in flour; cook for 3 minutes, stirring constantly. Stir in hot milk, stirring constantly until sauce has thickened. **2** Reduce heat to low. Stir in salt, mustard and hot pepper sauce; simmer for 10 minutes. **3** Meanwhile, in a large pot of boiling salted water, cook penne until al dente. Drain. **4** Butter an 8-inch (2 L) square baking dish. Arrange half the penne, half the sauce and half the cheese in baking dish. Make another layer with remaining ingredients. Top with bread crumbs. **5** Bake at 350°F (180°C) for 25 minutes or until crumbs are golden. Serve hot.

CAPPELLETTI WITH MASCARPONE AND SWEET ITALIAN SAUSAGE

SERVES FOUR   National Cheese Company Ltd. — Concord, Ontario

NATIONAL CHEESE COMPANY LTD. was founded in 1960, selling their products under the Tre Stelle brand name. At that time the plant was a mere 3,500 square feet, with sales in the first week reaching a total of $5. This was far from a setback for these determined partners, who knew that Ontario's Italian immigrants were in search of the quality cheeses they were accustomed to "back home." For the first few years National's mozzarella, provolone and ricotta were sold through Italian grocery stores. In less than four years they had opened a branch office in Montreal; by 1977, another in Vancouver. At a mere eight years old, National had outgrown its site and needed a larger production facility. A 25,000-square-foot plant was built in Concord; it has now been expanded to five times that size.

Vineland Estates St. Urban Premium Dry Riesling

Vineland, Ontario

Though the sweet sausage and spinach offer some flavour, this dish is dominated by its rich mascarpone cheese sauce. Vineland's Premium dry Riesling is a good choice, as it equals the sauce in weight but offers grapefruit aromas and flavours and a good acidic spine that offsets the rich creamy taste.

Other Choices:
Ontario dry Gewürztraminer

Mascarpone and Parmesan

Made by National Cheese

½ lb	sweet Italian sausage, coarsely chopped	250 g
2	cloves garlic, chopped	2
2 tbsp	finely chopped fresh parsley	25 mL
1	small green onion, sliced	1
¼ cup	Vineland Estates St. Urban Premium dry Riesling (white wine)	50 mL
¼ cup	beef stock	50 mL
½ lb	fresh spinach, chopped	250 g
	Salt and pepper to taste	
1½ lb	cappelletti	750 g
¾ lb	mascarpone cheese	375 mL
⅔ cup	grated Parmesan cheese	150 mL

1 In a large skillet over medium heat, fry sausage until cooked through, about 15 minutes. Drain fat from skillet. Add garlic, parsley and green onion; sauté until garlic is tender, about 3 minutes. Add wine, beef stock, spinach, salt and pepper. **2** Cover skillet, reduce heat to low, and simmer until spinach is wilted, about 10 minutes. **3** Meanwhile, in a large pot of boiling salted water, cook cappelletti until al dente. Drain. **4** Toss pasta with sauce and mascarpone. Spoon onto serving plates and sprinkle with Parmesan cheese.

TWO-CHILI AND THREE-CHEESE RISOTTO

SERVES FOUR	Bright Cheese & Butter Manufacturing Co. Ltd. — Bright, Ontario

BRIGHT IS ONE OF THE OLDEST dairies in Ontario, founded in 1874 by a group of local farmers who decided to pool their surplus milk. Now using almost 2 million gallons of milk each year, Bright makes Monterey Jack, Colby, brick, marble, mozzarella and a variety of Cheddars. The medium, old and extra-old Cheddars are heat-treated instead of being made from pasteurized milk. The difference? To pasteurize, a temperature of 161°F must be reached and maintained for 16 seconds to destroy all bacteria, says cheesemaker Alan Smith. With heat treatment, the temperature reaches only 150°F for 16 seconds. This lower temperature kills bacteria while preserving enzymes that are important to the development of flavour. The Cheddars are then aged for at least 60 days to ensure that a natural pasteurization occurs. The extra-old Cheddar is aged up to four years.

Henry of Pelham Merlot

St. Catharines, Ontario

Ruby in colour with a blackberry bouquet and palate coupled with medium body and a spicy oak finish, this red equals the weight of this dish provided by the three cheese varieties and chili.

Other Choices:
B.C. Chancellor

Bright brand Monterey Jack, Bright brand Old Cheddar and Bright brand Mozzarella

Made by Bright Cheese & Butter Manufacturing

¼ cup	butter	50 mL
1	onion, finely chopped	1
1 cup	arborio rice	250 mL
2 cups	vegetable stock	500 mL
1 cup	Henry of Pelham Merlot (red wine)	250 mL
1	medium jalapeño pepper, seeded and chopped	1
1	small red chili, seeded and chopped	1
1	sweet red pepper, diced	1
1	sweet yellow pepper, diced	1
¼ cup	pitted black olives	50 mL
1	stalk celery, diced	1
½ cup	shredded Monterey Jack cheese	125 mL
½ cup	shredded extra-old Cheddar cheese	125 mL
½ cup	shredded mozzarella cheese	125 mL
1½ cups	sour cream	375 mL
	Salt and pepper to taste	

1 In a large oven-safe skillet over medium heat, melt butter; sauté onion until tender. Add rice, stirring until rice is glossy. Add stock, wine, jalapeño pepper, red chili, red pepper and yellow pepper. Bring mixture to a boil. **2** Cover skillet and bake at 350°F (180°C) for 20 minutes or until rice has absorbed all liquid. **3** Fold in olives, celery, Monterey Jack, Cheddar, mozzarella, sour cream, salt and pepper. **4** Butter a 9-inch (2.5 L) square baking dish. Turn rice mixture into dish. Bake at 400°F (200°C) for 20 minutes or until golden.

GOOD OL' LASAGNA

SERVES FOUR   Lactantia de Victoriaville — Victoriaville, Quebec

A DIVISION OF AULT FOODS, Lactantia dairy products (especially the butter) are well known throughout Quebec and Ontario. Until 1993, mozzarella was the only cheese produced at the Victoriaville plant. The company now offers a line of white Cheddars and brick.

½ lb	lasagna noodles	250 g

Meat Sauce:

⅔ lb	ground beef	350 g
2 tbsp	butter	25 mL
1	clove garlic, minced	1
2	medium tomatoes, peeled and diced	2
1	medium onion, diced	1
¼ cup	finely chopped mushrooms	50 mL
1 tbsp	tomato paste	15 mL
	Salt and pepper to taste	
1¼ cup	beef stock	300 mL
1¼ cup	Château des Charmes Cabernet Sauvignon (red wine)	300 mL

Cheese Sauce:

¼ cup	butter	50 mL
1 tbsp	all-purpose flour	15 mL
1⅔ cups	hot milk	400 mL
1 cup	shredded mozzarella cheese	250 mL
1 cup	grated Parmesan cheese	250 mL

Château des Charmes Paul Bosc Estate Cabernet Sauvignon

Niagara-on-the-Lake, Ontario
Available in Quebec (La Maison des Vins)
Available in Ottawa (Château des Charmes Wine Boutique, Minto Place, Laurier Ave., 613-783-2410)

Winemaker Paul Bosc Sr. changed the direction of Ontario's wine industry by being the first to plant his entire vineyard to European Vinifera grapes. Cabernet Sauvignon was one of the varieties planted. This red is well balanced, with a deep purple shade and aromas of tobacco, green peppers and berry fruit. The palate is just as complex, showing tobacco, blackberries and a touch of chocolate. Full-bodied to equal the meat sauce and heavy cheese sauce.

Other Choices:

B.C. Cabernet Sauvignon (International Blend)

1 *To make meat sauce*, in a large saucepan over medium heat, fry ground beef for 5 minutes or until most of meat is brown, not pink. Drain fat from pan. **2** Melt butter in pan. Add garlic, tomatoes, onion and mushrooms. Cook for 5 minutes or until meat is cooked and vegetables are tender. Drain liquid from pan. **3** Add tomato paste, salt, pepper, beef stock and red wine. Simmer, uncovered and stirring occasionally, for 45 minutes or until sauce is thick. **4** Meanwhile, in a large pot of boiling salted water, cook lasagna until al dente. Drain and keep warm. **5** *To make cheese sauce*, in a medium saucepan over medium heat, melt butter. Stir in flour; cook for 2 min-

utes, stirring constantly. Add milk slowly, stirring constantly. Stir in half the mozzarella cheese, making sure it is melted before adding the rest. Stir in half the Parmesan cheese. Bring sauce to a boil, stirring constantly. Reduce heat to low and stir until sauce thickens. **6** Place a layer of lasagna noodles in a 13- by 9-inch (3.5 L) baking dish. Cover with cheese sauce, then meat sauce. Repeat layers, ending with cheese sauce. Top with remaining Parmesan. **7** Bake at 375°F (190°C) for 30 minutes. Serve hot.

Mozzarella

Made by Lactantia de Victoriaville

Parmesan

Made by Saputo Cheeses

PROVOLONE BROCHETTES IN ANCHOVY-RICOTTA SAUCE

SERVES FOUR   Silani Sweet Cheese — Schomberg, Ontario

SILANI SWEET CHEESE opened in 1954 and has seen three generations of Lanzino and Talarico family members. Vince and Joseph Lanzino and Michael Talarico are now running the company, which manufactures and imports 40 cheeses. At the Schomberg factory, Italian-style varieties are made from pasteurized cow's milk, including ricotta, mozzarella, provolone, Friulano, bocconcini and Caciocavallo.

Colio Wines Cabernet Franc

Harrow, Ontario

Colio's wines are produced by a native Italian, Carlo Negri. Carlo makes a consistently good Cabernet Franc from year to year. This particular red has raspberry aromas and flavours and full body, making it an excellent partner for the provolone and bread. Its austere tannin balances the saltiness of anchovies as well.

Other Choices:
B.C. Maréchal Foch

Provolone and Ricotta

Made by Silani Sweet Cheese

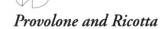

8	slices sourdough bread	8
½ lb	provolone cheese, sliced	250 g
½ cup	butter	125 mL
	Salt and pepper to taste	
16	anchovy fillets	16
¼ cup	ricotta cheese	50 mL

1 Cut bread slices into quarters. Cut provolone slices into equal-sized squares. Alternately thread bread slices and provolone onto eight skewers, using four pieces of bread per skewer. Place skewers over an oven-safe dish, supported by the rim. **2** Melt half the butter; brush over brochettes. Season with salt and pepper. Bake at 400°F (200°C) for 15 to 20 minutes or until brochettes are golden. **3** Meanwhile in a small saucepan over medium heat melt remaining butter. Mash anchovies and add to butter; sauté for 1 minute. Gradually add ricotta and, stirring constantly, bring to a boil. **4** In a food processor or blender purée sauce until smooth. **5** Return sauce to saucepan and reheat. Pour sauce over brochettes. Serve immediately.

FIDDLEHEAD AND OKA STRUDEL

SERVES FOUR   Agropur — Granby, Quebec

CHERRY HILL AND INGERSOLL, L'Extra, Oka and Corneville, Anco and Allegro and Delicrème — these are but a few of the many brand names given to the fine cheeses produced by Agropur. Canada's largest cheese manufacturer and dairy co-operative, Agropur markets their products under 1,000 different labels. Their cheese factories make close to 110 million lb of bulk cheese each year for industrial customers, as well as a wide variety of fine cheeses — soft, semi-soft and firm — for cheese-loving consumers. In 1981 Agropur acquired the famous Oka cheese plant, founded by Trappist monks more than a century ago.

Filling:

1 cup	fresh fiddleheads*	250 mL
2 tbsp	butter	25 mL
1	medium leek, white part only, thinly sliced	1
1 tbsp	chopped shallot	15 mL
1/4 lb	Oka cheese, shredded	125 g
1 tbsp	sliced toasted almonds	15 mL
1	large egg, beaten	1
1 tbsp	finely chopped fresh parsley	15 mL
1 tbsp	finely chopped fresh chives	15 mL
1/2 tsp	salt	2 mL
1/2 tsp	pepper	2 mL
Dash	cayenne	Dash
Dash	paprika	Dash
1/2 tsp	freshly squeezed lemon juice	2 mL

Strudel:

1/2 cup	butter, melted	125 mL
6	sheets phyllo pastry	6
1/2 cup	grated Romano cheese	125 mL

Vignoble de L'Orpailleur Vin Blanc

Dunham, Quebec

The fiddleheads and delicate pastry go nicely with this wine's vegetative aromas, light body and crisp acidity.

Other Choices:

Ontario Sauvignon or B.C. dry Kerner

*If fiddleheads are not in season, use asparagus.

1 Plunge fiddleheads into boiling water and blanch until bright green and tender-crisp. Immediately refresh fiddleheads under cold water; drain. **2** To make filling, in a large saucepan over medium heat melt butter; sauté leek and shallot until translucent. **3** In a large bowl toss together fiddleheads and remaining filling ingredients. **4** To make strudel, grease a baking sheet with some of the melted butter. Lay one phyllo sheet on baking sheet and quickly brush with some melted butter. Sprinkle with 1 tbsp (15 mL) Romano cheese. Place another phyllo sheet over cheese. Brush with butter and sprinkle with cheese. Continue until all phyllo sheets are used. **5** Spread fiddlehead filling evenly over phyllo, leaving 1-inch (2.5 cm) border on all sides. **6** Fold in borders over filling. Beginning with long end, roll up phyllo in jelly-roll fashion. Lay strudel seam side down on baking sheet. Brush entire surface with remaining melted butter. **7** Bake at 350°F (180°C) for 20 to 25 minutes or until strudel is golden. Cool slightly and slice. Serve immediately.

Oka

Made by Agropur

Romano

Made by Saputo Cheeses

TALARICO'S PESTO AND BLACK OLIVE PIZZA WITH PARMESAN AND MOZZARELLA

SERVES FOUR   Alberta Cheese Company Ltd. — Calgary, Alberta

A NATIVE OF CALABRIA, ITALY, cheesemaker Frank Talarico has been dedicated to the Canadian cheese industry since 1959. He began at his father's factory, Silani Sweet Cheese, in Toronto, then went on to open Alberta Cheese in 1976. Now a thriving factory supplying restaurants across three provinces, Alberta Cheese Company is the only cheesemaker in the province to specialize in the Italian cheeses, mozzarella, ricotta, provolone, bocconcini and Caciocavallo. Their Caciocavallo, a mild cheese with smooth texture and a buttery-almond taste, is still made in the traditional Italian way of being stretched by hand in warm water.

1 oz	dried porcini mushrooms	25 g
¼ cup	lukewarm water	50 mL

Dough:

1¼ cup	self-raising flour	300 mL
Pinch	salt	Pinch
3 tbsp	olive oil	50 mL

Pesto:

½ cup	fresh basil leaves	125 mL
3	cloves garlic, peeled	3
2 tbsp	pine nuts	25 mL
1 cup	grated Parmesan cheese	250 mL
⅓ cup	olive oil	75 mL
	Salt and pepper to taste	

Toppings:

½ cup	pitted sliced black olives	125 mL
¼ lb	hot Italian sausage, thinly sliced	125 g
1 cup	shredded mozzarella cheese	250 mL

Mission Hill Vineyards Coolman Cabernet

Available in Alberta
(selected wine shops)

A blend of Washington State Cabernet Sauvignon and B.C. Maréchal Foch, this red has light to medium body with raspberry aromas and flavours and just a hint of spicy oak on the finish. A good choice for this dish, as it works with the combined flavours of mozzarella, Parmesan and Italian sausage.

Other Choices:

Ontario Merlot

1 Soak porcini mushrooms in lukewarm water for 30 minutes. **2** Meanwhile, to make dough, sift flour and salt into a bowl. Stir in oil and sufficient water to mix to a moist dough. **3** On a well-floured work surface, roll out dough 1/8 inch (3 mm) thick. Fit dough into a greased baking sheet. Pinch up edges to make a ridge. **4** *To make pesto,* in a food processor or blender purée basil, garlic, pine nuts and Parmesan with 2 tbsp

(25 mL) oil. With motor running add remaining oil until sauce emulsifies. Season with salt and pepper. **5** Brush pizza dough with pesto. Top with drained porcini mushrooms, black olives, and sausage. Sprinkle with mozzarella. **6** Bake at 375°F (190°C) for 20 to 25 minutes or until crust is golden.

Tre Stelle Parmesan

Made by National Cheese

Mozzarella

Made by Alberta Cheese

CLASSIC CHEDDAR SOUFFLÉ

SERVES FOUR — Albert Perron Inc. — Saint-Prime, Quebec

SINCE ADÉLARD PERRON founded Albert Perron Inc. in 1889, the company has seen four generations of Perrons. Adélard's grandson, Albert, now runs the company and is training son Jean-Marc to follow in the family's tradition. Though still a small enterprise, with only 30 employees, Albert Perron has a notable reputation for making consistently good Cheddars. Some are exported to England, but most are distributed throughout Quebec and Eastern Ontario.

*Brights Wines
President
Canadian
Champagne Brut*

Available in Quebec (Société des Alcools Québec)

This clean, crisp sparkler offers enough simplicity for a souffle.

Other Choices:

Quebec Canadian Champagne

Old Cheddar

Made by Albert Perron

5 tbsp	butter	75 mL
¼ cup	all-purpose flour	50 mL
2¼ cups	warm milk	550 mL
	Salt and pepper to taste	
¼ lb	old Cheddar cheese, shredded	125 g
4	eggs, at room temperature, separated	4

1 Grease a 7-inch (18 cm) soufflé dish with 1 tbsp (25 mL) butter. **2** In a medium saucepan over medium heat, melt remaining butter. Stir in flour. Cook for 1 minute, stirring constantly without browning. Add warm milk, stirring constantly until sauce thickens. Season with salt and pepper. Remove from heat. Stir in cheese until melted. **3** In a small bowl, lightly beat egg yolks. Stir a little sauce into egg yolks. Stir egg yolks into sauce. **4** Beat egg whites to soft peaks. Fold a quarter of the whites into sauce. Gently add remaining egg whites; blend with a whisk. Pour mixture into soufflé dish. **5** Bake in the middle of a 400°F (200°C) oven for 25 minutes or until soufflé is golden. Serve immediately.

PUFF PASTRY PIE WITH POTATOES AND HAVARTI

SERVES FOUR   Millbank Cheese & Butter — Millbank, Ontario

SINCE 1908 MILLBANK CHEESE & BUTTER has been supplying Ontario's cheese lovers with such varieties as Cheddar, Gouda, brick, Colby, Edam and Havarti. All the Cheddars are aged at 42°F in cold storage. The mild version is up to two months old; the medium is aged four to six months. Millbank's Old Cheddar spends nine to twelve months in cold storage, and Extra Old hangs around for at least another six months. Before any of the cheeses are shipped from the premises they have to be tested by Millbank's expert cheese grader and superintendent, Ken Krotz. Unlike some graders, Krotz relies on a traditional, fail-proof method of testing — the good ol' taste test. "When the cheeses are sharp enough for me," Krotz says, "then they're sharp enough for my customers." Millbank is a division of J.M. Schneider Inc.

Chef Jean-Claude Terrattaz, of Ottawa, Ontario, created this scrumptious dish for the Dairy Bureau of Canada.

¼ cup	butter	50 mL
¾ cup	julienned leeks	175 mL
1	pkg (1 lb/411g) frozen puff pastry	1
½ lb	potatoes	250 g
½ lb	Havarti cheese, sliced	250 g
	Eggwash, made with 1 egg yolk beaten with 1 tsp (5 mL) water	
	Salt and pepper to taste	

Peller Estates Vidal
Winona, Ontario

Andres Wines has established a successful line of varietal wines under the label Peller Estates, named after the owner Andrew Peller. Though potatoes and Havarti cheese share a heavy texture, both have a mild flavour, thus needing a fleshy wine with subtle fruit to match. Peller Estates Vidal is full bodied with ripe pear aromas and flavours.

Other Choices:
B.C. barrel-aged Chardonnay

PELLER ESTATES

Havarti

Made by Millbank Cheese & Butter

1 In a large saucepan over medium heat, melt butter; braise leeks until transparent. Set aside. **2** Place puff pastry dough on a lightly floured work surface. Dust dough with flour. Roll it out into a neat rectangle 11 by 12 inches (28 by 30 cm) and 1/8 inch (3 mm) thick. Transfer dough to a lightly greased baking sheet. Cover and refrigerate for at least 30 minutes. **3** Peel potatoes, thinly slice, sprinkle with salt and let dry. **4** Fold chilled dough in half lengthwise on the baking sheet to make a seam, then open. Arrange potato slices, leeks and Havarti slices on one half of the dough, leaving a 3/4-inch (2 cm) border around edges. Brush border with eggwash. Fold other half of dough over filling. Press edges together with a fork to seal. Trim edges with a pizza cutter. Lightly brush top of pie with remaining eggwash. Cut three steam vents in top of pie. Refrigerate for 1 hour or until dough is firm and edges are well sealed. **5** Place pie in a 400°F (200°C) oven. Reduce heat to 375°F (190°C) and bake for 20 to 25 minutes or until pie is puffed and golden. Let cool slightly before cutting. Serve hot.

OYSTER, BACON AND CHEDDAR PIE

SERVES FOUR TO SIX   Käsemann's Curds and Whey — New Hamburg, Ontario

CHEESE HAS BEEN A WAY OF LIFE for the Bast family. Although generations of family members had made cheese, George Bast III was the first to open a cheese stand in Kitchener's Farmers' Market. Son George Bast IV followed in his father's footsteps by opening Käsemann's Cheese Shop in Kitchener in 1967. George Bast IV's daughters, Mary Jane Bast and Sharon Hammer, eventually moved the shop to New Hamburg and renamed it Käsemann's Curds and Whey. Full of country-style charm, this shop features a wide assortment of Canadian and imported cheeses, flavoured vinegars, specialty jams and herbal teas.

Lakeview Cellars Gurinskas Vineyard Chardonnay

Vineland, Ontario

Before establishing Lakeview Cellars, Eddy Gurinskas was a prize-winning amateur winemaker. He now produces close to 1,300 cases of wine each year, consisting of such varieties as Cabernet Sauvignon, Chardonnay, Pinot Gris, Baco Noir and Vidal. Offering pear-like flavours and just a hint of vanilla, this Chardonnay complements the smoky flavour of the oysters and light Cheddar flavour.

Other Choices:

B.C. barrel-fermented Chardonnay

Lakeview Cellars
Estate Winery Ltd.

Ricotta

Made by Grande Cheese

7-year-old Cheddar

Cured by Käsemann's Curds and Whey

2	slices bacon, coarsely chopped	2
2 tbsp	minced shallots	25 mL
2 cups	ricotta cheese	500 mL
2	cans smoked oysters, drained (3½ oz/100 g each)	2
½ lb	old Cheddar, shredded	250 g
2	eggs, beaten	2
¼ tsp	hot pepper sauce	1 mL
	Salt and pepper to taste	
	Pastry for 9-inch (23 cm) double-crust pie	
1	egg, beaten	1

1 In a saucepan over medium heat fry bacon until crisp. Drain off fat. Add shallots and sauté until tender. **2** Add ricotta. Lower heat and cook, stirring constantly, for 5 minutes. **3** Fold in oysters. Remove from heat. Fold in Cheddar, 2 beaten eggs, hot pepper sauce, salt and pepper. **4** On a lightly floured work surface, roll out two-thirds of pastry and line bottom and sides of an 8-inch (2 L)) springform pan. Pour filling into pan. Roll out remaining pastry and cover filling, pinching edges together to seal. Brush top with 1 beaten egg; reserve remaining egg. **5** Place springform pan on a baking sheet. Bake at 400°F (200°C) for 30 minutes. **6** Remove sides of pan and brush sides of pie with remaining egg. Bake another 10 minutes or until top and sides are golden.

FOCACCIA WITH FIOR DI LATTE CHEESE

SERVES SIX — Shari Darling — Toronto, Ontario

FOCACCIA IS A TRADITIONAL Italian bread that can be topped with a variety of ingredients. This recipe uses an Italian-style cheese called Fior di Latte. Made from cow's milk, Fior di Latte has a springy texture and milky flavour and is similar to mozzarella but with a rich taste because of its higher fat content.

Hainle Vineyards Baco Noir

Peachland, British Columbia

Tilman Hainle produces delicious varietals that fall within organic standards. This means no insecticides or herbicides are used on the grapes and sulphite is avoided whenever possible in making the wine. This dedication to natural wine has proved successful, as Tilman has won awards for his White Riesling dry, Traminer Dry Estate and Riesling Icewine. The Baco Noir has a floral note on the nose, with berry fruit and good acidity on the mouth. Light to medium bodied, this wine can be chilled, giving a pleasant contrast to the warmth of melted Fior di Latte cheese.

Other Choices:

Ontario Pinot Noir

HAINLE VINEYARDS

Fior di Latte

Made by Saputo Cheeses

1 oz	active dry yeast	25 g
3½ cups	all-purpose flour	875 mL
1 tbsp	salt	15 mL
⅓ cup	olive oil	75 mL
2	cloves garlic, finely chopped	2
2 tbsp	finely chopped fresh sage	25 mL
½ lb	Fior di Latte cheese, shredded	250 g

1 Dissolve yeast in 1/2 cup (125 mL) warm water. Let stand for 10 minutes. **2** Pour flour onto a work surface. Add dissolved yeast, salt and 2 tbsp (25 mL) oil. Knead until smooth and elastic. Put dough in a floured bowl. Cover with plastic wrap; let stand for 3 hours. **3** On a lightly floured work surface, knead dough for 2 to 3 minutes. Pat into a circle and line a greased 10-inch (25 cm) tart pan. Let rise for 30 minutes. **4** Dimple dough with fingertips. Sprinkle with garlic, sage and Fior di Latte. Pour remaining oil over top. **5** Bake at 400°F (200°C) for 20 to 25 minutes or until crust is golden. Serve warm.

CAMEMBERT AND WILD MUSHROOM QUICHE

SERVES FOUR TO SIX   Fromagerie Cayer Inc. — Saint-Raymond, Quebec

THE CAYER FAMILY'S HISTORY is as old as the village of Saint-Raymond, Quebec. In fact, the Cayer clan was the first to settle in the area, having been granted land, a horse and a cow from the government. Eventually, son Henry took over the vegetable farm and converted it into a dairy in hopes of owning the greatest herd of Holsteins in Quebec. His dream came true with countless prizes for his Holsteins as proof of his success. In the late 1940s, Henry extended the dairy to include an ice cream company, another great accomplishment. He sold this company to a conglomerate in 1978 and began a third enterprise, Fromagerie Cayer. Today Henry is retired, but sons Denis and Dominique continue the family cheese factory, operating the same farm and using the original cabin as an ageing cellar for their fine Canadian cheeses. Some of these include Brie, Camembert, Havarti, Neufchatel and feta. Many of these varieties have captured awards.

Inniskillin Wines Pinot Noir

Niagara-on-the-Lake, Ontario
Available in Quebec (Le Marchand de Vin Inc., 514-481-2046)
Available in Ottawa (Inniskillin Wine Boutique, 11 Metcalf St., 613-563-3803)

Deep ruby with medium body and black cherry character and soft texture, Pinot Noir is wonderful with Camembert's mushroom flavour and Neufchatel's creamy consistency. The wine is also light enough not to overpower the egg base.

Other Choices:
B.C. Gamay Noir

Retro Camembert and Baron Roula Neufchatel

Made by Fromagerie Cayer

1 tbsp	unsalted butter	15 mL
1	clove garlic, minced	1
½ cup	coarsely chopped fresh shiitake mushrooms	125 mL
3 oz	Camembert, rind removed*	75 g
⅓ lb	Neufchatel cheese	175 g
4	eggs	4
	Salt and white pepper to taste	
Pinch	cayenne	Pinch
1 tbsp	finely chopped fresh basil	15 mL
1	unbaked 8-inch (20-cm) single-crust pie shell	1

Use a cheese plane or vegetable peeler to remove rind of Camembert.

1 In a small saucepan over medium heat, melt butter; sauté garlic and mushrooms until tender; set aside. **2** In a large bowl combine Camembert and Neufchatel. Using a fork, whip cheeses until all lumps are gone. **3** Beat in eggs until mixture is smooth. Add mushrooms and garlic, salt, pepper, cayenne and basil. **4** Turn mixture into pie shell. Bake at 375°F (190°C) for 25 minutes or until quiche is golden.

GOUDA AND BROCCOLI CALZONE

SERVES FOUR   Sunnyrose Cheese Factory — Lethbridge, Alberta

SUNNYROSE CHEESE, founded in 1984 by Sandi and Fran De Jong, produces 14 varieties, including a prize-winning Gouda, Havarti, Cheddar and Monterey Jack. All are preservative-free and additive-free. Sandi is cheesemaker, a self-taught artist who has had a love for cheese since he was 16. In 1984 he started making cheese as a hobby, and the art form has flourished into a full-time job for him. In 1991 Sandi brought home two medals for his Gouda from the Royal Winter Fair. The cheese not only took first prize in its own category but cleaned up overall, winning the Grand Championship that year.

Calzone:

1	envelope active dry yeast	1
4 cups	all-purpose flour	1 L
2 tbsp	olive oil	25 mL
Pinch	salt	Pinch

Filling:

1 head	broccoli (about 1 lb/500 g)	1
½ lb	Gouda cheese, shredded	250 g

1 Dissolve yeast in 1 1/2 cups (375 mL) warm water. Let stand for 10 minutes. **2** In a large bowl combine dissolved yeast, flour, olive oil and salt. Knead for 10 minutes until dough is elastic. Coat dough with oil and set in a greased bowl. Let stand for 1 hour or until doubled in size. **3** To make filling, steam broccoli until bright green and tender; let cool; dice. Divide broccoli and Gouda into four equal portions. **4** Divide dough into four balls. On a lightly floured work surface, roll out balls 6 inches (20 cm) wide, 1/4 inch (5 mm) thick. **5** Place one-quarter of broccoli and one-quarter of Gouda on one half of each circle, leaving a border. Brush border with water. Fold dough in half, pressing edges firmly together to seal. Lightly brush dough with oil; cut two steam vents. Place on a lightly floured baking sheet. **6** Bake at 450°F (230°C) for 25 to 30 minutes or until golden. Serve hot.

Gray Monk Cellars Kerner Dry

Okanagan Centre, British Columbia
Available in Alberta at independent liquor stores

Herbaceous notes in the bouquet and on the palate with plenty of citrus fruit, this dry, crisp white goes with broccoli and the piquant taste of Gouda.

Other Choices:
Ontario Sauvignon

GRAY·MONK

Gouda

Made by Sunnyrose Cheese Factory

BLUBRY AND MAPLE-CURED BACON FRITTATA

SERVES FOUR   Shari Darling — Toronto, Ontario

ALSO KNOWN AS "BLUE BRIE," Cambozola is an interior-ripened cheese with a bloomy rind and creamy interior, like Brie. Its flavour is much like a mild blue cheese. Of German origin, this cheese is made from pasteurized cow's milk with added cream. Fromagerie Cayer calls their version Blubry.

8	eggs	8
5	slices maple-cured bacon, cut into 1-inch (2.5 cm) squares	5
1/4 lb	Cambozola cheese, rind removed, diced	125 g
1/2 cup	sliced mushrooms	125 g
1 tbsp	finely chopped fresh rosemary	15 mL
3 tbsp	butter	50 mL
2	cloves garlic, minced	2

Konzelmann Estate Winery Pinot Noir
Niagara-on-the-Lake, Ontario

Herbert Konzelmann produces a wide range of German-style varietal wines. In 1993 his 1991 Pinot Blanc won a gold medal at VinItaly. The combined flavours of the mild blue cheese, maple-cured bacon and egg base call for a light, fruity red like Pinot Noir. Konzelmann's version displays fresh strawberries in the bouquet and palate that enhance the mild bite of Cambozola.

Other Choices:
B.C. Gamay Noir

Blubry
Made by Fromagerie Cayer

1 In a large bowl beat together eggs, bacon, Cambozola cheese, mushrooms and rosemary. **2** In a large skillet over medium heat, melt butter; sauté garlic until soft. **3** Increase heat to high. When butter begins to bubble, add egg mixture, shaking skillet to distribute ingredients evenly. Reduce heat to medium-low and cook for 6 to 7 minutes. **4** Using a spatula, loosen egg mixture from sides of skillet and gradually from bottom. When frittata can slip in pan, invert a serving plate over the skillet. Flip the skillet, letting frittata fall onto the plate. Slide frittata back into pan and cook the other side until eggs are set about 3 minutes.

SCALLOP CHEESECAKE WITH QUARK AND PIMIENTO

SERVES FOUR TO SIX   Say Cheese — London, Ontario

WHEN YOU VISIT Say Cheese you'll be guaranteed three things — an innovative and extensive selection of domestic and imported cheeses and specialty food items downstairs in the cheese shop; a creative and always changing menu and wine list featuring local cheeses and wines in the upstairs restaurant; and most of all an exploration of the senses every time you dine. Because of these combined elements, Say Cheese has enjoyed two and a half decades of success. Nigel Gamble has been executive chef at Say Cheese since 1974. He developed this wonderful cheesecake for this cookbook.

Crust:

1/3 cup	finely crushed Carr's Table Water Crackers with Cracked Pepper	75 mL
1/2 tsp	salt	2 mL
2 tsp	finely chopped fresh parsley	10 mL
3 tbsp	clarified butter	50 mL
1 1/2 tsp	Patak's Tikka Curry Paste	7 mL

Filling:

2/3 lb	small scallops	350 g
	Milk for simmering	
3 cups	cream-based Quark cheese, at room temperature	750 mL
1 1/2 tsp	salt	7 mL
3 tbsp	all-purpose flour	50 mL
3	large eggs	3
1	egg yolk	1
3 tbsp	chopped pimiento	50 mL
1/3 cup	milk	75 mL
3 1/2 oz	creamed coconut, grated*	100 g

Creamed coconut is available at Indian supermarkets and specialty food shops.

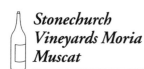

Stonechurch Vineyards Moria Muscat

Niagara-on-the-Lake, Ontario

With light body, this white does not overpower the delicate taste of Quark cheese and scallops, while offering lots of spice to complement the curry flavour of the crust.

Other Choices:

B.C. dry Gewürztraminer

1 To make crust, in a bowl combine crushed crackers, salt, parsley, butter and curry paste. Rub mixture between fingertips until well blended. **2** Line an 8-inch (2 L) springform pan with parchment paper. Lightly butter parchment paper. Press crust mixture into bottom of springform pan. **3** Bake at 400°F (200°C) for 5 minutes; let cool. **4** To make filling, in a saucepan combine scallops with just enough milk to cover. Simmer for 2 minutes or until scallops are white; drain on paper towels. **5** In a large bowl blend Quark cheese, salt and flour. Add eggs and egg yolk, one at a time, blending well after each addition. Stir in pimiento. **6** Fold scallops into Quark mixture. **7** In a small saucepan over medium heat, heat milk. Add coconut, stirring until melted. Blend coconut mixture into Quark mixture. **8** Pour filling into prepared crust. Bake on centre rack at 300°F (180°C) for 1 hour and 10 minutes or until centre is set. **9** Serve warm or cold with a light curry sauce.

Quark

Made by Pinneau Dairy

CRAB CHEESECAKE

SERVES FOUR TO SIX   Island Farms Dairy — Vancouver Island, British Columbia

ISLAND FARMS DAIRY opened in 1944 and continues to make a wide range of dairy products, among them sour cream, cottage cheese, ice cream and a "Victoria style" cream cheese.

Crust:

2 tbsp	butter, melted	25 mL
1/2 cup	dried bread crumbs	125 mL
1/2 cup	shredded brick cheese	125 mL
1/2 tsp	poppy seeds	2 mL
2 tbsp	butter	25 mL

Filling:

2 cups	cream cheese	500 mL
4	eggs	4
1/2 cup	half-and-half cream	125 mL
1/2 cup	finely chopped onion	125 mL
1/3 cup	cooked crabmeat	75 mL

1 *To make crust,* in a large bowl combine melted butter, bread crumbs, brick cheese and poppy seeds. **2** With 2 tbsp (25 mL) butter, grease a 9-inch (2.5 L) springform pan. Press crust into bottom and up sides of pan. Chill crust while preparing filling. **3** *To make filling,* in the cleaned bowl beat together cream cheese, eggs and cream until smooth. Fold in onion and crabmeat. Pour filling into crust. **4** Bake at 325°F (160°C) for 1 hour and 15 minutes or until centre is set. Turn off oven, prop open oven door, and let cheesecake stand in oven for 1 hour. **5** Cool to room temperature. Chill for 1 hour before serving.

Summerhill Estate Cipes NV Brut

Kelowna, British Columbia

Stephen Cipes puts his champagne in a pyramid-shaped cellar. Though no one understands what exactly occurs to the wines under these conditions, many wine authorities admit that there's a positive difference. Vinified in the traditional méthode champenoise style used in Champagne, France, this sparkler has forward pear and apricot aromas and flavours, with a light yeasty note and good acidity that offsets the richness of crab without overpowering the cream cheese base.

Other Choices:

Ontario Canadian champagne

Cream cheese

Made by Island Farms Dairy

HERBED QUARK CHEESECAKE

SERVES FOUR TO SIX   Pinneau Dairy Limited — Cambridge, Ontario

PINNEAU DAIRY has been producing Quark, a delicious German-style cheese, since 1969. In 1972 brothers Artur and Eduard Pinneau broadened their product line to include yogurt and sour cream. All products are free of preservatives and additives. Artur uses a traditional cheesemaking method, having been schooled in butter- and cheesemaking in Hannover, Germany. He furthered his dairy education by working as a butter- and cheesemaker in Chile before immigrating to Canada, where he obtained a diploma in dairy technology from the University of Guelph.

Magnotta Wines
Podamer Brut
Champagne

Vaughan, Ontario

With so many flavours featured, this recipe is best served with a sparkler. Podamer Brut Champagne, done in the méthode champenoise (second fermentation in the bottle) is made mostly from the Riesling grape, giving the bubbly a pear-like character and a good dose of acidity. Refreshes the palate without overpowering all the delicate flavours here.

Other Choices:
B.C. Canadian champagne

Quark (Cream-based)

Made by Pinneau Dairy
Ermite

Made by L'Abbaye de Saint-Benoît-du-Lac

⅓ lb	butter	175 g
1½ lb	Quark cheese (cream-based)*	750 g
2 oz	blue cheese (Ermite)	50 g
2 tbsp	sesame seeds	25 mL
3	stalks celery, finely chopped	3
Pinch	cayenne	Pinch
1	sweet red pepper, diced	1
2 tbsp	sweet paprika	25 mL
1	clove garlic, minced	1
	Salt and white pepper to taste	
¼ lb	cooked ham, diced	125 g
1 tbsp	finely chopped fresh chives	15 mL
2 tbsp	dry sherry	25 mL
	Prosciutto slices (for garnish)	
	Fresh parsley sprigs (for garnish)	

Note: Be careful when selecting Quark. If using a skim-milk version for this recipe, the Quark will have to be drained in a sieve overnight.

1 In a bowl, cream butter with Quark cheese. Divide evenly among three bowls. **2** In first bowl, combine Quark with blue cheese, sesame seeds, celery and cayenne. **3** In second bowl, combine Quark with red pepper, paprika, garlic, salt and pepper. **4** In third bowl, combine Quark with ham, chives and sherry. **5** Place a 9-inch (2.5 L) springform pan on a serving plate. Line sides of pan with a strip of aluminum foil. **6** Pour blue cheese mixture into pan. **7** Pour red pepper mixture into pan. **8** Pour ham mixture into pan. Refrigerate for at least 3 hours. **9** One hour before serving, remove sides and foil. Garnish top with curled strips of prosciutto and fresh parsley sprigs.

THREE-CHEESE BUNDLES

SERVES FOUR   Olympic Food & Cheese — St. Lawrence Farmers' Market
(South Building), Toronto, Ontario

GEORGE TSIOROS WAS ONLY 16 when he started at his brother-in-law's fresh cheese and meat shop in 1960. Now he is an integral part of the shop's success. This shop offers some 400 cheeses, 100 of them Canadian. Cherry Hill, Balderson, Ivanhoe, Forfar and Albert Perron are some of the brand-name Cheddars to be found here, along with most of Agropur's domestic specialty varieties. George also makes scrumptious homemade Greek savouries, such as tzatziki (a yogurt sauce), taramasalata (caviar spread) and hummus (crushed chick-peas with tahini sauce), and his own Boursin — a spreadable cheese made with cream cheese, herbs and spices. George says cheese-loving Torontonians keep his store busy from Tuesday to Saturday because his prices average 20 percent lower than the competitors'.

Reif Estate Winery Chardonnay

Niagara-on-the-Lake, Ontario

Reif is situated on the Niagara Parkway, a romantic road along the meandering Niagara River. It is a section of the Niagara Wine Route that prepares wine enthusiasts for an enjoyable tour of a winery with Germanic charm and Old World appeal. Winemaker Klaus Reif's Chardonnay is dry, crisp and lean, offsetting the heavy weight of the combined three cheeses, while not overpowering the delicate flavour of the tarts. Displays excellent apple fruit on the nose and palate.

Other Choices:
B.C. Chardonnay

Cheese Filling:

4 oz	mozzarella cheese, grated	125 g
4 oz	feta cheese, crumbled	100 g
1/3 cup	cottage cheese	75 mL
1/4 cup	unsalted butter, at room temperature, cubed	50 mL
1	small egg	1
	Salt and pepper to taste	

Crusts:

1 1/4 cups	all-purpose flour	300 mL
1/4 tsp	salt	1 mL
1	small egg, lightly beaten	1
1 tbsp	vegetable oil	15 mL
1/4 cup	club soda, at room temperature	50 mL
6 tbsp	unsalted butter, melted	90 mL

1 *To make cheese filling*, in a large bowl stir together well mozzarella, feta, cottage cheese, butter, egg, salt and pepper. Set aside. **2** *To make crusts*, in a large bowl sift flour with salt. Make a well in the centre. Pour in egg, oil and club soda. Stir, adding more club soda if needed to make a soft dough. Knead until smooth and elastic, about 10 minutes. Shape into a ball. Cover with a cloth and let stand for 1 hour. **3** Divide dough in two. Shape halves into balls, cover with cloth, and let stand for 15 minutes. **4** On a lightly floured work surface, roll out one ball to 1/8-inch (3 mm) thick square. Brush dough with some of the melted butter. Brush fingers with butter; pull edges of dough in different directions until paper-thin. (Do not worry if dough tears slightly.) **5** Trim edges of dough to form an even square. Fold square in half. Brush surface with butter; fold in half again to form a 6-inch (15 cm) square. If square is too small, pull edges slightly. Brush square with butter. **6** Shape half the cheese filling into a ball. Place ball in centre of square. Fold corners of square toward centre, covering filling. **7** Flatten bundle to 1 inch (2.5 cm) thick. Brush top with butter. **8** With remaining dough and cheese filling, make second bundle. **9** Transfer bundles to a buttered baking sheet. Bake at 350°F (180°C) for 35 minutes or until golden.

Feta

Made by Fromagerie Cayer

BLOOMSBURY BLUE CHEESECAKE

Bloomsbury Edible Flowers & Herbs — Apsley, Ontario

CHEFS CAN SNIFF OUT quality food suppliers like hogs can sniff out truffles. Bloomsbury is one of the gems that many chefs have dug up in their search for fresh herbs and edible flowers. Located in an old barn in the hamlet of Apsley, Bloomsbury was created by bon vivants Carmel Morrison and Linda Fierheller. These women have made a name for themselves by providing Ontario's finest restaurants with delicacies such as fresh tarragon, lemon and cinnamon basil, pogonias, nasturtiums, pansies and calendula (a great substitute for saffron). And although herbs and flowers may be this duo's business, they're avid cheese lovers to boot. This scrumptious savoury is one of their creations.

Base:

2 tbsp	butter	25 mL
½ cup	fine dry bread crumbs	125 mL
2 tbsp	finely chopped fresh tarragon	25 mL

Filling:

3 cups	Quark	750 mL
¾ lb	blue cheese (Ermite)	375 g
½ cup	sour cream	125 mL
4	eggs	4
½ cup	finely chopped onion	125 mL
2	cloves garlic, minced	2
Pinch	white pepper	Pinch
½ tsp	dry mustard	2 mL
2 tbsp	finely chopped fresh Greek oregano	25 mL
2 tbsp	finely chopped fresh rosemary	25 mL

Topping:

2 cups	sour cream	500 mL
2 tbsp	finely chopped fresh parsley	25 mL
2 tbsp	finely chopped fresh garlic chives	25 mL

Marynissen Estates Lot 31A Cabernet Sauvignon

Aged in American oak, this full-bodied Cabernet Sauvignon has ripe raspberry fruit and spicy oak tones. It is an ideal partner for this blue cheese cheesecake.

Other Choices:

B.C. port

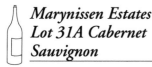

MARYNISSEN
E S T A T E S

1 *To make base*, rub sides and bottom of a 10-inch (3 L) springform pan with butter. In a bowl combine breadcrumbs with tarragon. Evenly coat pan with breadcrumb mixture. **2** *To make filling*, in a large bowl combine Quark and blue cheese. Add sour cream; whip mixture with a fork until smooth, about 30 seconds. **3** Add eggs, one at a time, until well incorporated. Beat in onions, garlic, pepper, mustard, oregano and rosemary. Pour mixture into pan. **4** Bake at 350°F (180°C) for 1 1/2 hours or until centre is set. **5** Meanwhile, make topping. In a bowl stir together sour cream, parsley and garlic chives. **6** When cheesecake is done let stand for 10 minutes. Spread with topping. Bake cheesecake another 5 to 10 minutes or until topping is set. **7** Chill for 2 hours before serving. (Tastes better if chilled overnight. Let stand at room temperature for 30 minutes before serving.)

Ermite

Made by L'Abbaye de Saint-Benoît-du-Lac

Cream-based Quark

Made by Pinneau Dairy

CANADIAN FONDUE

SERVES FOUR   Our Lady of the Prairies Abbey

TRAPPIST CHEESE is similar to Oka, though it is made from unpasteurized milk. On the Our Lady of the Prairies Abbey in Holland, Manitoba, a herd of Holsteins are fed a diet conducive to producing a rich milk, used in the making of this cheese. Trappist is made by hand, which means the curd is cut and stirred in warm water by hand, a time-consuming process that allows the curd to lose its watery whey and gain firmness. When the curd has developed a desired firmness, most of the whey is drained. The curd is then transferred to a mould and pressed for 24 hours to extract more whey. Once salted, the 5-lb wheels of Trappist cheese are cured in the Abbey's cellar for eight weeks. The cellar's humidity is kept as high as 95% to induce bacteria growth on the surface in order to form the rind. Every day the cheese is washed with salt water and a sponge to keep from ripening too quickly.

Hillebrand Mounier Brut

Niagara-on-the-Lake, Ontario

Mounier Brut Champagne, done in the traditional méthode champenoise (second fermentation in the bottle), is straw yellow with fine bubbles and a long mousseux. Not overly toasty or yeasty, Mounier Brut Champagne is clean, crisp and refreshing, making it the consummate beverage to serve with this fondue.

Other Choices:

B.C. Canadian champagne

Trappist cheese

Made by Our Lady of the Prairies Abbey

Montasio

Made by Paron Dairy

1	clove garlic, sliced	1
2 cups	Hillebrand Estates Le Baron Blanc (white wine)	500 mL
½ lb	Trappist cheese, shredded	250 g
½ lb	Montasio cheese, shredded	250 g
3 tbsp	kirsch	50 mL
1 tsp	cornstarch	5 mL
Pinch	nutmeg	Pinch
	White pepper to taste	
1	loaf Italian bread, cubed (for dunking)	1

1 Rub inside of fondue pot with garlic. **2** Pour in white wine. **3** Over medium heat, heat until bubbly, about 3 minutes. Add cheeses a handful at a time, stirring constantly until smooth. Stir in kirsch and cornstarch. **4** Cook, stirring constantly, until mixture has thickened. Season to taste with nutmeg and pepper.

OYSTER AND GOUDA RAREBIT ON TOASTED SODA BREAD

SERVES FOUR   Gort's Gouda Cheese Farm — Salmon Arm, British Columbia

ESTABLISHED IN 1983, Gort's Gouda Cheese Farm is the only cottage dairy farm left in western Canada that makes raw-milk Gouda. With this method, the Gouda must be stored for a minimum of 60 days to make sure a natural pasteurization takes place to destroy any pathogens that could be left in the cheese. This technique produces a Gouda with longer ageing potential and, as most cheese lovers believe, a superior, distinctive taste, says cheesemaker and owner Arie Gort. He also produces a whole-milk Quark and a low-fat (10%) Gouda.

Some English say "rarebit" (pronounced "rabbit") derived from the word "rearbit," a term used for the delicious savouries served at the end of a British meal. This recipe is an adaptation from the traditional version, "Welsh Rarebit."

Soda Bread:

6 tbsp	whey butter	90 mL
3 cups	unbleached all-purpose flour	750 mL
1½ tsp	salt	7 mL
1 tbsp	baking powder	15 mL
1 tsp	baking soda	5 mL
¾ cup	sugar	175 mL
1¾ cups	buttermilk	425 mL
2	eggs	2

Oyster Sauce:

3 tbsp	butter	50 mL
1 lb	Gouda cheese, shredded	500 g
½ tsp	salt	2 mL
Dash	hot pepper sauce	Dash
3	eggs, beaten	3
2	cans (3½ oz/100 g each) smoked oysters	2
3 tbsp	dry sherry	50 mL
	Finely chopped fresh parsley (for garnish)	

CedarCreek Estate Winery Proprietor's Blush

Kelowna, British Columbia

This light dish featuring the tangy, nutty flavour of Gouda deserves a refreshing blush like CedarCreek's. Berry fruit comes through in the aromas and flavours with a hint of vanilla at the end.

Other Choices:
Ontario Pinot Noir

CEDARCREEK
Estate Winery

1 *To make soda bread,* grease a 10- by 6-inch (3 L) loaf pan with 2 tbsp (25 mL) butter. **2** In a large bowl sift together flour, salt, baking powder, baking soda and sugar. **3** Melt 2 tbsp (25 mL) butter. In another bowl whisk together melted butter, buttermilk and eggs. **4** Pour wet ingredients over dry ingredients, stirring until blended. Do not overmix.

5 Transfer batter to pan. Dot batter with remaining butter. Bake on centre rack at 350°F (180°C) for 60 minutes or until golden and puffed. Let cool. **6** *To make oyster sauce*, in a medium saucepan over low heat, melt butter. Add Gouda cheese, salt and hot pepper sauce, stirring constantly until cheese melts and mixture is smooth. Stir a little of the warm cheese mixture into beaten eggs; pour egg mixture into saucepan, stirring constantly. Stir in oysters and sherry. **7** Toast four slices soda bread. Place one slice on each plate. Top toast with oyster sauce. Sprinkle with chopped parsley.

Gort's Gouda

Made by Gort's Gouda Cheese Farm

BAKED CHESHIRE CHEESE FONDUE

SERVES FOUR   Buttercup Farms Inc. — Bridgewater, Nova Scotia

BUTTERCUP FARMS, established in 1989, is owned by cheesemaker Maarten Winkelman, a native of the Netherlands. Maarten produces Cheddar, Havarti, Cheshire, Monterey Jack and Gouda, all sold in the farm's retail shops, the Buttercup Farm and Piping Hot Bake Shop in downtown Bridgewater and at the Brewery Market in Halifax. Though Buttercup Farm cheeses are the focus here, the shop also carries an array of Canadian and imported cheeses and specialty food items.

Inniskillin Wines Pinot Noir

Niagara-on-the-Lake, Ontario
Available in Nova Scotia
(Liquor Commission)

Light and fruity with soft texture and cherry fruit with a hint of oak in the background, this red complements Cheshire cheese.

Other Choices:
B.C. Gamay Noir

Cheshire

Made by Buttercup Farms

6	eggs	6
1 cup	milk	250 mL
¾ lb	Cheshire cheese, shredded	375 g
2 tbsp	finely chopped fresh parsley	25 mL
	Salt and pepper to taste	
	Hot red pepper sauce to taste	

1 In a bowl beat together eggs and milk. **2** Fold in cheese and parsley. Season with salt, pepper and hot pepper sauce. **3** Butter four individual custard cups. Fill each with mixture. Bake at 350°F (180°C) for 30 minutes or until fondues are puffy.

MONTREAL MONKEY WITH OKA

SERVES SIX   La Fromagerie du Marché Atwater — Montreal, Quebec

TWENTY YEARS AGO Fernand Jourdenais's tiny shop offered little more than fresh eggs and honey. Now it's a going concern in Montreal's Atwater Market, offering a vast assortment of domestic and imported cheeses, 475 varieties in total. Of these, 35 are domestic types, many from Quebec, but all bearing a handful of company names. Son Gilles Jourdenais says value and consistency from week to week are priorities for him, and he finds this only with a few specific cheesemakers. Labels you're sure to spot here are Albert Perron for Cheddar, Fromagerie Fritz Kaiser for Swiss types and Fromagerie Tournevent for goat's milk cheeses. Imported pastas, homemade sauces and condiments, gourmet coffees and fresh bread also embellish this shop.

What the fondue is to Switzerland and raclette is to France, so rarebit is to England. The English monkey or white monkey are close relatives. What all these classic dishes have in common are two ingredients — bread and melted cheese. Here's Montreal's version of a monkey.

Cave Spring Cellars Chardonnay

Jordan, Ontario
Available in Quebec (Le Maison des Vins)

A simple Chardonnay with sweet apple aromas and flavours that complement the sauce, while being light enough for this luncheon dish.

Other Choices:
B.C. Pinot Blanc

Tommes de Monsieur Séguin (Oka-style cheese)

Made by Fromagerie Fritz Kaiser

2 cups	stale bread crumbs	500 mL
2 cups	milk	500 mL
2 tbsp	butter	25 mL
½ lb	Oka-style cheese (Tommes de Monsieur Seguin), shredded	250 g
2	eggs, lightly beaten	2
Pinch	salt	Pinch
Pinch	cayenne	Pinch
6	slices buttered toast	6

1 In a large bowl, soak bread crumbs in milk for 15 minutes.
2 In a medium saucepan over medium heat, melt butter. Gradually add cheese, stirring constantly until melted. Add soaked bread crumbs, eggs, salt and cayenne. Cook, stirring constantly, for 3 to 5 minutes until well heated. Serve over buttered toast.

MIRANDA FONDUE WITH SEAFOOD AND DILL

SERVES FOUR   Fromagerie Fritz Kaiser Inc. — Noyan, Quebec

WHEN THE KAISER FAMILY left Switzerland and immigrated to Canada in 1975, Fritz Kaiser stayed behind to finish his cheesemaking apprenticeship in Oron and Zurich. Upon arriving in Canada in 1978, he established Fromagerie Fritz Kaiser. Using knowledge and experience acquired back home, Fritz now produces four Swiss-style cheeses, Vacherin, raclette, Miranda and Saint Paulin. Kaiser says his cheeses lean toward the semi-firm types, though they are generally classified in the semi-soft category. Except Miranda, they are made from pasteurized cow's milk and have subtle interiors and washed rinds. These particular cheeses are washed with a culture that promotes the growth of bacteria on the outside and forms a brownish or reddish rind. Unlike his other varieties, Miranda is a Gruyère-style cheese made from unpasteurized cow's milk obtained from the family farm in Noyan. Miranda is aged from six to eight months, giving it a dry texture, nutty aroma and sweet flavour. It melts well, making it an ideal cooking cheese.

Cave Spring Cellars Barrel-Fermented Chardonay

Jordan, Ontario
Available in Quebec (La Maison des Vins)

A forward toasty nose and a citrus spicy palate make this white a good choice for the nutty flavours of the cheese. The wine's weight can stand up to a fondue, while its acidity offers contrast to the richness of cheese.

Other Choices:
Ontario or B.C. barrel-fermented and/or -aged Chardonnay

1	clove garlic, halved	1
½ cup	Cave Spring Cellars Riesling dry (white wine)	125 mL
1 tsp	fresh lemon juice	5 mL
½ lb	Miranda cheese, shredded	250 g
½ lb	Vacherin cheese, shredded	250 g
1 tsp	cornstarch	5 mL
2 tbsp	brandy	25 mL
1 tsp	finely chopped fresh dill	5 mL
1 lb	cooked scallops (for dunking)	500 g
1 lb	cooked shrimp, peeled and deveined (for dunking)	500 g

1 Rub inside of fondue pot with garlic. **2** Pour in wine and lemon juice. Over medium heat, heat until bubbly. Add cheeses, a handful at a time, stirring constantly until melted. **3** In a small bowl, whisk cornstarch into brandy. Stir into fondue, stirring for another 2 to 3 minutes. **4** Stir in dill.

Miranda and Vacherin

Made by Fromagerie Fritz Kaiser

CHICKEN AND RACLETTE FONDUE

SERVES SIX   Fromagerie Marché Village Inc. — Brossard, Quebec

FRANCESCO AND MICKIE Gaudio's specialty cheese shop, in Brossard's busy farmers' market, has a collection of close to 800 imported and Canadian cheeses. The 50 or so domestic versions boast the labels National Cheese, Fromagerie Cayer, Agropur and Fritz Kaiser, to name a few. Italian pastas and French vinegars, mustards and foie gras make this shop a popular stop with market shoppers.

1 lb	raclette cheese, shredded	500 g
2 tbsp	all-purpose flour	25 mL
2 tbsp	butter	25 mL
1¼ cups	Cave Spring Cellars Indian Summer Riesling (white wine)	300 mL
¼ cup	brandy	50 mL
1 lb	chicken breasts, cooked and cubed (for dunking)	500 g

1 Toss raclette cheese with flour; set aside. **2** Coat inside of fondue pot with butter. Pour in wine and brandy. Heat until wine just bubbles. **3** Set pot over spirit lamp. Slowly add cheese, a handful at a time, stirring constantly until melted.

Cave Spring Cellars Indian Summer Riesling

Jordan, Ontario
Available in Quebec (La Maison des Vins)

A medium sweet Riesling showing a honeyed, apricot nose with ripe pear and apricot flavours that complement chicken and the nutty character of raclette. With good Riesling acidity and full body, this white balances raclette's heavy weight and richness.

Other Choices:
Ontario or B.C. dry Riesling

Anco Raclette

Made by Agropur

CAMEMBERT FONDUE

SERVES FOUR   Smith Cheese Inc. — London, Ontario

THERE'S NOTHING FOOD AFICIONADOS and chefs love more than perusing the local farmers' market for fresh meats, seasonal harvests and locally made cheeses. In London, food devotees head to the Covent Garden Market, where Smith Cheese has been operating since 1950. Glenda Smith runs the family business with its 220 domestic and imported varieties. Although Glenda buys Cheddars locally, she ages them herself; some have had her tender, loving care for more than eight years. Gourmet gift baskets and made-to-order cheese trays are also popular items here.

1	clove garlic, halved	1
1/2 cup	Marynissen Estates Riesling (white wine)	125 mL
2/3 cup	half-and-half cream	150 mL
1 lb	Camembert, rind removed	500 g
1 tbsp	cornstarch	15 mL
1/4 cup	brandy	50 mL
1	loaf French bread, cubed (for dunking)	1
4	apples, peeled and cubed (for dunking)	4

1 Rub inside of fondue pot with garlic. **2** Pour in wine and cream. Heat over spirit lamp until bubbly. Over low flame, add Camembert, stirring constantly until cheese is completely melted. **3** In a bowl whisk cornstarch into brandy. Add to cheese mixture, stirring for another 2 to 3 minutes.

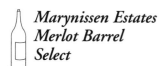

Marynissen Estates Merlot Barrel Select

Niagara-on-the-Lake, Ontario

This medium-bodied red offers an earthy aroma that resembles the mushroom taste of this Canadian Camembert. The wine's blackberry palate and long spicy finish also complement the cheese and the apple chunks.

Other Choices:
B.C. Chancellor

MARYNISSEN
E S T A T E S

Corneville Camembert

Made by Agropur

SCAMPI WRAPPED IN LEEKS WITH TOMATO, BASIL AND RICOTTA SAUCE

SERVES FOUR — Chef Zdravko Kalabric — Toronto, Ontario

THIS DELICIOUS RECIPE was developed by the executive chef of the York Downs Golf and Country Club for the Dairy Bureau of Canada.

12	leeks, white part only	12
4 tsp	butter	20 mL
2 tbsp	finely chopped fresh basil	25 mL
24	scampi, peeled and deveined	24
2 tbsp	Calona Wines Pinot Blanc (white wine)	25 mL
1	clove garlic, minced	1
1	shallot, minced	1
3	tomatoes, peeled, seeded and diced	3
¼ cup	ricotta cheese	50 mL
	Salt and pepper to taste	

Calona Wines Pinot Blanc (dry)

Kelowna, British Columbia

Calona Wines' Pinot Blanc is dry, delicate and refreshing, with apple aromas and flavours, making it a great partner for scampi and the mild sauce.

Other Choices:
Ontario Chardonnay

CALONA VINEYARDS

Ricotta

Made by Saputo Cheeses

1 Wash leeks well. In a pot of boiling water, blanch leeks to soften, about 2 minutes. Drain and let cool. Cut leeks in half lengthwise and separate layers. **2** In a saucepan over medium heat, melt 4 tsp (20 mL) butter; sauté basil and scampi until scampi are tender, about 2 minutes. Remove from heat. With slotted spoon remove scampi from pan. **3** Roll a strip of leek around the centre of each scampi. Set on a plate, seam side down; cover and keep warm. **4** Return saucepan to medium-high heat; deglaze pan with white wine, scraping up any brown bits. Add garlic; sauté until brown. Reduce heat to low; add shallot and tomatoes. Simmer until tender, about 1 minute. Add ricotta cheese, stirring constantly until mixture is well blended. Season with salt and pepper. **5** Carefully return leek-wrapped scampi to saucepan; simmer gently for 2 to 3 minutes. **6** On each plate arrange six scampi in a fan shape. Surround scampi with sauce. Serve very hot.

GRILLED SALMON WITH BIQUET RÉMOULADE

SERVES FOUR   Fromagerie Tournevent — Chesterville, Quebec

CANADIANS DEVOUR GOAT CHEESE — some fresh and tangy, others firm and ripened. Canada's love affair with goat cheese has made Fromagerie Tournevent a lasting success. Since 1979 they have produced a medley of goat cheeses that please the palates of Quebeckers. Biquet and Tournevent are their most celebrated varieties, both soft and unripened, with mild flavours and light textures. Gourmands take a fancy to their Chevrino (mild and medium Cheddars), while Quebec's Greek communities favour the prize-winning Capriati Trio, three Mediterranean-style cheeses. All their varieties are made from Swiss Saanen goat's milk produced by a four-farm co-operative just outside Victoriaville, Quebec's dairy-producing region. Some goat cheese producers are forced to use frozen curds because the farms are so far away. But Tournevent has their milk delivered to them from the co-operative three times a week. This advantage gives Fromagerie Tournevent cheeses a rich, fresh flavour.

Inniskillin Wines Pinot Noir

Niagara-on-the-Lake, Ontario
Available in Quebec (Le Marchand de
Vin Inc., 514-481-2046)
Available in Ottawa (Inniskillin Wine
Boutique, 11 Metcalf St.,
613-563-3803)

Exhibiting a deep ruby shade and black cherry fruit, Inniskillin's Pinot Noir has soft texture that complements the creamy consistency of this goat cheese mayonnaise without overpowering this meaty fish.

Other Choices:
B.C. Pinot Noir

Biquet (fresh goat cheese)
Made by Fromagerie Tournevent

Rémoulade:

1	egg yolk	1
2 tbsp	extra virgin olive oil	25 mL
2 tbsp	vegetable oil	25 mL
½ lb	fresh goat cheese (Biquet), crumbled	250 g
1 tsp	dry mustard	5 mL
1 tsp	lemon juice	5 mL
1	clove garlic, minced	1
	Salt and pepper to taste	
1 tsp	finely chopped fresh dill	5 mL
1 tsp	finely chopped fresh chives	5 mL
4	salmon fillets (6 oz/150 g each)	4

1 In a food processor or blender, blend egg yolk, olive oil, vegetable oil and goat cheese. Add mustard, lemon juice, garlic, salt, pepper, dill and chives. Blend until well combined. Refrigerate until needed. **2** On a hot barbecue or under broiler, grill salmon for 2 to 3 minutes on each side or until firm. **3** Arrange salmon on plates. Garnish with a generous dollop of the rémoulade. Serve remaining rémoulade on the side.

PORTUGUESE CASSEROLE WITH SALT COD AND REQUEIJÃO

SERVES SIX   Portuguese Cheese Co. Ltd. — Mimico, Ontario

MANUAL JORGE OPENED his factory in 1966 to serve Toronto's Portuguese communities. His client base now spans Montreal, Toronto, London and Windsor. Though still actively involved in the business, Manual has handed the cheesemaking task to John Dutra. John's cheesemaking apprenticeship began at the Cooperativa Leiteira Santima Trindade, in the town of Almagreira, Portugal, where he specialized in making a cheese called São Jorge (St. George). He now produces five varieties. Portuguese Cheese Company's São Jorge and Sae Miguel taste like mild Cheddars; Montana is similar in flavour to Pico. A favourite is Serra, a soft cheese with a mild, refreshing taste. And whereas Portugal's traditional Requeijão is a farmer's cheese made from boiled sheep's or goat's milk, this company's version is closer in texture and taste to ricotta.

De Sousa Cellars
Dois Amigos Red

Beamsville, Ontario

John and Mary De Sousa opened their winery in 1987 and now produce a variety of varietal and blended wines. In the traditional Portuguese manner, this creamed salt cod casserole is married to red wine. Dois Amigos Red is a blend of de Chaunac, Villard Noir and Maréchal Foch. Delicate, dry and soft, it matches the delicate taste and texture of the casserole.

Other Choices:
 B.C. Merlot

Requeijão cheese

Made by Portuguese Cheese

1½ lb	dried salt cod, quartered	750 g
4 tbsp	extra virgin olive oil	50 mL
1	large yellow onion, thinly sliced	1
1¾ cups	milk	425 mL
1½ lb	potatoes, diced	750 g
¼ cup	water	75 mL
3 tbsp	unsalted butter	50 mL
3 tbsp	all-purpose flour	50 mL
½ tsp	white pepper	2 mL
1½ cups	Requeijão or ricotta cheese	375 mL

1 Soak salt cod, covered, for 48 hours, changing water daily. Drain and rinse. **2** Shred cod; set aside. **3** In a large skillet over low heat, heat 2 tbsp (25 mL) oil; sauté onions until soft. **4** Add cod and 1/2 cup (125 mL) milk. Simmer, covered, for 30 minutes, stirring occasionally. **5** Meanwhile, in another skillet over low heat, fry potatoes in remaining oil for 2 minutes. Add water; simmer, covered, for 15 minutes. Set aside, still covered. **6** In a medium saucepan over medium heat, melt butter; stir in flour. Cook, stirring, for 2 minutes. Pour in remaining milk, stirring constantly until sauce is smooth, about 3 minutes. Season with pepper. **7** In a shallow 13- by 9-inch (3.5 L) baking dish combine cod mixture, potato mixture and sauce. Top with cheese. Bake at 450°F (230°C) for 15 minutes. Lower heat to 350°F (180°C); bake another 25 minutes or until casserole is bubbly.

QUENELLES IN SAUCE LE MOINE

SERVES FOUR   Shari Darling — Toronto, Ontario

LE MOINE CHEESE, made by L'Abbaye de Saint-Benoît-du-Lac, in Quebec, is a pasteurized cow's milk Gruyère-type cheese, aged for two months. Its nutty flavour makes it suitable for cheese trays, nibbling and cooking.

2 lb	boneless pike fillets (or any freshwater fish)	1 kg
3	egg whites	3
1/2 cup (approx)	whipping cream	125 mL

Le Moine Sauce:

1/4 cup	butter	50 mL
1/2 cup	finely chopped button mushrooms	125 mL
3/4 cup	Gehringer Brothers Müller-Thurgau (white wine)	175 mL
1 1/4 cups	whipping cream	300 mL
1/3 lb	Gruyère-style cheese (Le Moine), diced	175 g
1	egg yolk, lightly beaten (if needed)	1
	Salt and pepper to taste	

Gehringer Brothers Müller-Thurgau

Oliver, British Columbia

Johannisberg Riesling, Verdelet, Pinot Auxerrois and Müller-Thurgau are a few of the wines produced by Walter and Gordon Gehringer. Light and dry, their Müller-Thurgau is an appropriate accompaniment for the melt-in-your mouth quenelles. It has melon and apple aromas, grapefruit and lime flavours and enough crisp acidity to cut through the richness of the cheese sauce.

Gehringer Brothers

Other Choices:
Vigneti Zanatta

Duncan, British Columbia
Vancouver Island's first winery, Vigneti Zanatta vinifies such grape varieties as Ortega, Pinot Gris and Pinot Noir. Ortega is a good choice for those who like peach and apricot character. Full-bodied, dry and crisp, the wine offsets the rich cheese sauce.

Other Choice:
Ontario Chardonnay

1 In a food processor or blender purée fillets. Push puréed fish through a sieve held over a bowl to extract bones. Chill bowl over ice for about 30 minutes or until purée has stiffened. **2** Beat egg whites until stiff. Gradually fold egg whites into puréed fish, a little at a time. **3** Add whipping cream, folding gently until mixture is moist enough to be fluffy but stiff enough to mould quenelles in your hands. Fold in additional cream if mixture is too stiff. If mixture is too runny, chill until stiff enough to work with. **4** With a tablespoon dipped in a large pot of boiling salted water, scoop out a heaping spoonful of the mixture. Dip another tablespoon into the boiling water and use both spoons to mould mixture into an egg shape. **5** Drop the quenelle into the boiling water and poach for 8 to 10 minutes or until firm when touched. If quenelle breaks up, beat another egg white into the mixture and chill for 30 minutes. **6** Drain quenelles on paper towels;

keep warm. **7** *To make Le Moine Sauce*, in a medium saucepan over medium heat melt butter; sauté mushrooms until tender. Add wine; bring to a boil. Stir in cream; return sauce to a boil, stirring constantly. When sauce just starts to boil, reduce heat. **8** Stirring constantly, add cheese, a few bits at a time, until melted. Remove sauce from heat. If sauce needs to be thickened, blend in egg yolk. **9** Strain sauce through a sieve. Season with salt and pepper. **10** Arrange quenelles on hot plates; top with sauce.

Le Moine

Made by L'Abbaye de Saint-Benoît-du-Lac

ZESTY SEAFOOD CASSEROLE WITH CHEDDAR AND SWISS CHEESE

SERVES FOUR TO SIX   Fitz-Henri Fine Foods — North York, Ontario

A FEW YEARS AGO the city of North York was just an unassuming suburb called Willowdale. Fitz-Henri's is one of Willowdale's original stores, established in 1964. It's now considered one of North York's finest speciality food shops, a place cheese lovers frequent to stock up on natural cheeses from near and far. All are cut to order. Among their assemblage of Canadian and imported cheeses, you'll find such mouth-watering delights as homemade jams, sauces and salad dressings and fresh and frozen appetizers, entrees, pâtés and desserts. A popular item is their pâté called Pesto Crème, a combination of cream cheese and homemade pesto sauce. John Fitzhenri still runs the shop while Judith operates their successful catering business, Fitz-Henri Catering Kitchen. This recipe is one of their more sublime entrees.

Lauro & Burden Cabernet Rosé

Mississauga, Ontario

A blend of California Cabernet Sauvignon and Ontario Maréchal Foch and de Chaunac, this rosé is refreshingly light and so does not overpower the seafood. With sweet raspberry character, the wine complements the cheese in this dish.

Other Choices:
B.C. Pinot Noir

LAURO & BURDEN WINERY

2 tbsp	butter	25 mL
2/3 lb	mushrooms, sliced	350 g
1 oz	thinly sliced green onions	25 g
1 lb	salmon fillet	500 g
2 tsp	lemon juice	10 mL
1 tsp	salt	5 mL
2½ cups	water	625 mL
1½ cups	Lauro & Burden Dry White (white wine)	375 mL
1 lb	scallops	500 g
1 lb	shrimp, peeled, deveined and coarsely chopped	500 g
½ cup	butter	125 mL
½ cup	all-purpose flour	125 mL
1½ cups	whipping cream	375 mL
¼ lb	old Cheddar cheese, shredded	125 g
¼ lb	Swiss cheese, shredded	125 g
½ tsp	hot pepper sauce	2 mL
	Salt and pepper to taste	

1 In a large saucepan over medium heat, melt 2 tbsp (25 mL) butter; sauté mushrooms and green onions until mushrooms are soft. Transfer vegetables to a large bowl. **2** Rub fish with lemon juice and salt. Wrap fish in cheesecloth or wide band of aluminum foil, leaving loose ends to lift easily. **3** In the same saucepan over high heat bring water and wine to a boil. Reduce heat to a simmer. **4** Poach wrapped salmon, covered, for 10 minutes per inch (2.5 cm) of thickness. Remove from liquid, unwrap and cut into chunks. Add to vegetables. **5** Poach scallops in poaching liquid, covered, for 1 minute or until white; remove with a slotted spoon and add to vegetables. **6** Poach shrimp, covered, about 2 minutes; remove with a slotted spoon and add to vegetables. Reserve poaching liquid. **7** In a large saucepan over medium heat melt 1/2 cup (125 mL) butter. Add flour; cook, stirring constantly, for 2 minutes without browning. Pour in poaching liquid, stirring constantly until smooth. Remove from heat. **8** Blend in cream, Cheddar and Swiss cheese, stirring constantly until sauce thickens. Stir in hot pepper sauce, salt and pepper. Stir in reserved vegetables, salmon and seafood. Return to low heat until heated through. Serve over basmati rice.

Old Cheddar

Made by Jenson Cheese

Grubec Swiss

Made by Agropur

HALIBUT AND ROMANO CAKES WITH BASIL BUTTER

SERVES FOUR   Shari Darling — Toronto, Ontario

THE ITALIANS PRODUCE three varieties of Romano — Pecorino Romano (sheep's milk), Caprino Romano (sharp goat's milk) and Vacchino Romano (mild cow's milk). In Canada, our dairies produce the latter version with a firm texture for grating and a mild flavour.

Cakes:

1 lb	halibut fillets	500 g
½ cup	milk	125 mL
½ cup	butter	125 mL
2	small onions, finely chopped	2
½ cup	all-purpose flour	125 mL
2	eggs, lightly beaten	2
½ lb	Romano cheese, grated	250 g
1 cup	dried bread crumbs	250 mL
	Salt and pepper to taste	
	Vegetable oil for shallow frying	

Basil Butter:

¼ cup	butter	50 mL
¼ cup	fresh basil	50 mL
1	clove garlic	1

Gray Monk Cellars Gewürztraminer (Broderson Vineyard)

Okanagan Centre, British Columbia

This Gewürztraminer is dry and well balanced, with floral, grapefruit and lime aromas and grapefruit flavours, accompanied by a long, spicy finish. Light but flavourful, this white is a good choice for fish and piquant Romano cheese.

Other Choices:

Ontario dry Gewürztraminer

GRAY·MONK

1 *To make fish cakes*, in a large skillet combine halibut and milk. Simmer over medium heat for 10 minutes or until halibut is tender. Drain halibut and transfer fish to a large bowl; mash fish. **2** In same skillet over medium heat melt butter; sauté onions until tender. Add flour; cook another minute until onions are well coated with flour. **3** Combine fish with onions, eggs, Romano cheese, bread crumbs, salt and pepper; stir together well. Spread mixture on a plate and refrigerate for 2 hours or until firm. **4** Divide mixture into eight balls; flatten into patties about 1/2 inch (1 cm) thick. **5** In a large skillet over medium-high heat, heat 1/4 inch (5 mm) vegetable oil until almost smoking. Fry cakes for 3 to 5 minutes on each side until golden. Drain cakes on paper towels; keep warm. **6** *To make basil butter*, in a food processor or blender blend butter, basil and garlic until smooth. **7** Transfer mixture to a saucepan. Over low heat, melt mixture; simmer for 5 minutes. **8** Arrange two cakes on each plate and drizzle with basil butter.

Romano

Made by Saputo Cheeses

GRILLED SWORDFISH STEAKS WITH ERMITE SAUCE

| *SERVES FOUR* | Shari Darling — Toronto, Ontario |

Côtes d'Ardoise (red), Domaine des Côtes d'Ardoise

Dunham, Quebec

Owned by Dr. Jacques Papillon, this winery produces a red that combines Gamay and Maréchal Foch. Oak-aged for six months, the wine is ruby in colour, light and easy drinking, with soft tannin, berries and a hint of spice on the nose and berry-like flavours. Delicate enough for this meaty fish yet possesses berry fruit that complements blue cheese.

Other Choices:
Ontario Pinot Noir or B.C. Gamay Noir

Ermite

Made by L'Abbaye de Saint-Benoît-du-Lac

Sauce:

3 tbsp	butter	50 mL
¼ cup	Carte d'Or Seyval by Domaine des Côtes d'Ardoise (white wine)	50 mL
¾ cup	whipping cream	175 mL
¼ lb	blue cheese (Ermite), crumbled	125 g
1	egg yolk, lightly beaten (if needed)	1
4	swordfish steaks, 1 inch/2.5 cm thick	4

1 To make sauce, in a medium saucepan over medium heat melt butter. Add wine and bring to a boil. Add cream, stirring constantly until sauce thickens slightly. Add Ermite cheese, a few bits at a time, stirring constantly until melted. Blend in egg yolk, if needed, to bind sauce. Keep warm. **2** On a well-oiled rack, grill swordfish on barbecue or under broiler for 5 minutes on each side or until meat is white. **3** Arrange steaks on serving plates and drizzle with sauce. Serve remaining sauce on the side.

ORANGE ROUGHY PAUPIETTES IN HAVARTI CREAM

SERVES FOUR   Kitchen Kuttings — Elmira, Ontario

ELMIRA, A SMALL TOWN in Ontario's Mennonite country, is home to farmers and craftsmen alike. Many of these townfolk buy locally made products, including cheese. The best varieties are displayed in a cosy shop in the heart of downtown. Its name? Kitchen Kuttings. Owned and operated by Lydia, Elmeda and Nancy Shantz, Kitchen Kuttings is decorated in country charm and highlights about 21 varieties of domestic cheeses and imports, all cut fresh on the premises.

Culotta Wines Gewürztraminer

Oakville, Ontario

Winemaker Bob Claremont produces a Gewürztraminer dry that is delicate enough for fish. Possessing lychee aromas and flavours with a slight vegetative note and soft texture, this white marries well with the sauce's butter-like smell, creamy consistency and mild flavour. By the same token, this Gewürztraminer carries enough acidity to cut through the cream's richness.

Other Choices:
B.C. dry Müller-Thurgau or dry Kerner

Sauce:

2 tbsp	cognac	25 mL
1/2 cup	Culotta Wines Gewürztraminer (white wine)	125 mL
1 1/4 cups	fish stock	300 mL
3/4 cup	half-and-half cream	175 mL
1/4 lb	Havarti cheese, shredded	125 g
1	egg yolk, beaten (if needed)	1

Stuffing:

1/2 cup	finely chopped cooked crabmeat	125 mL
1/2 cup	dried bread crumbs	125 mL
1	egg	1
1 tbsp	lemon juice	15 mL
1 tbsp	finely chopped fresh parsley	15 mL
Pinch	each salt and pepper	Pinch

4	orange roughy fillets (5 oz/100 g each)	4

1 *To make sauce*, in a medium saucepan over high heat boil cognac with white wine until reduced by half. Reduce heat to medium; add fish stock. Simmer until liquid is reduced by half again. Reduce heat to low; add cream. Simmer for 5 minutes, stirring constantly. Add cheese, stirring until well blended. Remove pan from heat. If sauce needs to be thickened, blend in egg yolk. Strain sauce through a sieve; keep warm. **2** *To make stuffing*, in a bowl combine crabmeat, bread crumbs, egg, lemon juice, parsley, salt and pepper; mix well. **3** Slice fillets lengthwise down centre, making two thinner fillets of each. Put one fillet on a strip of parchment paper; spread 2 tbsp (25 mL) of stuffing along its length. Roll up the fillet, peeling back parchment paper as you go. Wrap paupiette tightly in the paper, twisting the ends. **4** In a pot of boiling water, poach paupiettes for 12 to 15 minutes. Drain. Allow to cool slightly; remove paper. **5** Spoon sauce onto each plate. Arrange paupiettes on sauce and slice into medallions. Serve hot.

Havarti

Made by Fromagerie Cayer

LOBSTER STUFFED CABBAGE ROLLS, WITH MONTEREY JACK SAUCE

SERVES FOUR   Cheese Magic — Toronto, Ontario

CHEESE MAGIC HAS BEEN OWNED and operated by Ping Chiu since 1987. With a need for additional retail and storage space, Ping recently moved the shop to Baldwin Street, in the centre of Kensington Market. At this location customers will enjoy more of the same — 100-plus varieties of domestic and imported cheeses, a wide selection of pâtés and cold cuts and gift baskets handmade to order.

Created by chef Zdravko Kalabric, of Toronto, this dish calls for Savoy cabbage, which is crinkled and delicate in texture.

1	head Savoy cabbage	1
¾ tsp	butter	4 mL
1	shallot, minced	1
1½ cups	chopped lobster meat	375 mL
2 tbsp	brandy	25 mL
⅓ cup	white wine	75 mL
¾ tsp	paprika	4 mL
⅓ cup	fish stock	75 mL
¼ cup	whipping cream	50 mL
	Salt and pepper to taste	
3 oz	Monterey Jack cheese, shredded	75 g

Summerhill Estate Cipes NV Brut

British Columbia
Available in Ontario at Vintages

Owners Stephen and Wendy Cipes and Eric von Krosigk produce a champagne, made in the traditional méthode champenoise (second fermentation in the bottle), is aged in a pyramid-shaped cellar. It is believed that the pyramid produces energy that benefits the wine's flavours. The result is a wonderful bubbly with forward pear and apricot aromas and flavours, with light yeasty character and good acidity. Both lobster and Monterey Jack are delicate foods and can be easily overpowered by a wine with too much body or character. Cipes NV Brut is delicate with good effervescence — perfect elements to marry to this dish.

Other Choices:
Ontario Canadian champagne

SUMMERHILL

1 Remove tough outer leaves from cabbage and trim stalk. Tie cabbage with kitchen string to keep it whole while cooking. In a large bowl of lightly salted water, soak cabbage for 30 minutes. In a large pot of boiling water, boil cabbage for 8 to 10 minutes or until outer leaves are tender. Drain cabbage; set aside to cool. **2** In a medium saucepan over medium heat melt butter; sauté shallots until tender. Add lobster meat; cook until heated through, about 1 minute. **3** Increase heat to medium-high; deglaze saucepan with brandy, scraping up brown bits. **4** Add white wine and paprika. Simmer mixture gently until reduced by half. **5** Add fish stock; simmer 2 to 3 minutes, until reduced by half. Remove from heat. **6** With a spoon remove lobster from sauce. Reserve sauce. **7** On a work surface, spread out four cabbage leaves, stem end toward you. Spoon lobster mixture onto each cabbage leaf, about 1 inch (2.5 cm) from stem end. Fold in sides and roll up tightly in jelly-roll fashion. **8** Set stuffed leaves in a small baking dish, seam side down. Keep warm in a 300°F (150°C) oven. **9** Over high heat, bring sauce to a boil. Add whipping cream, salt and pepper. Boil, stirring constantly, until reduced by half. Reduce heat to low. **10** Add cheese, stirring constantly until cheese is melted. Remove from heat. **11** Arrange a lobster roll on each plate. Spoon sauce around roll and serve immediately.

Monterey Jack

Made by Riverside Cheese and Butter

LOBSTER AND PARMESAN RAMEKINS

SERVES FOUR   Paron Dairy Ltd. — Hannon, Ontario

BUTTERY CASATA, nutty Montasio and delicate Friulano are just some of the delicious cheeses produced by Paron Dairy. But it's Paron's exceptional Black Parmesan that has brought this company national recognition. Cheesemaker/owner Louis Paron uses only cow's milk produced during the winter to make his Parmesan. Winter milk is higher in calcium and protein and contains less water, making it richer in flavour, says Paron. He then ages the cheese for a minimum of two years. This cheesemaking style has won Paron countless awards in the Pacific National Exhibition and the Royal Winter Fair cheese competitions. In 1993 his Parmesan, casata and large old Montasio captured gold medals in their categories, and the Black Parmesan took the Grand Canadian Championship (overall grand prize) at the Royal Winter Fair.

Béchamel Sauce:

2 tbsp	butter	25 mL
2 tbsp	all-purpose flour	25 mL
¾ cup	milk, scalded	175 mL
	Salt and pepper	
Pinch	nutmeg	Pinch

Ramekins:

6 tbsp	butter	100 mL
14	large button mushrooms, sliced	14
1 lb	fillet of sole, cubed	500 g
½ cup	Cedar Springs Chardonnay (white wine)	125 mL
1½ cups	whipping cream	375 mL
1½ cups	cooked lobster meat	375 mL
	Salt and pepper to taste	
	Juice of ½ lemon	
¾ lb	Parmesan cheese, grated (for garnish)	175 g

Cedar Springs Global Selection Chardonnay

London, Ontario

A full-bodied Chardonnay with a toasty nose and flinty palate dominating subtle pear fruit, this white is big enough for lobster and cream.

Other Choices:

CedarCreek Estate Winery Chardonnay, Kelowna, British Columbia

1 *To make béchamel sauce*, in a small saucepan over medium heat melt butter. Add flour and cook, stirring constantly, for 3 minutes. Remove from heat. Add scalded milk, stirring constantly. Return pan to heat; simmer until sauce thickens, about 10 minutes. Season to taste with salt, pepper and nutmeg. **2** *To make ramekins*, in a large saucepan over medium heat, melt 3 tbsp (50 mL) butter; sauté mushrooms until tender, about 10 minutes. Transfer mushrooms to a bowl. **3** In same saucepan, melt remaining 3 tbsp (50 mL) butter; sauté sole until flaky, about 6 minutes. Transfer fish to bowl with mushrooms. **4** Add wine to saucepan. Over high heat, bring to a boil; reduce by half. Add cream; reduce by half. **5** Stir fish, mushrooms and lobster into saucepan. Season to taste with salt, pepper and lemon juice. **6** Divide mixture between four 1-cup (250 mL) ramekins. Spoon 2 tbsp (25 mL) sauce over each ramekin. Sprinkle generously with Parmesan. **7** Bake at 400°F (200°C) for 7 to 8 minutes or until mixture is bubbling and cheese is golden. Serve hot.

Black Parmesan

Made by Paron Dairy

BEGGAR'S BAGS WITH SCALLOPS AND NEUFCHATEL CHEESE

SERVES FOUR   Chef Dominique Jamain — Montreal, Quebec

A DELICIOUS APPETIZER or entree, this dish was created by Chef Dominique Jamain for the Dairy Bureau of Canada.

Fish Velouté: (Makes 4 cups/1 L)

5 cups	water	1.25 L
	Bones and heads of 4 sole or flounder	
	Juice of 1/2 lemon	
1 cup	finely chopped yellow onions	250 mL
	Bouquet garni	
	(made with thyme, peppercorns, bay leaves, and garlic)	
1 cup	Vignoble de l'Orpailleur Vin Blanc (white wine)	250 mL
2 tbsp	whey butter	25 mL
2 tbsp	all-purpose flour	25 mL

Neufchatel Sauce:

2 tbsp	whey butter	25 mL
1	shallot, chopped	1
1/3 cup	whipping cream	75 mL
1/3 cup	Neufchatel cheese	75 mL

Beggar's Bags:

24	large scallops	24
1/2 cup	Neufchatel cheese	125 mL
2 tbsp	finely chopped fresh chives	25 mL
2 tbsp	finely chopped fresh parsley	25 mL
	Salt and pepper to taste	
12	sheets phyllo pastry	12
1/4 cup	clarified butter, melted and cooled	50 mL
20	chives (for tying)	20

Vignoble de l'Orpailleur Mousse d'Or Brut

Made from 100 percent Seyval grapes and done in the traditional méthode champenoise, this bubbly is light, dry and refreshing, with delicate green apple aromas and flavours. With good effervesce, Mousse d'Or Brut cuts through the richness of scallops and Neufchatel cheese.

Other Choices:
Ontario or B.C. Canadian champagne

1 *To make fish velouté*, in a large pot combine water, fish bones, lemon juice, onions and bouquet garni. Bring to a boil; simmer, uncovered, for 45 minutes. Strain stock through a sieve lined with cheesecloth. Return stock to pot. Add white wine; simmer until reduced by half. Reserve 1/3 cup (75 mL) fish stock for Neufchatel sauce. **2** In a medium saucepan over medium heat melt butter; stir in flour. Cook for 2 minutes, stirring constantly. Gradually pour in fish stock, stirring constantly. Simmer until reduced by half and velvety smooth. Reserve 1/3 cup (75 mL) fish velouté for beggar's bags; freeze remainder. **3** *To make Neufchatel sauce*, in the cleaned saucepan over low heat melt butter; sweat shallot for 2 minutes or until translucent. **4** Add reserved fishstock; simmer until reduced by half. **5** Add cream; simmer until reduced by half. **6** Stir in Neufchatel cheese until cheese is melted. If sauce is too thin, whisk in butter 1 tbsp (15 mL) at a time until thickened. Remove from heat. **7** In a blender or food processor, purée sauce; keep warm. **8** *To make beggar's bags*, slice scallops crosswise into three coins each. **9** Grill scallops until light golden, about 30 seconds each side. Do not burn. **10** In a medium bowl stir together Neufchatel cheese, reserved fish velouté, chives, parsley, salt and pepper. Fold scallops into cheese mixture, being careful not to break them. **11** Divide 12 sheets of phyllo into four sets of three sheets. Working with first set, on a work surface lay out one sheet of phyllo; brush with clarified butter. Top with one sheet; brush with butter. Top with remaining sheet; brush with butter. **12** With a 4-inch (20 cm) round cookie cutter, cut out five circles.

13 Spoon 1 tbsp (15 mL) scallop mixture into the centre of each circle. Gather up edges to form a purse; tie each with a chive. Cut off long ends of chives. **14** Repeat process with remaining three sets until 20 purses are made. **15** Place purses on a buttered baking sheet. Brush purses lightly with butter. **16** Bake at 350°F (180°C) for 4 to 5 minutes or until golden. Remove chives. **17** Spoon sauce onto heated plates. Arrange five purses in a circle on each plate.

Baron Roula Neufchatel

Made by Fromagerie Cayer

MEDITERRANEAN PARMESAN STUFFED SQUID IN CHAMPAGNE SAUCE

SERVES FOUR   Shari Darling — Toronto, Ontario

Château des Charmes NV Brut

Niagara-on-the-Lake, Ontario

A sparkler is the best choice for this dish, as it works with the delicate squid, its Parmesan stuffing and, of course, the champagne sauce. Made from Pinot Noir and Chardonnay grapes, this bubbly was done in the méthode champenoise (second fermentation in the bottle) and aged on its lees (yeast) for two years. Medium-bodied and well-balanced, NV Brut is a good partner for all dishes, including this one.

Other Choices:

B.C. Canadian champagne

Black Parmesan

Made by Paron Dairy

Stuffing:

16	cleaned small squid (2 oz/50 g ea)	16
2 tbsp	finely chopped fresh parsley	25 mL
1¼ cups	grated Parmesan cheese	300 mL
2 tbsp	olive oil	25 mL
1	large shallot, finely chopped	1
	Salt and pepper to taste	

Sauce:

2 tbsp	olive oil	25 mL
2 lb	tomatoes, peeled, seeded and chopped	1 kg
1	clove garlic, minced	1
Pinch	each salt and pepper	Pinch
2 tbsp	finely chopped fresh basil	25 mL
¼ cup	Château des Charmes Brut Champagne	50 mL

1 *To make stuffing,* dice tentacles and fins; in a bowl, combine diced squid with parsley and parmesan. **2** In a medium saucepan over medium heat, heat olive oil; sauté shallot until soft. Add to diced squid; mix well. Season with salt and pepper. **3** Using a small spoon, stuff squid pouches with stuffing. Secure each pouch with a toothpick. **4** *To make sauce,* in the same saucepan over medium heat, heat olive oil. Add tomatoes, garlic, salt and pepper; simmer for 2 minutes. **5** Reduce heat to low. Add squid pouches; baste. Simmer, covered, for 30 minutes or until squid is very tender. Remove pouches; keep warm. **6** Stir basil and champagne into sauce; simmer for 10 minutes or until reduced by one-quarter. **7** Spoon sauce onto four serving plates. Place four squid pouches on each plate. Slice the pouches into medallions. Serve hot.

PARSLEY SHRIMPS AND SCALLOPS WITH FETA

SERVES FOUR TO SIX   Kawartha Goat Cheese — Indian River, Ontario

SOFT AND CREAMY or firm and crumbly, feta is the national cheese of Greece. And because of its distinctive, tangy flavour, it is an important part of the country's gastronomy. In fact, feta connoisseurs and lovers of Mediterranean cuisine will eat only mature versions made from unpasteurized goat's or sheep's milk. Outside of those produced in Greece, the real McCoys are hard to find. (Most imitation feta is made from pasteurized cow's milk, giving the cheese a mild flavour.) Fortunately, Canada is lucky enough to have a couple of cheesemakers who produce their feta in the traditional way. One of these is Greta Strain, of Kawartha Goat Cheese. Since 1983 Greta has been singlehandedly running her farm, milking 40 Nubian goats to supply Kawartha's local supermarkets with her delicious matured feta. She has won several awards for this cheese at the British Empire Cheese Show held in Belleville, Ontario, each year.

Cave Spring Cellars Chardonnay Reserve

Jordan, Ontario

Any one of Cave Spring Cellars' barrel-fermented Chardonnays would work with this dish. The Reserve has a spicy character to the nose with full apple flavours, buttery texture and a touch of spice to the finish. All these elements carry enough weight to match the wine to the seafood's rich taste and the tangy flavour of this aged feta.

Other Choices:
B.C. barrel-fermented and/or - aged Chardonnay

Kawartha brand Feta
Made by Kawartha Goat Cheese

3 tbsp	extra virgin olive oil	50 mL
3	cloves garlic, minced	3
2 small	onions, chopped	2
4	tomatoes, peeled and chopped	4
¼ cup	finely chopped fresh parsley	50 mL
¼ cup	Cave Spring Cellars Chardonnay (white wine)	50 mL
	Salt and pepper to taste	
¼ lb	cooked shrimped, peeled and deveined	125 g
¼ lb	scallops	125 g
1	tomato, thinly sliced	1
¼ lb	feta cheese, thinly sliced	125 g

1 In a large skillet over medium heat, heat oil; sauté garlic and onions until soft, about 3 minutes. Add tomatoes; simmer for 10 minutes. **2** Stir in 2 tbsp (25 mL) parsley. Pour in wine. Simmer 10 minutes until wine is reduced. Season sauce with salt and pepper. **3** Pour sauce into an 11- by 7-inch (2 L) baking dish. Arrange shrimp and scallops over sauce. Lay tomato slices over seafood and top with feta slices. **4** Bake at 450°F (230°C) for 8 minutes or until scallops are cooked and feta is melted. Sprinkle with remaining parsley and serve immediately.

EMMENTHAL-COATED CHICKEN BREASTS SAUTÉED IN L'ORPAILLEUR

SERVES FOUR   Fromagerie Coté — Warwick, Quebec

IN 1976 GEORGES COTÉ decided to buy a cheese factory. That he possessed absolutely no cheese-making skills did not pose a problem for this entrepreneur. A mere passion for food was enough. Today, under his direction, the company produces a variety of cheeses, including Cheddar, brick and ricotta. Coté's Swiss-style cheeses — Vacherin, raclette and emmenthal — are renowned throughout Quebec. In 1993 the raclette took first prize and the Vacherin second at the Pacific National Exhibition Cheese Competition in Vancouver. His Vacherin also captured first place in the Variety Cheese Category at the 1993 Royal Winter Fair in Toronto. These varieties are made by Swiss-born cheesemaker Stephane Richoz.

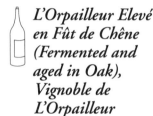

L'Orpailleur Elevé en Fût de Chêne (Fermented and aged in Oak), Vignoble de L'Orpailleur

Dunham, Quebec

Established in 1982, this winery makes four wines from the Seyval Blanc grape. This white is made from 100 percent Seyval. Full-bodied and refreshing with a smoky aroma and prominent vanilla and spice palate, this white tastes absolutely heavenly with the combined flavour of nutty Emmenthal cooked in white wine.

Other Choices:

Ontario or B.C. barrel-fermented and/or -aged Chardonnay

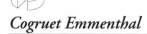

Cogruet Emmenthal

Made by Fromagerie Coté

4	boneless chicken breasts	4
	Flour for dredging	
2	egg whites, beaten until stiff	2
	Dried bread crumbs for dredging	
3 tbsp	butter	50 mL
2	cloves garlic, minced	2
1 cup	L'Orpailleur oak-aged (white wine)	250 mL
1/2 lb	Emmenthal cheese, thickly sliced	250 g

1 Dredge chicken breasts in flour. Dip in beaten egg whites; roll in bread crumbs. **2** In a large skillet over medium heat, melt butter; sauté garlic until tender. **3** Add chicken; sauté until both sides are golden, about 3 minutes each side. **4** Pour in wine. Cover skillet and simmer breasts for 15 to 20 minutes or until meat is white and tender. **5** Lay Emmenthal slices over chicken. Cover skillet until cheese has melted.

CHICKEN STUFFED WITH GOUDA IN GEWÜRZTRAMINER CREAM

SERVES FOUR   Crystal Spring Cheese Farm — Bluffton, Alberta

MORE THAN 28 CHEESES are made at Crystal Spring Cheese Farm, among them Gouda, Swiss and mozzarella. All are preservative-free. Owner and cheesemaker Johan Broere, a graduate in dairy and cheesemaking from Dronten University in Holland, follows a Dutch method for making his Gouda. As with all cheese, a culture starter is added to ripen (sour) the milk to promote the development of acid and to begin curdling. Rennet is then added to stimulate the coagulation of the milk so it becomes jelly-like in texture. The coagulum is cut into cubes to expel its liquid, called whey. The resulting curds are then heated in warm water and stirred until they develop Johan's desired firmness. Johan repeats this washing process because it helps to expel most of the curds' moisture, he says. Although this double washing method is time consuming, Johan says his Gouda contain less moisture, giving them longer ripening potential and therefore more flavour. The curd is then allowed to settle into one large block. The block is cut into cubes that are transferred to cylindrical moulds. Once covered with a piece of salted cloth, the curds are pressed for three to four hours. The resulting Gouda are salted in a brine solution to preserve them in storage.

Sumac Ridge Estate Winery Gewürztraminer Private Reserve

Summerland, British Columbia
Available in Alberta

No wine is better suited for this dish. The aromas show forward white grapefruit and background spice, while its grapefruit flavour is softened by a touch of sweetness, complementing the citrus sauce and nutty flavour of Gouda.

Other Choices:

B.C. off-dry Ehrenfelser

2	whole boneless skinless chicken breasts	2
1 lb	Gouda, shredded	500 g
1/2 cup	all-purpose flour	125 mL
1/2 tsp	salt	2 mL
1/2 tsp	pepper	2 mL

Sauce:

3/4 cup	Sumac Ridge Gewürztraminer Private Reserve (white wine)	175 mL
1/4 cup	orange juice	50 mL
1/4 cup	grapefruit juice	50 mL
1 cup	whipping cream	250 mL
1	egg yolk, beaten (if needed)	1
2	oranges, peeled and sectioned (for garnish)	2
	Pink peppercorns (for garnish)	

1 Place chicken breasts between two sheets of waxed paper and, using a mallet, pound to 1/4 inch (5 mm) thick. Place 1/2 cup (125 mL) shredded cheese on one half of each double breast. Fold over breast; tie with kitchen string. **2** In a small bowl, mix flour with 1/4 tsp (1 mL) of each salt and pepper;

coat all sides of breasts with seasoned flour. **3** Arrange chicken breasts in a buttered 12 1/2- by 8 1/2-inch (3.5 L) baking dish. Bake at 400°F (200°C) for 20 to 25 minutes or until chicken is tender and no longer pink. **4** Meanwhile, make sauce. In a large saucepan over high heat, bring wine to a boil. Reduce heat to medium; stir in orange juice, grapefruit juice and remaining 1/4 tsp (1 mL) each salt and pepper. Simmer gently for 2 minutes. **5** Add cream; stir well. Remove from heat. Blend in egg yolk, stirring constantly, if sauce needs to be thickened. **6** Remove string from chicken and cut breasts into four slices. **7** Place two slices on each plate. Pour sauce over slices. Garnish with orange sections and pink peppercorns.

Old Gouda
(aged 1 year)

Made by Crystal Spring Cheese Farm

CHICKEN LIVER, PROSCIUTTO AND CHEDDAR CRÊPES

SERVES FOUR   Dutchmen Dairy Ltd. — Sicamous, British Columbia

NELLIE DEWITT of Dutchmen Dairy has tantalized the tastebuds of British Columbians for more than 15 years with her natural Cheddars. They range from mild (aged six months) to sharp (aged two years). Homemade ice creams are also featured here, consisting of some 57 flavours. Though cheese lovers visit the dairy to stock up on a few of these specialty items, most of the Cheddars are distributed to local restaurants, hotels and supermarkets.

Filling:

3 tbsp	butter	50 mL
1 cup	chopped button mushrooms	250 mL
1	small onion, chopped	1
½ cup	coarsely chopped chicken livers	125 mL
	Salt and pepper to taste	

Crêpes:

⅔ cup	all-purpose flour	150 mL
Pinch	salt	Pinch
2	eggs	2
1½ cups	beer	375 mL
	Vegetable oil for shallow frying	

6	slices prosciutto	6
½ cup	Baker's White cheese	125 mL
½ cup	shredded Cheddar cheese	125 mL
2 tbsp	finely chopped fresh parsley	25 mL

CedarCreek Estate Winery Chancellor

Kelowna, British Columbia

Ruby red and medium-bodied, Chancellor boasts a raspberry nose and palate with just a hint of spice lurking behind. Though not a heavy wine, it has enough flavour to contend with the prosciutto and Cheddar. Its velvet smoothness provides a pleasant contrast to the meaty texture of chicken livers.

Other Choices:

Ontario Merlot

1 *To make filling*, in a small saucepan over medium heat, melt butter; sauté mushrooms and onion for 5 minutes. Add livers; sauté another 3 to 4 minutes. Season with salt and pepper. Set aside. **2** *To make crêpes*, in a bowl sift flour with salt. Make a well in centre and add eggs and beer. Beat to a smooth batter. **3** Brush an 8-inch (20 cm) crêpe pan with 2 tsp (10 mL) oil. Set over medium heat. Spoon in 2 tbsp (25 mL) batter; cook crêpe until surface looks dry, about 30 seconds. Make 12 crêpes. Set aside. **4** Cut prosciutto slices in half. Place one half on each crêpe. Divide liver mixture between crêpes. Roll up crêpes. Place side by side in a greased baking dish. Coat crêpes with Baker's White cheese; sprinkle with Cheddar and parsley. **5** Bake at 400°F (200°C) for 15 to 20 minutes or until Cheddar is melted and crêpes are heated through. Serve hot.

Baker's White Cheese

Made by Armstrong Cheese

White Cheddar

Made by Dutchmen Dairy

SOUTH AMERICAN CHICKEN IN A SPICY PARMESAN SAUCE

SERVES SIX   Leslie Cheese Shoppe — Stratford, Ontario

EVERY SUMMER the acclaimed Stratford Festival lures thousands of Canadians and tourists to its theatre. During off-times, theatregoers flock to the town's hub to shop, browse and dine. On Saturdays you'll spot the same faces at the Stratford Farmers' Market, where handmade crafts, gourmet fare and fresh produce take centre stage. Bob and Joan Smith, owners of the local Leslie Cheese Shoppe, have been at the market since 1990 selling their imported and locally made cheeses. Here, such names as Bright Cheese & Butter, Millbank Cheese and Oak Grove Cheese have become a priority for the loyal clientele. Part of the couple's success can be attributed to the imagination they pour into the creation of their gift baskets. And exquisite these baskets are. Hundreds are sold each year and shipped to loved ones throughout North America and Europe.

Cave Spring Cellars Merlot

Jordan, Ontario

Cave Spring Cellars has just opened a restaurant called On The Twenty adjacent to the winery. Here you can enjoy delicious food and a whole list of Cave Spring and Niagara wines. This recipe is a perfect example of why the rule about white wine and chicken must be broken. The sauce has powerful flavours of walnut and Parmesan, with spice that makes the forehead perspire, and a heavy potato base. These elements demand a red. Cave Spring Cellars Merlot can hold here. It is light bodied enough for chicken, but exhibits heavy spice on the nose and full raspberry fruit and sweet oak on the mouth.

Other Choices:

B.C. Baco Noir

5	large potatoes	5
8	slices white bread	8
2 cups	milk	500 mL
1/2 cup	olive oil	125 mL
1	clove garlic, minced	1
1	large yellow onion, finely chopped	1
2 tbsp	ground dried red Thai chilies*	25 mL
1 cup	walnuts, ground	250 mL
1/4 tsp	salt	1 mL
1/4 tsp	freshly ground black pepper	1 mL
2 tbsp	olive oil	25 mL
1	roasted chicken (4 lb/2 kg), skinned, boned and meat shredded	1
1/2 cup	grated Parmesan cheese	125 mL
3	hard-cooked eggs, each sliced into 6 wedges	3
12	black olives	12
2	fresh hot red chilies, seeded and cut in thin strips	2

Dried red Thai chilies are available in Asian supermarkets. Grind them between your fingers. Be sure to wash your hands afterwards.

1 In a large pot of boiling salted water, boil potatoes until tender. Peel and cut into 1/4-inch (5 mm) slices. Arrange slices side by side in a 13- by 9-inch (3.5 L) baking dish. **2** Cut crusts from bread. In a bowl soak bread in 1 cup (250 mL) milk for 5 minutes. Mash bread and milk into a thick paste. **3** In a large skillet over medium heat, heat oil; sauté garlic and onions until soft. Add ground chilies, walnuts, salt and pepper. Reduce heat; simmer for 5 minutes. **4** Stir in oil and bread paste. Gradually stir in remaining milk. Cook, stirring constantly, until sauce thickens. **5** Add chicken and Parmesan cheese; simmer for 5 minutes, until chicken is heated through. **6** Spoon chicken mixture over potatoes. Decorate with egg wedges, olives and fresh chili strips. **7** Bake at 350°F (180°C) for 5 minutes. Serve immediately.

Grated Parmesan

Made by Oak Grove Cheese Factory

CHICKEN AND GOUDA MOUSSAKA

SERVES SIX TO EIGHT   Island Farmhouse Gouda Inc. — Winslow, P.E.I.

IN HOLLAND THE BEST GOUDA come from farms where the cheesemaker takes a hands-on approach during production. The same holds true in Canada, and Island Farmhouse Gouda is a case in point. Following a Dutch recipe, owner and cheesemaker Martina Terbeek makes only 150 Baby Gouda or 30 Big Wheel Gouda each day. (Large manufacturers can make as many as 50,000 Gouda wheels a day.) Island Farmhouse offers a variety of Gouda, ranging in size, strength and taste. Young Gouda is aged up to six weeks, while the medium version spends four to ten months in cold storage to achieve a mild, buttery flavour. To be considered mature, Old Gouda must be aged for at least ten months, giving it a full, rich, tangy quality. Herb and Garlic, Red Chili, Pepper and Mustard Seed, and Cumin are a few of the spiced varieties produced at this farm. The farm, by the way, is open for public tours, and visitors can see how the cheeses are made.

Inniskillin Wines Chardonnay

Niagara-on-the-Lake, Ontario
Available in P.E.I. (Liquor Control Commission)

Inniskillin Wines produces more than 27 varietal wines, emphasizing VQA standards. Straw yellow, this Chardonnay has prominent green apple aromas with an easy-drinking approach full of citrus flavour. Works quite well with the tangy, nutty taste of Gouda without overpowering the eggplant or cinnamon.

Other Choices:
B.C. Pinot Blanc

White Sauce:

4 tbsp	butter	50 mL
4 tbsp	flour	50 mL
1½ cups	milk	375 mL
	Salt and pepper to taste	

Casserole:

4 tbsp	vegetable oil	50 mL
1 lb	eggplant, thinly sliced	500 g
1 lb	ground chicken	500 g
½ cup	chopped onion	125 mL
1½ cups	chopped tomatoes	375 mL
½ cup	water	125 mL
1	clove garlic, crushed	1
1 tsp	salt	5 mL
½ tsp	pepper	2 mL
¼ tsp	cinnamon	1 mL
½ tsp	finely chopped fresh thyme	2 mL
½ tsp	finely chopped fresh rosemary	2 mL
1 tbsp	finely chopped fresh parsley	15 mL
⅔ lb	Old Gouda, shredded	350 g

1 *To make white sauce*, in a medium saucepan over medium heat melt butter. Add flour; cook, stirring constantly, for 2 minutes. Gradually pour in milk, stirring constantly until sauce is smooth and thick. Remove from heat. Season with salt and pepper. **2** *To make casserole*, in a large saucepan over medium heat, heat 2 tbsp (25 mL) oil; sauté eggplant until tender. With a slotted spoon remove eggplant and drain on paper towels. **3** In same saucepan, sauté chicken until golden. Remove and set aside. **4** Add remaining oil to the saucepan; sauté onions until soft. Stir in tomatoes, water, garlic, salt, pepper, cinnamon, thyme, rosemary and parsley. Simmer for 15 minutes, stirring occasionally, until sauce thickens. **5** In an 11- by 7-inch (2 L) baking dish, layer half the eggplant. Spread half the chicken on the eggplant. Spoon half the white sauce over the chicken. Repeat with remaining eggplant and chicken, ending with a layer of white sauce. Sprinkle with Gouda cheese. **6** Bake, covered, at 350°F (180°C) for 1 hour. Let cool slightly before serving.

Old Gouda

Made by Island Farmhouse Gouda

CORNISH GAME HENS STUFFED WITH MASCARPONE, PRUNES AND PECANS

SERVES FOUR   Shari Darling — Toronto, Ontario

ORIGINALLY FROM ITALY'S Lombardy region, mascarpone is a double- or triple-cream cheese made from cow's milk. Though its texture may vary between producers, it's always ivory with a buttery rich flavour ideally suited for main dishes or desserts containing fruit.

4	Cornish game hens (2 lb/1 kg each)	4
Marinade:		
1 cup	Wild Goose Vineyards Johannisberg Riesling (white wine)	250 mL
½ cup	olive oil	125 mL
4	cloves garlic, minced	4
Pinch	pepper	Pinch
6	prunes, pitted and diced	6
Stuffing:		
6 slices	bread, shredded	6
¼ cup	chopped pecans	50 mL
½ lb	mascarpone cheese	250 g
Basting Ingredients:		
2	small stalks celery, diced	2
2	carrot, chopped	2
2	shallots, chopped	2
	Salt and pepper to taste	

1 Remove necks from hens; set aside. Rinse hens; pat dry. Set in a baking dish just large enough to hold them. **2** *To make marinade*, in a bowl whisk together wine, oil, garlic and pepper. Stir in prunes. Pour marinade over hens; marinate for 1 hour, basting frequently. Drain hens, reserving marinade. **3** *To make stuffing*, in a large bowl combine marinade with bread, pecans and mascarpone cheese; mix well. Stuff hens with stuffing. **4** In the baking dish combine celery, carrots and shallots. Set hens on vegetables. Season hens with salt and pepper. **5** Roast at 350°F (180°C) for 1 1/2 hours, basting frequently with pan juices, until hens are tender and golden.

Mascarpone

Made by Salerno Dairy Products

Transfer hens to a cutting board and keep warm. **6** In a food processor or blender, purée pan juices and vegetables until smooth. **7** Slice hens in half. Place two halves, stuffing side down, on each plate. Drizzle hens with sauce and serve.

Wild Goose Vineyards Johannisberg Riesling Dry

Okanagan Falls, British Columbia

Wild Goose Vineyards is owned and operated by winemaker Adolf Kruger. This particular Riesling, produced from A.F. Kruger Vineyard grapes in Okanagan Falls, has a bouquet reminiscent of apple blossoms and oranges and a white grapefruit flavour with medium body. The wine's tart acidity is opposite to the rich, creamy stuffing, bringing harmony to this marriage.

Other Choices:
Le Blanc Estate Winery Riesling

Harrow, Ontario
Established in 1993, Le Blanc Estate Winery is operated by Lyse Le Blanc, an amateur winemaker turned pro. Lyse is already earning respect in the industry with her Riesling, Vidal and Icewine. Other varieties will include Chardonnay, Pinot Blanc and a couple of Cabernets. Offering full body and a good balance of acid and sweetness and pear-like character, this Riesling is a good choice for those who prefer to match the wine's texture with the texture of the dish. This wine has enough body to match the heavy texture and rich flavours of the dressing.

GUINEA FOWL WITH BRIE AND HAZELNUTS

SERVES FOUR Chef Thomas Dietzel — Vancouver, British Columbia

THIS GORGEOUS DISH was created by the executive chef at the Waterfront Centre Hotel for the Dairy Bureau of Canada.

Filling:

1	medium pear, peeled	1
1	slice white bread, crust removed, diced	1
3 oz	Brie, diced	75 g
3 tbsp	chopped hazelnuts	50 g
Pinch	pepper	Pinch

4	boneless, skinless guinea fowl breasts (¼ lb/125 g each)	4
3 tbsp	butter, melted	50 g
16	sheets phyllo pastry, 6 by 4 inches (15 by 10 cm)	16

Sauce:

1	medium shallot, sliced	1
½	clove garlic, sliced	½
1 cup	Hainle Vineyards White Riesling dry (white wine)	250 mL
1 cup	whipping cream	250 mL
5 oz	Brie, diced	125 g
	Salt and pepper to taste	

1 In a pot of boiling water poach pear until tender-crisp. Drain; core and dice. **2** *To make the filling,* in a bowl mix pear, bread, Brie, hazelnuts and pepper. **3** In each guinea fowl breast, cut a pocket 2 inches (5 cm) long and 1/4 inch (5 mm) deep. Stuff each pocket with one-quarter of the filling. **4** On a work surface, lay out a phyllo sheet; brush with melted butter. Top with another sheet; brush with butter. Continue until four sheets have been used. Place a stuffed

Hainle Vineyards Baco Noir

Peachland, British Columbia

Tilman Hainle makes more than 10,000 gallons of wine each year, all within organic standards. This approach has brought this winery critical acclaim. Hainle Vineyards won four international gold medals for their 1987 Icewine. Tilman also produces an excellent Baco Noir, ideal for this dish. Smoky, floral nose precedes a raspberry palate with good acidity and light body, making it a good match in weight for guinea fowl while offering berry fruit that enhances the creamy Brie sauce.

Other Choices:

Ontario Pinot Noir

HAINLE VINEYARDS

breast at one end of pastry. Fold in sides; roll breast until wrapped in pastry. Repeat procedure until all breasts are wrapped in pastry. **5** Place wrapped breasts on baking sheet. Brust phyllo pouches lightly with butter. Bake at 325°F (160°C) for 15 to 20 minutes or until phyllo is golden and crispy; set aside. **6** *To make sauce*, in a medium saucepan over medium heat, combine shallot, garlic and wine; reduce to one-quarter. Stir in cream; reduce by half. Stirring constantly, slowly add diced Brie. **7** Strain sauce through a sieve. Return to saucepan. Season with salt and pepper; keep hot. **8** Spoon sauce onto each warm plate. Set wrapped breast on sauce. Slice into four slices.

Rocky Mountain Brie

Made by Neapolis Dairy Products

CHICKEN BREASTS WITH BLUE CHEESE AND GRAPES

SERVES FOUR   Chef Thomas Dietzel — Vancouver, British Columbia

Stuffing:

3 oz	baked focaccia bread, cubed	75 g
¼ lb	Havarti cheese, shredded	125 g
¼ cup	coarsely chopped macadamia nuts	50 mL
¼ tsp	finely chopped fresh thyme	1 mL
¼ tsp	salt	1 mL
Pinch	white pepper	Pinch

Chicken Breasts:

4	boneless, skinless chicken breasts (¼ lb/125 g)	4
	Salt and pepper to taste	
¼ cup	Quails' Gate Riesling (white wine)	50 mL

Sauce:

1	medium shallot, sliced	1
1 cup	Quails' Gate Riesling (white wine)	250 mL
1 cup	whipping cream	250 mL
3 oz	blue cheese (Ermite), crumbled	75 mL
16	small red seedless grapes (for garnish)	16

Quails' Gate Vineyards Riesling

Westbank, British Columbia

Quails' Gate Riesling offers citrus character on the nose and mouth and a good dose of acidity that contrasts nicely with the heavy cheese stuffing and subtle flavour of blue cheese in the sauce.

Other Choices:

Ontario dry Riesling

Quails' Gate®

Havarti

Made by Armstrong Cheese

Ermite

Made by L'Abbaye de Saint-Benoît-du-Lac

1 *To make stuffing*, in a medium bowl mix together focaccia bread, Havarti cheese, macadamia nuts, thyme, salt and pepper. **2** In each chicken breast, cut a 2-inch (5 cm) long and 1/4-inch (5 mm) deep pocket. Stuff each pocket with one-quarter of stuffing. Season breasts with salt and pepper. **3** Butter a roasting pan. Place breasts in pan, pocket side up. Pour in wine. Roast at 325°F (160°C) for 15 minutes or until breasts are white and tender; keep warm. **4** *To make sauce*, in a medium saucepan over high heat combine shallot and wine. Reduce to one-quarter. **5** Reduce heat to medium; add cream and blue cheese. Stirring constantly, reduce by half. **6** Strain sauce through a sieve. **7** Spoon sauce onto each plate. Set breasts on sauce. Slice breasts into four slices. Garnish each plate with four grapes.

APRICOT-POACHED DUCK BREASTS AND ROMANO CHEESE

SERVES FOUR   Oak Grove Cheese Factory Ltd. — New Hamburg, Ontario

OAK GROVE CHEESE, born in 1927, is owned and operated by Tristano and Reta Langenegger and Tristano's brothers, Mark and Anthony. Brick, Parmesan and Old Bra are their primary varieties, all distributed to restaurants, wholesalers and a few specialty shops in Canada. Old Bra, also known as Romano, is made from partly skimmed cow's milk and is a wheel-shaped hard, dry cheese. With a strong aroma and pronounced sharp, tangy and salty taste, Old Bra is a cheese lover's cheese.

Hernder Estates Vidal

St. Catharines, Ontario

One of Niagara's newest wineries, Hernder Estates concentrates their efforts on producing four varietal wines. One of these is the Vidal (semi-dry), a light white that works well with duck breasts. The wine's tropical fruit aromas and flavours enhance the concentrated sweetness of poached apricots, while its good backbone of acidity complements the piquant taste of Old Bra.

Other Choices:
B.C. off-dry Bacchus

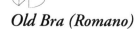

Old Bra (Romano)

Made by Oak Grove Cheese Factory

Poached Apricots:

¼ cup	brown sugar	50 mL
1¼ cups	Hernder Estate Vidal (white wine)	300 mL
12	fresh apricots, quartered	12

Duck Breasts:

4	duck breasts	4
½	lemon	½
	Seasoned flour for dredging	
¼ cup	butter	50 mL
3 oz	Romano cheese, shredded	75 g
	Salt and white pepper to taste	
½ cup	chicken stock	125 mL

1 In a medium saucepan over medium-high heat, blend sugar and wine. Simmer, until reduced by two-thirds. **2** Reduce heat to low. Add apricot quarters. Simmer, turning apricots periodically, until fruit is soft. Set aside to cool. **3** *To prepare duck breasts*, flatten them with the side of a knife. Rub cut lemon over breasts; coat with seasoned flour. **4** In a large saucepan over medium heat melt butter; sauté breasts for 10 minutes or until golden on both sides. **5** Pour poached apricots and liquid around breasts. Boil sauce for 1 minute. Reduce heat to low. Sprinkle breasts thickly with Romano cheese; season with salt and pepper. **6** Pour chicken stock into saucepan. Cover, and cook breasts for 5 to 10 minutes or until they are tender and cheese has softened. Remove breasts from saucepan. **7** Spoon sauce onto each plate. Lay breasts on sauce.

ROAST BREAST OF CHICKEN WITH ONTARIO GOAT CHEESE AND OLIVE STUFFING

SERVES SIX   Sebastian's Splendid Foods — London, Ontario

SEBASTIAN'S, WITH THREE BUSY LOCATIONS, is a gastronomic paradise for those who love to cook, those who hate to cook and for everyone who enjoys dishes like Indonesian chicken satay, herbed smoked duckling and chocolate raspberry truffle. Owners Ed Healy and chef Norbert Herreias have carved a special niche for themselves in London's food industry by incorporating a gourmet deli and catering business, European bakery and specialty food shop all under one roof. It is in the shop that a whole assortment of domestic specialty cheese can be found. Cheeses such as Woolwich Chevrai and L'Extra Brie have also found their way into Norbert's kitchen where they're transformed into heavenly creations for Sebastian's deli and catering menu.

Southbrook Farms Pinot Noir Vin Gris

Maple, Ontario

Southbrook Farms Winery, Farms and Market Garden attracts more than 100,000 visitors a year. This award-winning rosé is produced from only Ontario grapes. Full-bodied with a smoky aroma and raspberry and vanilla flavours, its characteristics marry well with chicken and enhance the creamy goat cheese stuffing.

Other Choices:
B.C. Cabernet Sauvignon (International Blend)

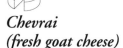

Chevrai (fresh goat cheese)

Made by Woolwich Dairy

Stuffing:

1/2 lb	fresh goat cheese, crumbled	250 g
1/3 cup	pitted black olives, chopped	75 mL
2 tbsp	finely chopped fresh chives	25 mL
1	clove garlic, chopped	1
2 tbsp	finely chopped fresh oregano	25 mL
2 tbsp	finely chopped fresh basil	25 mL
1/2 tsp	pepper	2 mL
6	boneless skinless chicken breasts	6
	Salt and pepper to taste	
2 tbsp	olive oil	25 mL
1 tbsp	finely chopped garlic	15 mL

1 In a bowl, mix together goat cheese, black olives, chives, garlic, oregano, basil and pepper. **2** Cut a slit 2 inches (5 cm) long and 1/4 inch (5 mm) deep in the backs of the chicken breasts. (If breasts are narrow and thick, cut a shorter, but deeper slit.) **3** Stuff each slit with stuffing. Tie breasts with kitchen string to seal slits. Season breasts with salt and pepper. **4** In a large skillet over medium heat, heat olive oil; sauté garlic until soft. Add chicken breasts; sauté until golden, about 3 minutes each side. **5** Transfer breasts to roasting pan, reserving oil in skillet. Bake at 375°F (190°C) for 10 minutes. Baste breasts with garlic and oil from skillet. Bake another 10 to 15 minutes, or until breasts are white throughout.

VEAL IN A GOAT CHEESE CRUST

SERVES SIX TO EIGHT   La Fromagerie de l'Ouest — Dollard-des-Ormeaux, Quebec

MARCHÉ DE L'OUEST, on Montreal's West Island, is an alluring farmers' market brimming with specialty food shops that spark the imaginations of chefs and home cooks alike. La Fromagerie de l'Ouest is a cheese shop with lots of Italian gusto. Owners Anna and Maher Helal offer their customers more than 200 imported and Canadian cheeses. Some of the domestic ones bear the labels Fromagerie Cayer, Fromagerie Clement and Agropur.

Inniskillin Wines Pinot Noir

Niagara-on-the-Lake, Ontario
Available in Quebec (Le Marchand de
Vin Inc., 514-481-2046)
Available in Ottawa (Inniskillin Wine
Boutique, 11 Metcalf St.,
613-563-3803)

A light-bodied red with ripe cherry aromas and flavours. With enough character to enhance veal, this red has enough acidity to complement the tangy flavour of the goat cheese crust.

Other Choices:

Chèvre des Neiges

Made by Fromagerie Cayer

Crust:

1 tsp	finely chopped fresh basil	5 mL
5	cloves garlic, minced	4
2 cups	fresh bread crumbs	500 mL
⅓ lb	fresh goat cheese, crumbled	175 mL
2 tbsp	olive oil	25 mL
Pinch	each salt and pepper	Pinch
1	veal loin (4 lb/2 kg)	1

1 In a food processor or blender combine all crust ingredients; blend until mixture is a moist dough. **2** Place loin in a covered roasting pan. Press crust dough over top and sides of loin. **3** Roast, covered at 475°F (240°C) for 30 minutes. Remove cover, and roast 30 minutes more. Let rest for 10 minutes before carving.

VEAL SADDLE GRATIN WITH ASIAGO CHEESE

SERVES FOUR   Chef Martin Boucher — Calgary, Alberta

YOU NEED ONLY ONE BITE of this dish to realize that Martin Boucher is a culinary artist. Chef de parties at the Palliser Hotel, Martin received his chef training at the Institut d' Hôtellerie de Québec in Montreal. This is a recipe for those who find joy in spending a few hours in the kitchen. Though time consuming, the recipe is easy to follow.

1½ lb	saddle milk-fed veal, boned	750 g
1	piece of pork back fat (3 oz/75 g) for barding*	1
3 tbsp	butter	50 mL
1	small carrot, thinly sliced	1
1	small onion, thinly sliced	1
4 tsp	Inniskillin Wines Cabernet Franc (red wine)	20 mL
2	small Paris mushrooms, thinly sliced	2
Pinch	salt	Pinch
½ tsp	black peppercorns	2 mL
1	Bouquet garni (made with 2 sprigs fresh parsley, 1 bay leaf and 1 sprig fresh thyme)	1
	Water as needed	
	Cornstarch as needed	

*Have your butcher cut a piece of pork back fat large enough to fit around the entire veal saddle.

Duxelle:

4 tsp	butter	20 mL
1 cup	sliced, wild mushrooms	250 mL
¼ tsp	flour	1 mL
	Salt and pepper to taste	

Onion Compote:

4 tsp	butter	20 mL
1 cup	diced onions	250 mL
2 tbsp	water	25 mL
	Salt and pepper to taste	

Inniskillin Wines Cabernet Franc

Niagara-on-the-Lake, Ontario
Available in Alberta (Vintage Consultants Ltd., 403-244-0324)

This medium-bodied red goes with veal without overpowering all the intricate flavours found in this layered dish. The wine's sweet pepper aroma and spicy character also complements the red pepper coulis.

Other Choices:
B.C. Chancellor

Mornay Sauce with Asiago:

2 tsp	butter	10 mL
2 tsp	all-purpose flour	10 mL
1 cup	milk	250 mL
2 oz	Swiss cheese, diced	50 g
2 oz	Asiago cheese, diced	50 g
Pinch	nutmeg	Pinch
	Salt and pepper to taste	

Red Pepper Coulis:

1	sweet red pepper	1
½ tsp	butter	2 mL
1	shallot, minced	1
2 tsp	Inniskillin Wines Cabernet Franc (red wine)	10 mL
2	bocconcini cheese (3 oz/75 g each)	2
	Salt and pepper to taste	

Basil and Parsley Coulis:

2	sprigs fresh basil	2
2	sprigs fresh parsley	2
3 tbsp	vegetable oil	50 mL
1 tsp	balsamic vinegar	5 mL
	Salt and pepper to taste	

1 Bard veal saddle by wrapping back fat around the whole saddle. Loop kitchen string around one end of the meat; tie a knot. Wind the string around the saddle to secure fat; knot the end. **2** In a large saucepan over medium-high heat, melt 1 tbsp (15 mL) of the butter and sear the barded saddle on all sides until golden. Transfer veal to a heatproof baking dish. **3** Drain fat from saucepan. Add remaining 2 tbsp (25 mL) butter; melt over medium heat. Sweat carrots and onions until onions are transparent. Add wine, mushrooms, salt and black peppercorns. Simmer until mushrooms are tender, about one minute. Transfer vegetables and bouquet garni to baking dish. **4** Add water until half of saddle is covered. **5** Set baking dish on high heat; bring to a boil. Transfer dish to oven and roast at 400°F (200°C) for 20 minutes or until veal is pink. Remove veal from baking dish; let cool. **6** Over high heat reduce stock by one-quarter. Strain stock through a sieve. Return stock to baking dish. Over medium heat simmer until stock is thin sauce. If needed, thicken sauce with cornstarch to desired consistency; keep warm. **7** *To make duxelle*, in a saucepan over medium heat, melt butter; sauté mushrooms until tender, about 2 minutes. Reduce heat to low; stir in flour. Simmer for 20 minutes, stirring occasionally, until liquid has almost evaporated. Season with salt and pepper. Set aside. **8** Meanwhile, *make onion compote*. In a saucepan over low heat melt butter; sweat onions until transparent, about 1 minute. Add water; simmer until all liquid has evaporated, about 20 minutes. Season with salt and pepper; set aside. **9** *To make Mornay sauce*, in a medium saucepan over low heat melt butter. Add flour; cook stirring, for 10 minutes. Pour in milk, stirring constantly; cook, stirring for 20 minutes. Slowly add Asiago cheese and Swiss cheese, stirring constantly until well blended. Season with nutmeg, salt and pepper. Strain sauce through a sieve; set aside. **10** *To make red pepper coulis*, grill pepper until blackened. Wrap in plastic wrap and let cool to room temperature. Under cold water, peel pepper. Mince pepper. In a saucepan over medium heat, melt butter; sweat shallot until tender, about 1 minute. Add pepper; cook another 2 minutes. Add wine. Cook another minute. Mix in bocconcini cheese. Season with salt and pepper. In a a food processor or blender purée until smooth. If coulis is too thick, add a little water until sauce consistency. Strain through a sieve; keep warm. **11** *To make basil and parsley coulis*, in a small pot of boiling water blanch parsley and basil for 5 seconds. Remove basil and parsley; reserve water. In a food processor or blender purée basil, parsley, oil and vinegar until smooth. If needed, add a little blanching water until consistency is liquidy. Strain through a sieve. Season with salt and pepper; set aside. **12** To assemble gratins, remove bard from the saddle. Cut saddle into thin slices. Place four (4-inch/10 cm) cookie cutters on a baking sheet. Place one slice of veal inside each cookie cutter. Top with a layer of duxelle. Place another slice of veal on duxelle. Top with with some onion compote. Place another slice of veal on compote. Continue until all duxelle and compote is used ending with a slice of veal. Top with Mornay sauce. **13** Bake gratins at 325°F (160°C) until Mornay sauce is golden, about 5 minutes. **14** With a metal spatula, transfer veal cakes inside their cookie cutters to four plates. Gently remove cookie cutters. Garnish each plate with a spoonful of red pepper coulis and basil and parsley coulis. Serve with Yorkshire Pudding with Canadian Blue (recipe on page 70).

Asiago and Bocconcini

Made by Salerno Dairy Products

Fromage Suisse

Made by Crystal Spring Cheese Farm

VEAL CORDON BLEU WITH EMMENTHAL CHEESE

SERVES FOUR
Towne & Country Cheese Shoppe — St. Marys, Ontario

NESTLED IN THE VALLEY at the junction of Trout Creek and the Thames River is St. Marys, a handsome town filled with waterways, Victorian and Gothic buildings and limestone quarries. Smack in the heart of town is a quaint cheese shop and deli called Towne & Country. A favourite eatery with locals, the shop features salads, soups and sandwiches that always satisfy without robbing the pocketbook. Owners Connie and Harold Douglas take pride in offering a wide selection of domestic cheeses. A majority of these are made locally at Pine River, Tavistock and Bright Cheese.

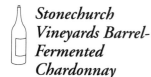

Stonechurch Vineyards Barrel-Fermented Chardonnay

Niagara-on-the-Lake, Ontario

Exhibiting a vanilla and apple bouquet that leads into a full-bodied mouth with buttery texture and oak flavours dominating pear-like fruit, this Chardonnay has enough character to equal the combined big flavour of veal, smoked ham and Emmenthal cheese.

Other Choices:

B.C. barrel-fermented and/or -aged Chardonnay

Anco Emmenthal

Made by Agropur

1½ lb	veal tenderloin, trimmed of fat	750 g
4	thin slices smoked ham	4
¼ lb	Emmenthal cheese, cut in 4 thin slices	125 g
2 tbsp	all-purpose flour	25 mL
½ tsp	salt	2 mL
¼ tsp	pepper	1 mL
¼ tsp	allspice	1 mL
1	egg, lightly beaten	1
½ cup	dry bread crumbs	125 mL
3 tbsp	vegetable shortening	50 mL
2 tbsp	water	25 mL

1 Cut veal lengthwise into four equal portions. Place a slice of ham and a slice of cheese on each piece of veal. Beginning at narrow end, roll up veal in jelly-roll fashion. Secure rolls with toothpicks. **2** In a small bowl mix flour, salt, pepper and allspice. Coat rolls in seasoned flour. Dip rolls in egg. Coat rolls in bread crumbs. **3** In a large skillet over medium heat, melt shortening; fry veal rolls about 5 minutes or until golden on all sides. 4. Reduce heat; add water. Cover skillet; simmer for 40 minutes or until veal is tender. Add more water if necessary. **4** Remove cover. Simmer another 5 minutes or until rolls are slightly crispy.

VEAL ROULADEN WITH PROVOLONE AND TRAPPIST CHEESE

SERVES FOUR   Our Lady of the Prairies Abbey — Holland, Manitoba

WHAT DO PORT SALUT, Oka and Trappist cheese all have in common? They are derivatives of one cheese that is believed to have originated in a monastery in Yugoslavia. After the French Revolution, Trappist monks returned to France from exile, bringing with them a secret recipe for a delicious surface-ripened cheese. The Abbey of Entrammes produced the cheese first, calling it Port Salut or Port du Salut (Port of Salvation). Over the centuries, the recipe travelled from monastery to monastery, country to country, taking on various names and characteristics. In 1890 Trappist monks in Oka, Quebec, developed Canada's famous Oka cheese, and in the early 1920s, the Trappist monks of Our Lady of the Prairies Abbey, in Manitoba started Fromage de la Trappé (Trappist cheese). Although Our Lady of the Prairies Abbey made the cheese only at various times since the 1920s, production has been steady since 1985. These Trappist monks are the sole producers of this unpasteurized handmade cheese. With a tawny rind, Trappist cheese has a springy interior, a nut-like aroma and a buttery, nutty taste.

Executive Chef Thomas Dietzel, of the Waterfront Centre Hotel in Vancouver, developed this delightful recipe for the Dairy Bureau of Canada.

Provolone

Made by Saputo Cheeses

Trappist cheese

Made by Our Lady of the Prairies Abbey

4	lean veal schnitzels (¹/₄ lb/125 g each)	4
Stuffing:		
¹/₄ cup	fresh spinach	50 mL
¹/₄ cup	radicchio	50 mL
¹/₄ lb	lean ground veal	125 g
¹/₄ lb	provolone cheese, shredded	125 g
1	egg, lightly beaten	1
1 tsp	shelled pistachios	5 mL
¹/₄ tsp	salt	1 mL
Pinch	white pepper	Pinch
2 tbsp	vegetable oil	25 mL
1 cup	dry vermouth	250 mL
Sauce:		
1	medium shallot, sliced	1
1 cup	whipping cream	250 mL
3 oz	Trappist cheese, diced	75 g
	Salt and pepper to taste	

1 Using a mallet, pound veal into thin steaks. **2** *To make stuffing*, in a pot of boiling salted water, blanch spinach and radicchio for 1 minute. Remove and plunge into cold water. Squeeze out excess water; chop coarsely. **3** In a large bowl mix together spinach, radicchio, ground veal, provolone cheese, egg, pistachios, salt and pepper. **4** *To make rouladen*, place one-quarter of stuffing on the end of each veal steak. Roll up tightly, tucking in ends. **5** In a large oven-safe skillet over medium heat, heat oil. Sear rouladen until golden on all sides. Remove from heat. Pour in vermouth. Cover skillet with aluminum foil. **6** Roast at 300°F (150°C) for 15 to 20 minutes. Remove rouladen; keep warm. **7** *To make sauce*, in same skillet over high heat bring pan juices to a boil; add shallots. Reduce to one-quarter. Reduce heat to medium; add cream and Trappist cheese, stirring constantly until cheese is melted. Season with salt and pepper. Simmer gently, stirring constantly, until sauce is reduced by half. Strain sauce through a sieve. **8** Spoon sauce onto each warmed plate. Place veal rouladen on sauce. Slice into four slices.

Sumac Ridge Estate Winery Stella's Jay Cuvée Dry

Summerland, British Columbia

Sumac Ridge produces three sparklers, a Blanc de Blanc, Blanc de Noir Brut Extra Dry and Stella's Jay Cuvée Dry. All three are perfect accompaniments to this dish. Stella's Jay Cuvée Dry is done in the traditional méthode champenoise (second fermentation in the bottle). Crisp with citrus notes in the nose and mouth, this simple bubbly works with veal and stuffing, while offering effervescence to offset the rich Trappist cheese sauce.

Other Choices:
Ontario Canadian champagne

OKA VEAL PAUPIETTES WITH SUN-DRIED TOMATOES

SERVES FOUR   Chef Thomas Dietze — Vancouver, British Columbia

---

THE WATERFRONT CENTRE HOTEL, in Vancouver, has an excellent executive chef in Thomas Dietzel. He developed this recipe for the Dairy Bureau of Canada.

Stuffing:

2 oz	lamb sweetbreads, cooked	50 g
2 tbsp	blanched arugula	25 mL
2 oz	lean ground veal	50 g
2 tbsp	diced button mushrooms	25 mL
¼ lb	Oka cheese, shredded	125 g
2 tsp	finely chopped fresh basil	10 mL
	Salt and pepper to taste	

Veal Paupiettes:

8	lean veal medallions (2 oz/50 g each)	8
2 tbsp	butter	25 mL
3 tbsp	Blue Mountain Vineyard and Cellars Pinot Blanc (white wine)	50 mL

Sauce:

1	medium shallot, sliced	1
1 cup	Blue Mountain Vineyard and Cellars Pinot Blanc (white wine)	250 mL
1 cup	whipping cream	250 mL
⅓ cup	cream cheese	75 mL
2 tsp	finely chopped fresh chives	10 mL
2 tsp	diced sun-dried tomatoes (packed in oil)	10 mL
	Salt and pepper to taste	

1 To make stuffing, break apart cooked sweetbreads; chop coarsely. **2** Gently squeeze out excess water from arugula; chop coarsely. **3** In a medium bowl mix together sweetbreads, arugula, ground veal, mushrooms, Oka cheese, basil, salt and pepper. **4** Using a mallet, flatten veal medallions until very thin. **5** Spoon one-eighth of stuffing onto each medallion; roll up tightly, tucking in ends. **6** In an oven-safe

---

Blue Mountain Vineyard and Cellars Sparkling Wine Brut

Okanagan Falls, British Columbia

This winery is operated by Ian and Jane Mavety. They produce Pinot Blanc, Pinot Gris, Pinot Noir and this tasty sparkler. The rich, cream-based sauce dominates this dish, requiring a white wine or bubbly to offset it. This bubbly was produced from 45 percent Pinot Noir, 45 percent Chardonnay and 10 percent Pinot Gris grapes. Made in the traditional méthode champenoise (second fermentation in the bottle), the wine is medium bodied, clean and crisp, making it an excellent companion to this dish.

Other Choices:

Ontario Canadian champagne

skillet over medium heat, melt butter; sear veal paupiettes until golden on all sides. Remove from heat. Pour in wine. Cover skillet with aluminum foil. **7** Roast at 300°F (150°C) for 15 minutes. Keep warm. **8** Meanwhile, make sauce. In a medium saucepan over high heat, bring shallots and wine to a boil; reduce to 1/4 cup (50 mL). **9** Reduce heat to medium. Stir in cream and cream cheese. Stirring constantly, reduce by half. Strain sauce through a sieve. Return to saucepan. Stir in chives, sun-dried tomatoes, salt and pepper. **10** Spoon sauce onto each plate. Place two veal paupiettes on the sauce. Slice each paupiette into three or four slices.

Oka

Made by Agropur

PORK ROULADEN "MONTEREY JACK"

SERVES FOUR   Chef Thomas Dietzel — Vancouver, British Columbia

EXECUTIVE CHEF at the Waterfront Centre Hotel, in Vancouver, Thomas is a native of West Germany. At age 17, he completed his chef's apprenticeship at Park Hotel Recklingloh, in West Germany, then travelled the world to further his education. Steigenberger Hotel in West Germany, a season in Lausanne at the Hotel Aualac and employment at Hotel Kempinski in Berlin are a few of the destinations in which he discovered and learned about German cuisine. Upon crossing the Atlantic, Thomas worked at the Princess Hotel in Bermuda, Maxims in Washington, D.C., the Queen Elizabeth Hotel in Montreal and the Hotel Vancouver. This is just one of the many recipes he developed for the Dairy Bureau of Canada.

Domaine de Chaberton Madeleine Angevine

Langley, British Columbia

Domaine de Chaberton is Langley's first farm-gate winery. Only a few years old, the winery has already won several awards for their varietal wines. No other white could be better suited for this pork dish than their Madeleine Angevine. Made from Muscat and Pinot Blanc, this white offers sweet apple aromas and spicy apple flavours that have a natural affinity with pork while allowing the mild flavour of Monterey Jack to come forth. Good acidity and lingering spice add pleasant contrast to the cream-based sauce.

Other Choices:

Ontario Chardonnay

4	lean pork schnitzels (1/4 lb/125 g each)	4

Stuffing:

1 cup	spinach, blanched	250 mL
1/2 lb	lean ground pork	250 g
1	egg white	1
1/4 tsp	salt	1 mL
1/4 tsp	paprika	1 mL
Pinch	white pepper	Pinch
1 tsp	Dijon mustard	5 mL
1/4 lb	Monterey Jack with Caraway, shredded	125 g
2 tbsp	vegetable oil	25 mL
1/4 cup	Domaine de Chaberton Madeleine Angevine (white wine)	50 mL

Sauce:

1/2 cup	whipping cream	125 mL
3/4 tsp	Dijon mustard	4 mL
	Salt and pepper to taste	
1/2	sweet red pepper	1/2

1 Using a mallet, pound pork schnitzels into very thin steaks. **2** *To make stuffing*, squeeze out excess water from spinach. Chop coarsely. **3** In a food processor or blender, blend ground pork, egg white, salt, paprika, pepper and mustard. Transfer mixture to a bowl; fold in spinach and Monterey Jack cheese. **4** Place one-quarter of stuffing on end of each pork steak. Roll up tightly to form rouladen. **5** In an oven-safe skillet over medium heat, heat oil; fry rouladen until golden on all sides. Remove from heat. Pour in wine. Cover skillet with aluminum foil. **6** Roast at 275°F (140°C) for 15 minutes or until pork is no longer pink. Remove rouladen; keep warm. **7** *To make sauce*, in the skillet over medium heat stir into cooking juices the cream, Dijon mustard, salt and pepper; reduce to two-thirds. **8** In a small pot of boiling salted water blanch red pepper for 1 minute. Drain and peel. Cut into four equal squares. **9** Spoon sauce onto each plate. Place rouladens on sauce. Slice rouladens into four slices. Garnish each with a red pepper square.

Monterey Jack

Made by Armstrong Cheese

PUFFED PORK ROLLS WITH FETA SALSA

SERVES FOUR   Chef Thomas Dietzel — Vancouver, British Columbia

THIS RECIPE, developed by the talented executive chef of the Waterfront Centre Hotel, in Vancouver, calls for Saint Paulin, a semi-soft cheese made from pasteurized cow's milk. It has an orange rind, a moist, springy centre with creamy consistency and a buttery flavour. An excellent cooking cheese.

Stuffing:

¼ lb	spinach, blanched	125 g
¼ lb	Saint Paulin cheese, shredded	125 g
¼ lb	ground lean pork	125 g
1	small egg, lightly beaten	1
¼ tsp	salt	1 mL
Pinch	pepper	Pinch

Pork Rolls:

4	lean pork schnitzels (¼ lb/125 g each)	4
4	prepared puff pastry squares (5 inches/12 cm square)	4
	Eggwash (1 egg beaten with 1 tsp/5 mL water)	

Salsa:

3 tbsp	tequila	50 mL
½	medium onion, diced	½
1 tbsp	tomato paste	25 mL
½ cup	canned peeled tomatoes, diced	125 mL
½	medium jalapeño pepper, diced	½
3 oz	feta cheese, crumbled	75 g
	Salt and pepper to taste	

Sumac Ridge Johannisberg Riesling

Summerland, British Columbia

Though the salsa has a tomato base, the majority of the recipe calls for a white wine — pork, puff pastry, Saint Paulin and feta cheeses. A full-bodied white with citrus aromas and flavours, this dry wine stands up to the weight of pork. With fine acidity, the wine offsets the buttery taste of puff pastry and the richness of the cheese stuffing. The acidity also works with the tangy feta flavour in the salsa.

Other Choices:

Ontario dry Gewürztraminer

1 *To make stuffing*, squeeze out excess water from blanched spinach. Chop coarsely. **2** In a large mixing bowl mix spinach, Saint Paulin cheese, ground pork, egg, salt and pepper. **3** *To make pork rolls*, using a mallet, pound pork schnitzels until very thin. Spread each schnitzel with one-quarter of the stuffing. Roll up tightly tucking in ends. **4** On a lightly floured work surface, roll out puff pastry squares until same length as pork rolls. Wrap pastry around each pork roll. Brush end of pastry with eggwash to seal. Place rolls on a baking sheet. **5** Bake at 350°F (180°C) for 20 to 25 minutes or until meat is cooked and pastry is golden. **6** *To make salsa,* in a small saucepan over medium heat combine tequila, onions and tomato paste; simmer for 1 minute. Stir in diced tomatoes, jalapeño, feta cheese, salt and pepper; simmer for 15 minutes. **7** Place a pork roll on each plate; slice into four slices. Pour a generous spoonful of salsa over each pork roll.

Anco Saint Paulin

Made by Agropur

Feta

Made by Woolwich Dairy

PORK CHOPS ROASTED IN GOAT CHEESE SAUCE WITH WILD MUSHROOMS AND BLUEBERRIES

SERVES FOUR   Budapest Delicatessen — Ottawa, Ontario

CHEESE, CHEESE AND MORE CHEESE — that's what you'll find at Budapest Deli in the Byward Farmers' Market. Owner André Vertes offers close to 100 Canadian varieties, among them Brie, Camembert, goat's milk varieties, Oka, Trappist and Cheddar. Cheddars are a big seller here, says André, because they're delicious and locally made by Balderson Cheese, Forfar Dairy and St. Albert Co-operative. At least 300 imported varieties are available here, too, with a minimum of eight raw-milk types on display at any one time. Although the name Budapest is now synonymous with quality cheese, the original shop, established in 1971 by André's father, Tibor, carried fresh produce and a few European cheeses. André left his father's business in 1978 to start Budapest Deli.

Hillebrand Estates Collector's Choice Cabernet-Merlot

Niagara-on-the-Lake, Ontario

A medium-bodied red with red currants and raspberries coming through in the bouquet. The palate offers raspberry flavour and a touch of vanilla. While having enough weight to match the texture of pork, this blend possesses enough acidity to match the tangy flavour of goat cheese. Its raspberry character also complements the berries in the sauce.

Other Choices:
B.C. Merlot

Chevrai

Made by Woolwich Dairy

1 tbsp	vegetable oil	15 mL
4	pork loin chops, 1 inch (2.5 cm) thick	4
2 tbsp	butter	25 mL
1	clove garlic, minced	1
½ cup	diced fresh shiitake mushrooms	125 mL
1 tsp	tomato paste	5 mL
1 cup	chicken OR beef stock	250 mL
½ lb	fresh goat cheese, crumbled	250 g
¼ cup	sour cream	50 mL
½ cup	fresh blueberries	125 mL

1 In a skillet over medium heat, heat oil; fry pork chops for 2 to 3 minutes on each side or until golden. **2** Meanwhile, in a saucepan over medium heat melt butter; sauté garlic and mushrooms until tender. **3** Remove saucepan from heat. Stir in tomato paste, and stock. **4** Return pan to high heat; bring to a boil. Reduce heat to medium; simmer for 5 minutes. **5** Meanwhile, in a food processor or blender blend goat cheese and sour cream until smooth. Stir into mushrooms until well combined. Fold in blueberries. **6** Transfer chops to a baking dish just large enough to hold them. Pour sauce over chops. Roast at 350°F (180°C) for 30 minutes or until chops are white throughout. **7** Spoon sauce onto each warm plate. Arrange chops on sauce and serve immediately. Serve extra sauce on the side.

SWEETBREAD AND CHEDDAR CASSEROLE

SERVES FOUR   Shari Darling — Toronto, Ontario

1 lb	prepared lamb sweetbreads, thickly sliced	500 g
¼ cup	all-purpose flour	50 mL
¼ cup	butter	50 mL
¼ lb	button mushrooms, sliced	125 g
¼ cup	Henry of Pelham Baco Noir (red wine)	50 mL
½ cup	chicken stock	125 mL
	Salt and pepper to taste	
2	small eggs	2
⅔ cup	plain yogurt	150 mL
¼ lb	extra-old Cheddar, shredded	125 g

1 In a bowl toss sweetbread slices with flour. **2** In a large saucepan over medium heat melt butter; fry sweetbreads and mushrooms for 10 minutes or until sweetbreads are golden. **3** Add wine. Simmer for 2 minutes. Add stock; season with salt and pepper. Simmer another 5 minutes. **4** Meanwhile, in a bowl beat eggs with yogurt. Stir in Cheddar cheese. **5** Transfer sweetbreads and mushrooms to a 13- by 9-inch (3.5 L) baking dish. Pour yogurt mixture on top. Bake at 375°F (190°C) for 20 minutes or until top is golden. Serve hot.

Henry of Pelham Baco Noir

St. Catharines, Ontario

Sweetbreads and Cheddar demand a full-bodied, showy red. Henry of Pelham's Baco Noir offers raspberry fruit overlaid by sweet tobacco and peppery spice. The palate also shares raspberry fruit with austere tannins. The raspberry character is wonderful alongside the Cheddar, while the wine in general is big enough to compete with this flavourful casserole.

Other Choices:

B.C. Cabernet Sauvignon (International Blend)

Extra-Old White Cheddar

Made by Tavistock

MEDALLIONS OF LAMB WITH SPINACH AND TRIPLE-CREAM BRIE

SERVES FOUR   Chef Zdravko Kalabric — Toronto, Ontario

THIS RECIPE WON a silver medal in the 5th Annual Food and Hotel Asia Culinary Competition in 1986.

2	lamb loins (2 lb/1 kg with bones each), bones and trimmings reserved*	2

Stock:

2/3 cup	mirepoix (diced carrots, onion, celery, leeks)	150 mL
1 tsp	tomato paste	5 mL
1/4 cup	cognac	50 mL
2 cups	water	500 mL
Pinch	salt	Pinch

Stuffing:

1 cup	fresh spinach	250 mL
3 oz	triple-cream Brie	75 g
	Salt and pepper to taste	
1 tbsp	finely chopped fresh rosemary	15 mL

Sauce:

1 tbsp	vegetable oil	15 mL
2	shallots, chopped	2
1/4 cup	Inniskillin Wines Brae Blanc (white wine)	50 mL
1/4 cup	whipping cream	50 mL
3 oz	triple-cream Brie	75 g

Have your butcher bone and trim the lamb.

Inniskillin Wines Klose Vineyard Cabernet Sauvignon

Niagara-on-the-Lake, Ontario

Add a rich triple-cream Brie sauce to lamb and you need a full-bodied red with lots of weight and flavour to match. This particular Cabernet Sauvignon is ideal, as it is full bodied with forward raspberry fruit on the nose and mouth accompanied by a slight herbaceous note and a long, delicious finish.

Other Choices:
B.C. Cabernet Sauvignon (International Blend)

1 *To make stock*, in a roasting pan roast lamb bones at 450°F (230°C) until burned, about 1 1/2 hours. Add mirepoix; cook for another 20 to 30 minutes. **2** Transfer bones and mirepoix to a large saucepan; stir in tomato paste. **3** Set roasting pan over high heat; deglaze with cognac, scraping up brown bits. Pour liquid over bones. Set aside roasting pan. **4** Pour water over bones. Bring stock to a boil; reduce heat and simmer, covered, for 2 hours. **5** Season stock to taste with salt. Strain stock through a sieve; set aside. **6** *To make stuffing*, in the rinsed saucepan blanch spinach; drain and cool. **7** In a food processor or blender, combine spinach, lamb trimmings, Brie, salt, pepper and rosemary. Process until smooth. **8** In the top of each lamb loin, cut an incision 2 inches (5 cm) long and as deep as possible. **9** Fill a piping bag or a plastic bag with one corner cut off with stuffing. Using a wooden spoon to hold open the incision, pipe stuffing into loins. **10** Tie loins with kitchen string to keep stuffing in place. Rub olive oil lightly over loins. **11** In a large skillet over medium heat, brown loins on all sides, about 90 seconds each side. **12** Arrange loins in the roasting pan; roast at 375°F (190°C) for 5 minutes for rare, 15 minutes for well-done; keep warm. **13** Meanwhile, make the sauce. In the same skillet over medium heat, heat oil; sauté shallots until soft. Increase heat to medium-high; add wine. Reduce heat. **14** Pour in stock; boil until reduced by half. **15** Stir in cream; reduce by one-quarter. Remove from heat. Add Brie, stirring constantly until cheese is melted. Strain sauce through a strainer. **16** Remove string from loins. Slice loins into medallions. **17** Arrange medallions on serving plates. Spoon sauce around lamb.

Damafro Triple-Cream Brie

Made by Fromagerie Clement

ONTARIO LAMB STEW WITH SPINACH AND FETA

SERVES FOUR   Forfar Dairy — Portland, Ontario

HISTORIC LEEDS COUNTY is home to Forfar Dairy, a small, independent company that has been making Cheddar, marble and brick for more than 128 years. The company continues to use an original method of wrapping their Cheddar in cheesecloth, then dipping it into hot wax for ripening. Unlike vacuum-sealed bags now used extensively, the hot-wax method allows their cheese to breathe, says Lloyd Steacy, Forfar's cheesemaker since 1982. Gentle air exposure can be beneficial if the cheese is retaining any unwanted gases that could possibly taint the flavour. Traditionally, the wax method sometimes left cheese vulnerable to unwanted moulds, which is why vacuum-sealed bags came into common use. Nowadays, however, technology permits Forfar to continue to use this age-old method without any of the inherent problems. The wax used is so hot it instantly kills any bacteria that may be apparent on the cheese. The 90-lb blocks are then stored in a curing room at 55°F and turned each day so ripening remains even. More than 450,000 lb of cheese are made each year at Forfar from locally produced milk. This commitment to the local farmers has created a significant local market for the company. But don't be surprised if you spot Forfar's cheeses in the independent supermarkets and specialty cheese shops throughout Ontario. Their reputation is widespread. Recently, they developed a Greek-style feta, Cheddar and mozzarella made from pasteurized goat's milk. All three varieties have met with great success.

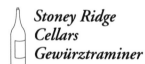

Stoney Ridge Cellars Gewürztraminer

Winona, Ontario

Add East Indian spice to this recipe's yogurt and feta base and you need a white wine with good weight and plenty of spice for balance. This Gewürztraminer is an excellent choice, as its bouquet offers lots of spice and its palate has a hint of sweetness to add weight and a spicy grapefruit flavour to complement the Indian spice. A good dose of acidity to clean the palate.

Other Choices:
B.C. off-dry Gewürztraminer

1½ lb	fresh spinach	750 g
3 tbsp	vegetable oil	50 mL
1½ lb	lean lamb, cubed	750 g
2	leeks, finely sliced	2
4	cloves garlic, crushed	4
1 tbsp	grated baby ginger	15 mL
1 tsp	ground coriander	5 mL
1 tsp	cumin	5 mL
½ tsp	turmeric	2 mL
1	bay leaf	1
2	tomatoes, peeled and chopped	2
2	green chilies, seeded and chopped	2
⅔ cup	plain yogurt	150 mL
1 cup	water	250 mL
⅓ lb	feta cheese, crumbled	175 g

1 Steam spinach until tender. Drain. In a blender or food processor, purée spinach until smooth. Set aside. **2** In a large skillet over high heat, heat oil; sear lamb on all sides. Transfer lamb to 13- by 9-inch (2.5 L) baking dish. **3** In the same skillet over medium heat, combine leeks, garlic, ginger, coriander, cumin, turmeric, bay leaf, tomatoes and chilies. Cook for 3 to 4 minutes, stirring occasionally. **4** Add yogurt and water; stir until well blended. **5** Pour mixture over lamb. Bake at 325°F (160°C) for 1 1/2 hours or until lamb is tender. Remove bay leaf. **6** Fold feta cheese into spinach purée and pour over lamb mixture. Bake 10 minutes. Serve hot.

Feta

Made by Forfar Dairy

RACKS OF LAMB WITH THREE CHEESES MEDITERRANEAN

SERVES FOUR   Chef Thomas Dietzel — Vancouver, British Columbia

CREATED FOR the Dairy Bureau of Canada, this recipe will tantalize your palate.

4	racks of lamb (¹/₂ lb/250 g each, or consisting of five ribs), trimmed and cut country-style*	4

Stuffing:

¹/₃ cup	blanched Swiss chard	75 mL
¹/₄ cup	pitted black olives, chopped	50 mL
3 oz	bocconcini cheese, diced	75 g
¹/₄ lb	feta cheese, diced	125 g
¹/₄ tsp	salt	1 mL
¹/₄ tsp	finely chopped fresh rosemary	1 mL
Pinch	pepper	Pinch

Sauce:

1	sweet red pepper	1
3 tbsp	plain yogurt	50 mL
1 tbsp	grated Romano cheese	25 mL
	Salt and pepper to taste	

4	sprigs fresh rosemary (for garnish)	4

Ask your butcher to trim and cut in a country-style the racks of lamb.

Mission Hill Vineyards Maréchal Foch (Organic)

Westbank, British Columbia

Dominated by lamb, this dish needs a full-bodied red. Aged in oak for six months, this red has blackberries and a background of spice in the nose and on the palate with soft tannin.

Other Choices:

Inniskillin Wines Cabernet Franc Available in B.C. (Vintage Consultants Ltd., 604-251-3366)

1 Open lamb racks away from ribs. Using a mallet, pound meat until flat. **2** *To make stuffing,* gently squeeze out excess water from Swiss chard; chop coarsely. In a bowl combine Swiss chard, olives, bocconcini, feta, salt, rosemary and pepper. **3** Spread one-quarter of stuffing along ribs of each rack. Fold over meat; secure meat to ribs with kitchen string. Season racks with salt and pepper. **4** Roast at 325°F (160°C) for 30 to 35 minutes or until medium rare. Keep warm. **5** *To make sauce,* roast whole red pepper at 400°F (200°C) for one hour or until blackened. Peel and seed. In a food processor or blender purée red pepper. With motor running, add yogurt and Romano cheese. Season with salt and pepper.

6 Transfer sauce to a saucepan. Over medium heat, warm sauce. **7** Cut lamb racks into ribs. **8** Lay a circle of sauce on each plate. Lay loins on the sauce. Garnish with fresh rosemary sprigs.

Bocconcini and Romano

Made by Saputo Cheeses

Feta

Made by Woolwich Dairy

CHEDDAR AND CHILI STUFFED FILETS MIGNON WITH MEXICANA SALSA

SERVES FOUR   Elm Hurst Carriage House — Ingersoll, Ontario

WHEN DRIVING ALONG Highway 401 at Ingersoll, it's easy to spot Elmhurst Inn, a Victorian Gothic manor nestled among century-old maples. Although now a welcoming spot featuring 49 guest rooms, dining and conference facilities and a gift shop, Elm Hurst, built in 1872, was once the home of the James Harris family. Much cheese history surrounds this inn and the Harris clan. In 1864 a cheese factory was built in Salford, a few miles from Ingersoll, by Vermont immigrants Lydia Chase and husband Hiram Ranney. It was Lydia who taught the cheese business to her son-in-law James Harris. In 1865 Harris constructed his own cheese factory on the family farm, where Elm Hurst Inn now stands. The family later added apple orchards to the land and prospered in both the cheese and apple industries for generations. Located on the Elm Hurst grounds is a historical plaque commemorating Oxford County as the birthplace of the commercial cheese industry in Canada. Whether visiting Ingersoll for a day or a weekend, stop by the Ingersoll Cheese Museum and Elm Hurst Inn. In the Elm Hurst Carriage House gift shop you'll find an assortment of locally made cheeses and wonderful trinkets and treasures.

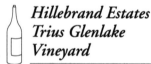

Hillebrand Estates Trius Glenlake Vineyard

Niagara-on-the-Lake, Ontario

Combining Cabernet Sauvignon, Merlot and Cabernet Franc and aged in French oak, this blend offers enough weight to marry with filet mignon, while having raspberry-like fruit on the nose and mouth with some vanilla tones and soft tannins that complement Cheddar. A spicy finish makes this red a good match for chilies and salsa.

Other Choices:

B.C. Cabernet Sauvignon (International Blend)

Salsa:

1 cup	finely diced tomatoes	250 mL
2 tbsp	finely chopped jalapeño peppers	25 mL
1 tbsp	lime juice	15 mL
2 tbsp	cold water	25 mL
3 tbsp	finely chopped onion	50 mL
1 tsp	finely chopped fresh oregano	5 mL

Stuffing:

2 tbsp	peanut oil	25 mL
1	clove garlic, thinly sliced	1
1	dried ancho chili, diced*	1
1	small onion, sliced	1
1/3 lb	old Cheddar, shredded	175 g

4	filets mignon (1/4 lb/125 g each)	4
	Salt and pepper to taste	

Dried ancho chilies are available in specialty food shops.

1 *To make salsa*, in a small bowl toss together tomatoes, jalapeño, lime juice, water, onion and oregano. Chill. **2** *To make stuffing*, in a small saucepan over medium heat, heat oil; sauté garlic, ancho chili and onion for 1 minute. Remove from heat. Stir in Cheddar cheese; mix well. **3** Slice filets crosswise; leaving one side attached. Open filets and pound both sides with a mallet to flatten. **4** Spoon one-quarter of stuffing onto each filet. Close, pressing to seal mixture inside. Set filets mignon on a baking sheet. Season with salt and pepper. **5** Grill 2 to 3 minutes per side. Serve with a dollop of salsa.

Cheddar

Made by Springbank Cheese

BISON OR BEEF VARIETY ON A ROASTED GARLIC AND BRIE SAUCE

SERVES FOUR   Chef Harald Bonkowski — Vancouver, British Columbia

A MORE EXTENSIVE version of this dish won the Main Course Category in the 1993 Annual Foodservice Awards held in Quebec City.

Medallions:

4	medallions of beef or bison (2 oz/50 g each)	4
	Salt and pepper to taste	
2 tsp	vegetable oil	10 mL

Rouladen:

2 tsp	vegetable oil	10 mL
1/4 cup	thin onion rings	50 mL
4	slices beef or bison (2 1/2 oz/60 g each)	4
1 tsp	Dijon mustard	5 mL
1 2/3 cup	brown stock OR beef stock	400 mL

Beef or Bison in Sweet Pepper Crust:

1/4 cup	mixed diced sweet green, yellow and red peppers	50 mL
2 tbsp	dried bread crumbs	25 mL
2 tbsp	egg whites	25 mL
	Salt and pepper to taste	
1/2 lb	beef or bison striploin	250 g
	Salt and pepper to taste	

Roasted Garlic and Brie Sauce:

1 tsp	olive oil	5 mL
1 tbsp	minced garlic	15 mL
1/4 cup	chicken stock	50 mL
1 1/2 oz	Brie, rind removed, cubed	40 g
	Salt and pepper to taste	

Marynissen Estates Merlot Barrel Select

Niagara-on-the-Lake, Ontario

Owner and winemaker John Marynissen specializes in producing fantastic reds: Cabernet Sauvignon, Merlot and red blends. This Merlot has a purple-ruby colour with earthy, flinty aromas. The palate has medium weight, blackberries and spice and austere tannins — ideal elements to marry to the beef and the flavourful sauce of Brie and garlic.

Other Choices:
B.C. Chancellor

MARYNISSEN
E S T A T E S

1 Season medallions with salt and pepper. In a medium oven-safe skillet over medium heat, heat oil; sauté medallions for 3 minutes on each side; keep warm. **2** *To make rouladen*, in same skillet over medium heat, heat oil; sweat onions for 3 minutes. Brush meat slices with mustard. Top meat slices with onion; roll up slices, securing each with kitchen string or a toothpick. In same skillet over medium heat, reheat oil; sear rouladen until golden on all sides, about 1 minute. Add brown stock; bring to a boil. **3** Transfer skillet to a 350°F (180°C) oven and braise meat for 40 minutes. **4** Transfer rouladen to a plate; remove string. Keep warm. **5** In skillet over medium-high heat, reduce stock to 1 cup (250 mL). Keep warm. **6** *To make sweet pepper crust*, in a small bowl stir together peppers, bread crumbs, egg whites, salt and pepper. **7** Season striploin with salt and pepper; place meat in a 13-by 9-inch (3.5 L) baking dish. Roast at 350°F (180°C) for 2 minutes for rare, longer for medium rare. **8** Press crust over meat. Bake another 8 minutes or until crust is light golden. Let rest for 5 minutes. Slice meat. Keep warm. **9** *To make sauce*, in a small skillet over medium heat, heat oil; sauté garlic until golden brown. Dry garlic on paper towels. In a blender or food processor blend garlic with chicken stock. With motor running, slowly add Brie, blending until smooth. Season with salt and pepper. **10** Spoon 1/4 cup (50 mL) reduced stock onto each plate. Pour 4 tsp (20 mL) sauce onto stock; swirl with a wooden skewer. Arrange medallions, rouladen and sliced crusted beef on sauce. Serve with Potato and Havarti Pudding (recipe on page 74).

Brie Corneville

Made by Agropur

BEEF AND VEAL TENDERLOIN WITH MOUSSE OF CRAB AND BRIE CHEESE WRAPPED IN A ROMANO CHEESE CRÊPE

SERVES SIX   Chef Yoerg Soltermann — Charlottetown, P.E.I.

SWISS-BORN YOERG SOLTERMANN is executive chef at the Prince Edward Hotel. Entering food competitions is a hobby for Yoerg, and his numerous awards are proof of his passion and talent. The recipe here won the Atlantic Region Prize in the 1993 Annual Foodservice Awards.

Inniskillin Wines Maréchal Foch

Niagara-on-the-Lake, Ontario
Available in P.E.I. (Liquor Control Commission)

A full-bodied, robust red with plenty of raspberry-like character on the nose and palate and hefty tannin. Big enough for beef and veal.

Other Choices:
B.C. Merlot

²/₃ lb	beef tenderloin ends	350 g
²/₃ lb	veal tenderloin ends	350 g
Mousse:		
2 oz	Brie cheese	50 g
¹/₃ cup	whipping cream	75 mL
1	egg white	1
6	crab legs, meat only (reserve shells for sauce)	6
	Salt and pepper to taste	
Crêpes:		
¹/₂ cup	all-purpose flour	125 g
1 cup	milk	250 g
2	eggs	2
¹/₂ cup	grated Romano cheese	125 mL
2 tbsp	butter, melted	25 mL
	Salt and pepper to taste	
3 tbsp	butter, melted	50 mL
Sauce:		
	Leftover crab shells	
4 tsp	olive oil	20 mL
²/₃ cup	mirepoix (diced carrots, onion, celery, leek)	150 mL
2 tbsp	tomato paste	25 mL
¹/₂ cup	Inniskillin Brae Blanc (white wine)	125 mL
1 cup	demiglace*	250 mL
¹/₄ cup	cognac	50 mL
¹/₄ cup	unsalted butter, softened and cubed	50 mL
	Salt and pepper to taste	
Dash	hot pepper sauce	Dash

<u>6 cooked crab claws (for garnish)</u>

Powdered and frozen demiglace is available at specialty food shops.

1 From the beef tenderloin ends cut six fillets about 4 inches (10 cm) long and 2 oz (50 g) in weight. From veal tenderloin ends cut six fillets about 4 inches (10 cm) long and 2 oz (50 g) in weight. Set aside. **2** *To make the mousse*, cut remaining meat into small chunks. In a food processor or blender grind meat. Add Brie, blend well. With motor running, slowly add cream; add egg white. **3** Pour mixture into a bowl. Fold in the crab meat from leg shells. Season with salt and pepper. Put bowl over ice and refrigerate until needed. **4** *To make crêpe batter*, put flour in a large bowl; push flour to one side. In a small bowl beat eggs with milk. Pour milk beside flour. Gradually whisk flour into milk until the batter is smooth. Stir in Romano cheese and 2 tbsp (25 mL) melted butter; season with salt and pepper. Refrigerate batter for 1 hour. **5** Meanwhile, *make sauce*. In a large saucepan over medium heat, combine crab leg shells and oil; roast shells at 350°F (180°C) for 15 minutes. Stir in mirepoix and tomato paste. Roast until paste turns brown but carrots are golden, about 15 minutes. Add white wine and demiglace. Simmer for 30 minutes, until mixture is reduced to one-third. Add cognac; simmer for 2 minutes. Strain sauce through a sieve. Keep warm. **6** *To cook crêpes*, brush a 6-inch (15 cm) nonstick crêpe pan or skillet with 2 tsp (10 mL) melted butter. Set pan over medium heat. Spoon in 2 tbsp (25 mL) batter; swirl pan until batter covers bottom. Cook until surface looks dry, about 30 seconds. Set crêpes on a plate and cover with a towel to keep from drying out while making five more crêpes. **7** On a work surface lay out crêpes. Using half the mousse, spread mousse down centre of each crêpe. Lay a beef and veal fillet side by side over mousse. Spread remaining mousse over fillets. Fold two sides tightly over filling. Brush tops of crêpes with 3 tbsp (50 mL) melted butter. **8** Lay crêpes on a baking sheet. Bake at 350°F (180 °C) for 10 to 15 minutes or until mousse is cooked through. **9** Meanwhile, whisk butter into sauce, one cube at a time. Season sauce with salt, pepper and hot pepper sauce. **10** Spoon sauce onto each plate. When crêpes have cooled slightly, slice in three lengthwise, and arrange on sauce. Garnish with a cooked crab claw.

L'Extra Brie

Made by Agropur

Romano

Made by Saputo Cheeses

ONTARIO FARM-RAISED RABBIT STUFFED WITH FETA

SERVES FOUR — The Wedge Cheese and Freeze House — Tillsonburg, Ontario

SET IN A PROVINCIAL CABIN on Highway 19 in the core of dairy country is The Wedge, as locals will always call it. Since 1979 Don and Sally Martin have appeased cheese-zealous minds and palates with their vast inventory of Canadian-made cheeses and Don's extensive knowledge on the subject. Before opening the shop, he was a licensed cheesemaker, milk grader, milk tester and cream grader. He is still active in the industry. Don is a past president of the Western Ontario Cheesemakers' Association, former director of the Ontario Cheddar Cheese Association and a member of the Dairyman's Association of Western Ontario. It's easy to believe this passion is an innate Martin family trait. Don's father, Glenn "Squire" Martin, was a cheesemaker for 50 years, as was Don's namesake, Donald Menzies, who manufactured cheese before the turn of the century and was one of the first federal cheese graders in Canada. In 1989 Don and Sally expanded their shop to include Le Connoisseur coffees, homemade sauces and relishes and frozen appetizers, meats and desserts. Hence the new name — The Wedge Cheese and Freeze House.

Stoney Ridge Cellars Pinot Noir

Winona, Ontario

Grape-grower Murray Puddicombe and winemaker Jim Warren have created a successful winery producing more than 30,000 gallons of wine with 25 labels every year. The wines are VQA listed. Their Pinot Noir is light bodied enough to not over-power rabbit. Sour cherries and a hint of chocolate are prominent in the aroma, with sour cherries commanding the mouth. These wonderful flavours and the wine's crisp acidity marry well with salty feta.

Other Choices:
B.C. Gamay Noir

1	rabbit (3 lb/1.5 kg)*	1

Marinade:

	Juice of 2¹/₂ lemons	
¹/₂ cup	Stoney Ridge Cellars Pinot Noir (red wine)	125 mL
3	cloves garlic, finely chopped	3
¹/₄ cup	olive oil	50 mL
	Salt and pepper to taste	
1 tbsp	finely chopped fresh thyme	15 mL
2 tsp	finely chopped fresh marjoram	10 mL

Stuffing:

¹/₃ lb	feta cheese, crumbled	175 g
1 tbsp	finely chopped fresh thyme	15 mL
¹/₃ cup	finely chopped fresh parsley	75 mL
2 tbsp	olive oil	25 mL
	Salt and pepper to taste	
	Flour for dredging	
2 cups	water	500 mL

*If using fresh rabbit, chop up liver and add to stuffing ingredients.

1 Wash rabbit well inside and out. Set in a bowl just large enough to hold it. **2** *To make marinade*, in a small bowl combine lemon juice, wine, garlic, olive oil, salt, pepper, thyme and marjoram. Pour marinade over rabbit; refrigerate, covered, for 6 hours, turning rabbit occasionally. **3** *To make stuffing*, in a food processor or blender combine feta, thyme, parsley and olive oil. Purée mixture to a thick paste. **4** Remove rabbit from marinade, reserving liquid. Fill cavity of rabbit with paste. Sew closed with string. **5** Season rabbit with salt and pepper; dredge lightly in flour. Place in a roasting pan. Pour in reserved marinade and water. **6** Roast at 350°F (180°C) for 1 hour, basting every 10 minutes with pan juices. Turn rabbit and roast, basting, another hour or until rabbit is tender.

Feta

Made by Ainos Dairy

VENISON IN STEAMED ROMANO PASTRY

SERVES FOUR   Ferrante Cheese Ltd. — Woodbridge, Ontario

OWNED AND OPERATED by Pippo Ferrante since 1981, Ferrante Cheese specializes in Italian-style cheeses. Cheesemaker Pippo also makes fresh cheeses such as ricotta and Tuma. The latter has a milky flavour and a firmer curd than its counterpart, ricotta. All Ferrante cheeses can be found in select independent supermarkets and at the factory's adjacent retail shop.

2 lb	venison, cut into 1-inch (2.5 cm) cubes	1 kg
1	large onion, thinly sliced	1
1 tbsp	finely chopped fresh oregano	15 mL
1 tbsp	finely chopped fresh basil	15 mL
	Salt and pepper to taste	
3 tbsp	all-purpose flour	50 mL
1¾ cups	self-raising flour	425 mL
1 tsp	salt	5 mL
¾ cup	shredded suet	175 mL
2 cups	grated Romano cheese	250 mL
6 tbsp (approx)	water	90 mL
1 cup	cold beef stock	250 mL
¼ cup	Château des Charmes Pinot Noir (red wine)	50 mL

Château des Charmes Wines Pinot Noir

Niagara-on-the-Lake, Ontario

Winemaker Paul Bosc Sr. has produced a delicate Pinot Noir with ripe cherry fruit on the nose and palate and a long finish. It's the best accompaniment for venison.

Other Choices:

B.C. Merlot

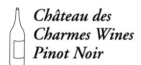

Romano

Made by Ferrante Cheese

1 In a bowl combine venison, onion, oregano, basil, salt and pepper. Toss with all-purpose flour. **2** Into another large bowl, sift the self-raising flour with salt. Stir in suet and Romano cheese. Add enough cold water to the mix to make a soft but sticky dough. Knead lightly until smooth. **3** Break off one-quarter of dough. Set aside. **4** On a lightly floured work surface, roll out large piece of dough into a 16-inch (40 cm) circle big enough to line a 14-inch (35 cm) pudding mould. Fit dough neatly into mould. **5** Pour meat mixture into mould. Pour in stock and wine. **6** Roll out remaining dough into a circle large enough to cover the mould. Brush edges of dough with water; cover pudding with dough lid. Seal edges well. **7** Cover pudding with aluminum foil, securing with string. Set mould in a deep kettle. Pour hot water about two-thirds of the way up side of mould. Steam, covered, for 5 hours, topping up with boiling water as required. **8** Just before serving, unmould pudding onto serving plate.

MARBLEIZED FRAMBOIS CHEESECAKE

SERVES SIX TO EIGHT   Shari Darling — Toronto, Ontario

½ cup	ground pecans	125 mL
⅓ cup	fresh raspberries	75 mL
1 tbsp	grated lemon rind	15 mL
3 cups	cream cheese, softened	750 mL
4	eggs	4
½ cup	sugar	125 mL
2 tbsp	all-purpose flour	25 mL
½ cup	whipping cream	125 mL
¾ cup	raspberry preserves	250 mL
¼ cup	Southbrook Farms Frambois (raspberry wine)	50 mL

Southbrook Farms Winery Frambois

Maple, Ontario

The only producers of this fresh-fruit wine in Canada. The juice from fresh raspberries is fermented to 2.5 percent alcohol, then fortified with young brandy. Frambois is delicious as an aperitif or as an accompaniment to desserts containing chocolate, cream or fresh fruit. It has a natural affinity with this cheesecake.

Other Choices:

B.C. Canadian champagne

Western cream cheese

Made by Westhill Dairy

1 Butter an 8-inch (2 L) springform pan. Coat with ground pecans. Chill. **2** In a saucepan over low heat, heat raspberries until tender. Stir in lemon rind. In a food processor or blender purée raspberries until smooth. Set aside. **3** In a large bowl, beat cream cheese with a fork until soft. Beat in eggs, one at a time, blending well after each addition. Add sugar, flour and cream; beat until smooth. **4** Reserve 1 cup (250 mL) of cheese mixture. Pour remaining cheese mixture into the pan. **5** Stir raspberry purée into reserved cheese mixture. Pour onto filling. Using a knife, cut raspberry cheese through plain cheese several times to create a marbled effect. **6** Bake at 350°F (180°C) for 50 minutes. Turn off oven, prop open door and let cheesecake stand for 30 minutes. Cool on a rack. **7** Meanwhile, in a small saucepan over high heat, bring raspberry preserves and Frambois to a boil; boil 1 minute, stirring constantly. Reduce heat to low; simmer gently for 3 to 4 minutes or until mixture is thick. Cool to lukewarm. Brush glaze over cooled cheesecake. Serve at room temperature.

WARM PEAR DUMPLINGS WITH CHILLED APRICOT COULIS AND RICOTTA CREAM

SERVES FOUR   Mannina Cheese Co. Ltd. — Windsor, Ontario

WHEN YOU HEAR THE NAME GALATI, only one style of cheese comes to mind. Cheesemaker Joe Galati has been making Italian-style cheeses for Southwestern Ontario's Italians since 1978, though the company was established in 1961. With the exception of ricotta, he makes pasta filata cheeses — mozzarella, bocconcini, Caciocavallo and Scamorza. Pasta filata means the curds are heated in water until they become elastic and form a thread (the pasta filata). This thread is stretched and wound into a ball, from which pieces are cut to make mozzarella or bocconcini or moulded to make Caciocavallo and Scamorza. Although considered a pasta filata and sometimes eaten fresh, Caciocavallo is dipped in a salt solution, which starts the formation of a rind. Aged up to six months, Caciocavallo has a dry, yellow rind and fibrous, milky interior. For most native Italians, tradition is a way of life; Joe is no exception. While large cheese factories have become fully mechanized to meet mass production, Joe remains dedicated to an age-old method of stretching his curds in hot water by hand, a time-consuming process. Is there a difference in the quality of the cheese? Most definitely. Mannina's pasta filatas are made and sold daily, thus having a fresh taste and buttery texture instead of being bland and rubbery like many others. Now that's Italian!

Henry of Pelham Estate Winery Riesling Icewine

St. Catharines, Ontario

There's only one match for this dessert — Icewine. This one has a concentrated nose of apples and pears with full apricot and peach flavours, all matching the fruit in this dessert. A good dose of acidity cleans the palate.

Other Choices:

B.C. Icewine

Apricot Coulis:

3	apricots, halved	3
1/4 cup	sugar	50 mL
4 tsp	water	20 mL

Dumplings:

2/3 lb	sifted all-purpose flour	350 g
1/4 tsp	salt	1 mL
3/4 cup	butter	175 mL
	Grated rind of 1 orange	
2 tbsp	sugar	25 mL
4	ripe pears	4
	Eggwash (1 egg beaten with 1 tsp/5 mL water)	

Ricotta Cream:

1/2 cup	ricotta cheese	125 mL
2 tbsp	whipping cream	25 mL

1 *To make apricot coulis*, in a saucepan over medium heat, combine apricots, sugar and water; cook 4 to 6 minutes, until apricots are tender. In a blender or food processor, purée apricots. Chill. **2** *To make dumplings*, in a bowl sift flour with salt. Rub in butter, orange rind, sugar and enough water to bind dough. Knead dough until smooth. Chill for 30 minutes. **3** On a lightly floured work surface, roll out dough to 1/8 inch (3 mm) thick. Cut dough into four 8-inch (20 cm) squares. **4** Peel and halve pears; core. Press pear halves back together. Place a whole pear on each dough square. Brush edges of dough with water. Bring corners of square together at the top of the pear, pinching seams closed. **5** Roll out dough trimmings; cut into four leaf shapes. Using the point of a sharp knife, make serrated cuts on the dumpling seams and leaves for decoration. **6** Brush eggwash over dumplings. Dip each leaf in eggwash and press against dumpling, as if hanging from the top. **7** Place dumplings on a well-greased baking sheet. Bake at 400°F (200°C) for 30 minutes or until dumplings are crisp and golden. **8** Arrange one dumpling on each plate. Spoon 3 tbsp (50 mL) apricot coulis in a semi-circle around each. **9** *To make ricotta cream*, whisk ricotta with cream. Spoon a generous dollop of ricotta cream on each dumpling.

Ricotta

Made by Mannina Cheese

A SWEET TRIO OF CHEESE WITH BLACK CURRANT SAUCE

SERVES FOUR   Rolf Runkel — Ottawa, Ontario

NOW PASTRY CHEF AT THE WESTIN HOTEL in Ottawa, Swiss-born Rolf Runkel completed his baking and pastry apprenticeship at the Switzerland Trade College and worked as pastry chef at the Bermudiana Hotel in Bermuda and the Four Seasons Hotel in Ottawa. No stranger to competitions, he won two silver medals in the Ottawa Culinary Show in 1990 and 1992. In 1993 he captured first place in both the Chocolate Carving Competition and The Silver Spoon Dessert Competition in Ottawa. This recipe was the grand prize winner in the Desserts and Pastries Category of the 1993 Foodservice Awards held by the Dairy Bureau of Canada.

Mounier Brut Champagne

Niagara-on-the-Lake, Ontario

With such a variety of flavours, this dessert is best served with a sparkler that simply refreshes the palate. Mounier is done in the traditional French method called méthode champenoise (second fermentation in the bottle). A dry bubbly with a hint of yeast on the nose, accompanied by a clean, fresh palate reminiscent of apricots. It's great with all desserts.

Other Choices:

B.C. Canadian champagne

Pears:

¼ cup	water	50 mL
1 cup	port wine	250 mL
2 tbsp	sugar	25 mL
¼	cinnamon stick	¼
	Rind of ¼ orange	
1 tbsp	black currants	15 mL
4	pears, peeled	4
3 oz	mascarpone cheese	75 g
1 tbsp	caramel flavouring	15 mL

Soufflés:

3 oz	Quark cheese	75 g
	Rind of ¼ lemon	
1	egg, separated	1
1 tbsp	all-purpose flour	15 mL
1 tbsp	sugar	15 mL
	Icing sugar for dusting	

Chocolate Swirls:*

5 oz	semisweet chocolate	140 g

Chocolate Swirl Filling:

3 tbsp	ricotta cheese	50 mL
1½ tsp	sugar	7 mL
1 tbsp	mango pulp	15 mL**

Sauce:

⅓ cup	black currants	75 mL
1 tbsp	sugar	25 mL
1 tbsp	orange juice	15 mL
Pinch	cinnamon	Pinch
½ tsp	cornstarch	2 mL
1 tbsp	water	15 mL
4	sprigs fresh mint (for garnish)	4

Some bakeries will sell chocolate swirls.
**Mango pulp is available at Asian supermarkets.*

1 *To prepare pears*, in a medium saucepan combine water, port, sugar, cinnamon stick, orange rind and black currants. Over high heat, bring to a boil; reduce heat to medium. Add pears. Simmer for 20 minutes or until pears are tender. **2** Transfer pears to a rack and cool to room temperature. Slice pears in half; core. Slice a small piece off the rounded side of four pear halves so they lie flat with the core side up. **3** In a small bowl combine mascarpone cheese and caramel flavouring. Fill hollow in each of the four pear halves with one-quarter of mascarpone mixture. Set aside. **4** Cut remaining four pear halves into pear fans: starting at the wide end, make fine, even slices lengthwise, leaving the narrow end attached. With the flat of your hand, carefully fan out the slices. Place one pear fan on each stuffed pear half. Set aside. **5** *To make soufflés*, in a bowl mix together Quark cheese, lemon rind and egg yolk. In a small bowl mix flour with sugar; fold into Quark mixture. Beat egg white until firm; fold into Quark mixture. Turn mixture into four well-greased individual soufflé cups. Bake at 325°F (160°C) for 15 to 20 minutes or until firm to the touch. Let cool. **6** *To make chocolate swirls*, melt chocolate in double boiler over hot water. Let cool until chocolate is thick and almost crystallized. Reheat again, until chocolate just begins to liquefy. Pour chocolate in an 8-inch (20 cm) wide strip on a marble surface. (If you do not have a marble surface, pour chocolate into an 8-inch wide baking sheet and smooth the top.) Let stand at room temperature until chocolate is firm. Using a long carving knife shave off a thin layer of chocolate, drawing blade toward you to form a swirl. Make four swirls. Chill. **7** *To* *make filling for chocolate swirls*, in a bowl mix together ricotta, sugar and mango pulp until smooth. Carefully fill chilled chocolate curls with filling. **8** *To make sauce*, in a small saucepan combine black currants, sugar, orange juice and cinnamon; bring to a boil. In a small bowl whisk cornstarch with water; stir into sauce. Cook for 1 minute or until sauce is thickened; let cool. **9** Pour a circle of sauce in the middle of each dessert plate. Place the chocolate swirl on the sauce. Set a pear on one side of the sauce. **10** Run a knife around the edge of the soufflé cups. Turn out onto the dessert plates, opposite the pears. Dust soufflés with icing sugar. Place a sprig of mint between pears and soufflés.

Mascarpone

Made by National Cheese

Quark

Made by Pinneau Dairy

Ricotta

Made by Grande Cheese

CHOCOLATE, CARAMEL AND MASCARPONE CHEESECAKE

SERVES SIX TO EIGHT National Cheese Company Ltd. — Concord, Ontario

AN INCREDIBLE recipe developed for National Cheese.

Crust:

1½ cups	vanilla wafer crumbs	375 mL
¼ cup	butter, melted	50 mL

Filling:

1	pkg (14 oz/400 g) caramels	1
⅔ cup	half-and-half cream	150 mL
1 cup	finely chopped toasted pecans	250 mL
2 cups	mascarpone cheese	500 mL
½ cup	sugar	125 mL
1	vanilla bean	1
2	eggs	2
½ cup	semisweet chocolate pieces, melted	125 mL

1 *To make crust,* combine vanilla wafer crumbs with butter. Press into the bottom of a 9-inch (2.5 L) springform pan. Bake at 350°F (180°C) for 10 minutes. **2** *To make filling,* in a saucepan over medium heat, melt caramels. Lower heat; add cream. Stir until smooth. Pour mixture over crust. Sprinkle with pecans. **3** In a large bowl beat together mascarpone and sugar. **4** Slit vanilla bean down one side and scrape seeds into mascarpone mixture. **5** Beat in eggs, one at a time, beating until well blended. **6** In a saucepan over low heat, melt chocolate. Stir melted chocolate into cheese mixture; spread evenly over pecans. **7** Bake at 350°F (180°C) for 50 minutes or until centre is set. Run knife around edge of cake to loosen. Chill overnight.

Calona Wines Late Bottled Vintage Port

Kelowna, British Columbia

A vintage port displaying a spicy, vanilla and cherry aroma and palate, making it an ideal partner for this dessert containing chocolate, caramel and nuts. This port won a bronze medal for Winemaster's Selection at the 1990 Okanagan Wine Festival.

Other Choices:
Ontario port

CALONA
VINEYARDS

Mascarpone

Made by National Cheese

RICOTTA CHEESE AND BLUEBERRY TARTS

MAKES TWENTY-FOUR

AN EASY BUT DELICIOUS recipe developed for the Dairy Bureau of Canada.

Velvet Sauce:

8	egg yolks	8
³/₄ cup	sugar	175 mL
2 tsp	vanilla extract	10 mL
2 cups	milk	500 mL

1	pkg (2 lbs/1 kg) frozen puff pastry dough, thawed	1
¹/₂ cup	plain cookie crumbs	125 mL

Filling:

2 lb	ricotta cheese	1 kg
4	egg yolks	4
1 cup	sugar	250 mL
2 tsp	grated lemon rind	10 mL

Glaze:

²/₃ cup	apricot jam	150 mL
¹/₄ cup	Calvados	50 mL

Fresh blueberries (or other fruit)	

1 *To make velvet sauce*, in a bowl beat together egg yolks, sugar and vanilla. In a saucepan over high heat, scald milk. Reduce heat to medium; gradually whisk in egg yolks. Cook over medium heat, stirring constantly, until mixture thickens and coats a metal spoon. Chill. **2** Cut puff pastry with a 4-inch (10 cm) cookie cutter; line tart pans, making 24 tart shells. Sprinkle each shell with 1 tsp (5 mL) cookie crumbs. **3** *To make filling*, in a bowl blend ricotta cheese, egg yolks, sugar and lemon rind. Spoon 1/4 cup (50 mL) filling into each tart shell. **4** Bake at 475°F (240°C) for 25 minutes or until pastry is golden. Remove tarts from pan; cool on a rack. **5** *To make glaze*, heat apricot jam; press through a sieve held

Vineland Estates Riesling Late Harvest

Vineland, Ontario

This winery produces excellent Rieslings, including this late harvest version. With tangerine in the aroma and dried apricots coming through in the mouth and only medium sweetness, this dessert wine goes hand-in-hand with the apricot glaze without dominating the dessert's delicate nature. Good Riesling acidity leaves the mouth clean.

Other Choices:

B.C. Late Harvest Ehrenfelser

over a small bowl. Stir in Calvados; let cool slightly. **6** Meanwhile, arrange four or five blueberries in a circle on each tart. **7** Brush tarts with glaze. Chill. **8** Spoon sauce onto a dessert plate and top with a tart.

Ricotta

Made by Quality Cheese

MANDARINS IN MAPLE GOAT CHEESE CREAM

SERVES SIX   Shari Darling — Toronto, Ontario

Domaine de Chaberton Ortega

Langley, British Columbia

A native grape of Germany named after Spanish philosopher José Ortega y Gasset, this dessert wine is medium sweet (8 sugar code) and full bodied with an intense nose and palate of peach and tangerine that works with the mandarins and maple syrup flavours of the dish. The wine also exhibits enough acidity to cut through the richness of the cream.

Other Choices:

Ontario Icewine

Chevrai

Made by Woolwich Dairy

6	mandarin oranges, peeled and divided into segments	6
¼ cup	maple syrup	50 mL
¼ cup	cold whey butter, cubed	50 mL
¼ lb	goat cheese, crumbled	125 g
½ cup	whipping cream	125 mL

1 Arrange mandarin wedges in a 13- by 9-inch (3.5 L) baking dish. Pour maple syrup over segments. Dot with butter. Bake at 400°F (200°C) for 20 minutes. **2** In a food processor or blender blend goat cheese with cream. Spread cheese mixture over oranges. Bake another 15 minutes, basting mandarin segments with cream every 5 minutes. **3** Let cool 10 minutes before serving.

FRAGRANT QUINCE AND CHEDDAR TORTE

Delapointe Farm — Bury, Quebec

IN THE EASTERN TOWNSHIPS near Mount Megantic, Delapointe is one of two organic Cheddar producers in North America and the only one of its kind in Canada. Made from raw milk, the cheeses are organic in that the farm's Holstein herd is fed organically grown grains, grass and hay, and the resulting Cheddars are free of preservatives and colouring agents. The Lapointe family manufactures in this way because, they say, the resulting products contain more easily assimilated proteins and calcium, and are more digestible. Once produced, the mild version is aged for a minimum of 60 days, the medium for 180 days, the old Cheddar for one year. Although Cheddar has brought the family national recognition through awards given at the Royal Winter Fair, they have been pleasing locals since 1975 with their organic vegetables, maple syrup and milk.

Aperid'Or,
Vignoble de
L'Orpailleur

Dunham, Quebec

Made from 100 percent Seyval, this aperitif is fortified with alcohol to 15 percent. Displaying apples on the nose and palate with good acidity, this wine goes great with quince and Cheddar. Serve at 7° to 10°C.

Other Choices:
Ontario or B.C. Late Harvest Riesling

Crust:

1 cup	all-purpose flour	250 mL
1/3 cup	sugar	75 mL
1/2 cup	butter	125 mL

Filling:

4	large quinces (bright yellow and firm), peeled, cored and sliced*	4
2 tbsp	sugar	25 mL
1 tsp	cinnamon	5 mL
1 cup	shredded extra-old Cheddar cheese	250 mL

Topping:

3/4 cup	sour cream	175 mL
1/2 cup	sugar	125 mL
2	eggs, beaten	2
2 tbsp	all-purpose flour	25 mL
1/4 cup	sliced almonds	50 mL
	Icing sugar (for dusting)	

Quinces are close in taste and texture to the pear and apple. Available in farmers' markets between September and November.

1 *To make crust,* in a medium bowl combine flour with sugar. Cut in butter until crumbly. Press into bottom and 1/2 inch (1 cm) up sides of a 9-inch (2.5 L) springform pan.

2 *To make filling,* toss quinces with sugar, cinnamon and Cheddar. Spoon filling into crust. **3** *To make topping,* in a medium bowl combine sour cream, sugar, eggs and flour; mix well. Pour evenly over filling. Sprinkle with almonds. **4** Bake at 450°F (230°C) for 10 minutes. Reduce heat to 400°F (200°C) and bake for 40 minutes or until quinces are tender. Serve warm or cold dusted with icing sugar.

Organic Old Cheddar

Made by Delapointe Farm

OLD-FASHIONED COEUR À LA CRÈME

SERVES FOUR   Farmers Dairy — Salmon River, Nova Scotia

FARMERS DAIRY believes in changing with the times. To this end they have just spent $2.5 million to upgrade their facility to include new vats and cutting tables. Full modernization will mean a substantial increase in production from the already enormous volume of 4.5 million lb of cheese per year. Their cheeses include Cheddar in mild, medium, old and marble versions, along with mozzarella and cream cheese.

Jost Vineyards Blush

Malagash, Nova Scotia

Jost Vineyards is operated by owner and winemaker Hans Christian Jost and produces more than 25,000 cases of wine each year. Produced from freshly pressed grapes and blueberries, this wine has a berry nose and palate that complements this simple dessert.

Other Choices:
Ontario blush or Canadian champagne

JOST Vineyards

½ cup	whipping cream	125 mL
½ lb	cream cheese, softened	250 g
⅓ cup	sugar	75 mL
1 tsp	vanilla	5 mL
½ cup	sour cream	125 mL

1 Whip cream until stiff. **2** In a large bowl, beat cream cheese with fork until fluffy; beat in sugar and vanilla. Fold in sour cream and whipped cream. **3** Line four individual heart-shaped coeur moulds with moistened cheesecloth. Pour cheese mixture into each mould. Set moulds on a large plate. Lay additional moistened cheesecloth over each mould; cover with plastic wrap. Refrigerate overnight. **4** Unmould onto dessert plates and serve with fresh fruit.

Cream Cheese

Made by Farmers Dairy

FLAN AUX POMMES ET AU CARAMEL (CARAMEL APPLE FLAN)

SERVES FOUR   Demi-chef Pastry Evelyn McManus

EVELYN MCMANUS graduated from the Stratford Chef School, where she also received, in 1993, the Eckhardt Award for Outstanding Achievement in Pastry. This is one of Evelyn's recipes that was featured in the Desserts and Pastries Category of the 10th Annual Foodservice Awards.

*Inniskillin Wines
L'Allemand
Canadian
Champagne*

Niagara-on-the-Lake, Ontario

Done in the Charmat method, this sparkling Riesling brut is inexpensive and elegant with a subtle earthy nose. The palate offers good fruit and medium acidity. A refreshing partner to all the flavours competing for attention in this dessert.

Other Choices:
B.C. Canadian champagne

Pastry:

1/2 lb	unsalted butter, softened	250 g
1/2 lb	cream cheese, softened	250 g
Pinch	salt	Pinch
	Finely grated rind of 1/2 lemon	
6 cups	cake-and-pastry flour, sifted	1.5 L

Filling:

5	medium Northern Spy apples	5
1/4 cup	unsalted butter	50 mL
1/4 cup	sugar	50 mL
2 tbsp	Calvados	25 mL

Caramel Sauce:

1 cup	sugar	250 mL
1/4 cup	whipping cream	50 mL
3/4 cup	mascarpone cheese	175 mL
1/2 cup	toasted sliced blanched almonds	125 mL
	Rind of 1 orange, removed with vegetable peeler	

Orange Sauce:

2 cups	water	500 mL
1 cup	sugar	250 mL
	Rind of 1 orange, cut in thin strips	

Candied Orange Rind:

	Rind of 1 orange, cut in thin strips	
1 cup	sugar	250 mL
2 cups	water	500 mL

1 *To make pastry*, in a large bowl cream together softened butter, softened cream cheese, salt and lemon rind until well mixed. Add flour all at once; knead mixture until dough forms a ball. Do not overwork. Wrap dough in plastic wrap and chill for 1 hour. **2** On a lightly floured work surface, roll out dough to 1/8 inch (3 mm) thick. Fit into a 9-inch (23 cm) flan pan; refrigerate for 1 hour. **3** Bake shell at 350°F (180°C) for 20 to 30 minutes or until shell is golden and flaky. **4** Meanwhile, *to make filling* peel apples and cut into 10 slices each. In a large saucepan over medium heat, melt butter; sauté apple slices until golden. Add sugar, stirring until apples caramelize. When apples are three-quarters cooked, add Calvados. Simmer for 3 minutes or until apples are soft. Cool to room temperature. **5** *To make caramel sauce*, place a heavy skillet over medium heat. Gradually add sugar to dry skillet, stirring constantly for 8 to 10 minutes or until sugar is completely melted and straw-coloured. Remove skillet from heat. Slowly add cream and mascarpone cheese, stirring constantly until smooth. Fold in almonds and orange rind. Let cool. **6** Arrange apples in the baked flan shell. Pour caramel sauce over apples. Set aside. **7** *To make orange sauce*, in a medium saucepan combine water, sugar and orange rind. Over high heat bring mixture to a boil. Reduce heat to low; simmer for 15 to 20 minutes or until mixture is thick and syrupy. Let cool. **8** *To make candied orange rind*, in a medium saucepan combine orange rind, sugar and water. Over high heat bring mixture to a boil. Reduce heat to low; simmer for 20 minutes or until mixture reaches the soft ball stage, or 239°F (115°C) on a candy thermometer. Remove mixture from heat. Pour cold water into saucepan (the rind will sink to the bottom). Drain, reserving rind. **9** Spoon a pool of orange sauce onto each plate. Set flan slice on sauce. Garnish with one-quarter of candied orange rind.

Mascarpone

Made by Salerno Dairy Products

PEACH AND CREAM CHEESE TART WITH PEACH WINE GLAZE

SERVES SIX TO EIGHT   Shari Darling — Toronto, Ontario

Crust:

1½ cups	all-purpose flour	375 mL
Pinch	salt	Pinch
¼ lb	cold whey butter, cubed	125 g
2 tbsp	cold vegetable shortening	25 mL
⅓ cup	ice water	75 mL

Filling:

4	large eggs	4
Pinch	salt	Pinch
½ tsp	grated lemon rind	2 mL
1 cup	cream cheese	250 mL
¼ cup	sugar	50 mL
¼ cup	ground pecans	50 mL

Topping:

4	peaches	4
¼ cup	sugar	50 mL
¼ cup	Konzelmann Estate Peach Wine	50 mL
Pinch	cinnamon	Pinch

Konzelmann Estate Winery Peach Wine

Niagara-on-the-Lake, Ontario

Vinified in stainless steel, this wine is swirling with fresh peaches in the bouquet and on the palate with just a hint of sweetness, making it a consummate partner for the peach topping.

Other Choices:

B.C. or Ontario Icewine

1 *To make crust*, in a large bowl combine flour with salt. Cut in butter and shortening until mixture is crumbly. Add half the water; knead until dough holds together. If too dry, add more water, a little at a time. Wrap dough in plastic wrap and refrigerate for 1 hour. **2** On a lightly floured work surface, roll out dough to fit a 10-inch (25 cm) pie plate. Bake crust at 400°F (200°C) for 10 to 12 minutes. Cool on a rack. **3** *To make filling*, in a food processor or blender combine eggs, salt, lemon rind, cream cheese and sugar. Blend until smooth. Fold in ground pecans. Pour filling into pie shell. Bake at 325°F (160°C) for 45 minutes or until filling is set. Let cool. **4** Meanwhile, *to make topping*, in a medium saucepan of boiling water, blanch peaches for 2 to 3 minutes. Drain peaches; peel and slice. **5** Return peach slices to saucepan; stir in sugar, wine and cinnamon. Over low heat, simmer until sugar dissolves. Increase heat; boil for 1 minute. Reduce heat to medium; simmer rapidly, stirring constantly, for 8 to 10 minutes, or until mixture is thick like jam. Chill. **6** Spoon topping over cooled tart. Chill for 30 minutes before serving.

Cream Cheese

Made by Westhill Dairy

LEBANESE KNAFI WITH RICOTTA

SERVES TEN TO TWELVE Grande Cheese Co. Ltd. — Weston, Ontario

ABOUT A HANDFUL of companies have captured the Italian cheese markets in Ontario, one of the first being Grande Cheese in 1963, owned by Albert Contardi. Grande makes pasta filatas (mozzarella, bocconcini) as well as ricotta. Cheesemaker at Grande since 1971, Dominic Barbuto uses a combination of whole milk and whey, which gives this ricotta body and more yield. The whey is heated to 185°F, then introduced to a lactic starter that causes curds to form and float to the surface. Once salted, the curds are dipped from the vat into draining cups, then transferred to a filling machine that fills individual containers. Sealed and cooled, Grande Ricotta is ready for shipment. Grande Cheese has made their cheeses more readily available to Ontario's Italian communities by opening four retail shops. Their name? Grande Cheese Factory Outlets.

My Lebanese neighbour, Ikhla Deebs, shared with me this traditional, easy-to-make dessert.

Château des Charmes Champagne Brut

Niagara-on-the-Lake, Ontario

A blend of estate-grown Chardonnay and Pinot Noir grapes done in the traditional méthode champenoise, the wine spent three years in the cellar before being released. A golden robe leads the way to a nose of firm Chardonnay fruit overlaid with creamy vanilla flavours. The dessert, light but overly sweet, needs a companion that simply refreshes the palate.

Other Choices:

B.C. Canadian champagne

Mozzarella and Ricotta

Made by Grande Cheese

Syrup:

3 cups	sugar	750 mL
1½ cups	water	375 mL
	Juice of ¼ lemon	

1 cup	butter, melted	250 mL
1	pkg (16 oz/454 g) phyllo pastry	1
1 cup	ricotta cheese	250 mL
½ lb	mozzarella cheese, shredded	250 g
½ cup	shelled pistachios, ground	125 mL

1 To make syrup, in a saucepan combine water, sugar and lemon juice. Over high heat, cook for 10 to 20 minutes, until mixture is thick and syrupy. Keep hot. **2** Brush a roasting pan with melted butter. Lay one sheet of phyllo in the pan; brush with melted butter. Continue layering, using one-third of phyllo. Spread ricotta cheese evenly over phyllo. **3** Spread next one-third of phyllo over ricotta, buttering each layer as you work. Sprinkle with mozzarella cheese. **4** Spread last one-third of phyllo over cheese, buttering each layer as you work. Generously butter top layer. Sprinkle with ground pistachios. **5** Bake at 350°F (180°C) for 20 minutes or until phyllo is golden. Cut into squares. Serve hot drizzled with syrup.

PUMPKIN RICOTTA CHEESECAKE

SERVES SIX TO EIGHT   Shari Darling — Toronto, Ontario

Crust:

¾ cup	graham cracker crumbs	175 mL
½ cup	chopped walnuts	125 mL
¼ cup	brown sugar	50 mL
¼ cup	butter, melted	50 mL

Filling:

1 cup	pumpkin purée	250 mL
3	large eggs	3
1 tsp	cinnamon	5 mL
½ tsp	nutmeg	2 mL
Pinch	salt	Pinch
3 cups	ricotta cheese	750 mL
½ cup	brown sugar	125 mL
2 tbsp	whipping cream	25 mL
1 tbsp	cornstarch	15 mL
1 tsp	vanilla extract	5 mL

Topping:

2 cups	sour cream	500 mL
2 tbsp	sugar	25 mL

Ground walnuts (for garnish)

Mission Hill Private Reserve Sherry (non-vintage)

Westbank, British Columbia

Produced from mostly 1974 wine, this sherry was fortified and stored in heavily charred whiskey barrels for 10 years. This golden sherry's creamy texture coincides with the creaminess of ricotta, while its nutty taste complements the pumpkin and draws attention to the mild walnut flavour.

Other Choices:

Ontario cream sherry

Ricotta

Made by Saputo Cheeses

1 *To make crust,* combine graham cracker crumbs, walnuts and sugar. Stir in butter. Press mixture into the bottom of a 9-inch (2.5 L) springform pan. Chill. **2** *To make filling,* whisk together pumpkin purée, eggs, cinnamon, nutmeg and salt. In a large bowl cream together ricotta cheese and brown sugar. Beat in cream, cornstarch and vanilla; beat in pumpkin mixture. Pour filling into crust. **3** Bake at 350°F (180°C) for 50 to 60 minutes or until centre is set. **4** Meanwhile, *to make topping,* beat together sour cream and sugar. **5** When cheesecake is done, cool on a rack for 5 minutes. Spread with topping. Bake cheesecake another 5 minutes. Cool in pan. **6** Chill a few hours or overnight. Before serving, sprinkle with ground walnuts.

WHITE CHOCOLATE CHEESECAKE

Westhill Dairy Inc. — Downsview, Ontario

IN THE LATE 1930s two family-owned companies, Birds Hill Dairy and Western Creamery, provided cream cheese, yogurt and sour cream to Southern Ontario's Jewish communities. Owners Leo Waldman and Lou Taichman amalgamated their businesses in 1970, and Westhill Dairy blossomed. Leo's son, Stephen, is now president, and under his direction the company continues to produce kosher dairy products. Made by the cold pack method, their Western cream cheese is of excellent quality (aroma, taste, body) and is all-natural, made of nothing more than milk, cream, enzyme culture and salt. (Mass-produced cream cheese is done in the hot pack method, which uses stabilizers and preservatives to lengthen shelf life, but quality is compromised.)

Created by Marci and Harold Rapp, this is one of the kosher desserts sold in the couple's Great Canadian Food Products shop in Toronto.

Crust:

1 1/2 cups	graham cracker crumbs	375 mL
6 tbsp	butter, softened	90 mL
2 tbsp	sugar	25 mL
1/2 tsp	cinnamon	2 mL

Filling:

1/3 lb	white chocolate	175 g
2 cups	cream cheese	500 mL
1/2 cup	sugar	125 mL
1 tsp	lemon juice	5 mL
2	eggs	2
3/4 cup	sour cream	175 mL

Topping:

1 cup	sour cream	250 mL
1 tsp	vanilla extract	5 mL

	White chocolate curls (for garnish)

London Wines
Cream Port

London, Ontario

Aged for 10 years in small oak barrels, this full-bodied tawny port is sweet enough (13 percent sugar code) to work with white chocolate. (Not kosher.)

Other Choices:
B.C. Canadian champagne or
B.C. port

1 *To make crust*, in a food processor or blender combine graham cracker crumbs, butter, sugar and cinnamon; blend well. Pat mixture into the bottom of a 9-inch (2.5 L) springform pan. **2** *To make filling*, in a double boiler set over barely simmering water, melt chocolate; keep warm. **3** In food processor or blender, combine cream cheese, sugar and lemon juice;

blend until well mixed. With motor running, add eggs, sour cream, and melted chocolate. Pour into crust. **4** Bake at 350°F (180°C) for 20 minutes or until centre is set. **5** Meanwhile, *to make topping*, stir together sour cream and vanilla. **6** Spread topping over cooked cheesecake. Bake another 15 to 20 minutes or until topping is set. Let cool. **7** Decorate top with white chocolate curls.

Western cream cheese

Made by Westhill Dairy

CLASSIC TIRAMISÙ

SERVES SIX TO EIGHT   Salerno Dairy Products Ltd. — Hamilton, Ontario

THREE DECADES OLD and still growing, Salerno is dedicated to the production of Italian-style cheeses. The family of the late founder Carmine Marzaro now operates the company and their newly acquired company, Gos & Gris Cheese Co., in Hannon, Ontario. Mozzarella, ricotta, Montasio, Parmesan, casata, Friulano, provolone and Romano, sold throughout Canada, are the company's mainstay. They also make a wonderful mascarpone. These cheeses are available in all of the chain supermarkets and Italian specialty shops throughout Canada.

Magnotta Wines Icewine Vidal Limited Edition

Vaughan, Ontario

With a golden robe, this rich dessert wine boasts tropical fruit aromas and flavours, making it an ideal match for Tiramisù.

Other Choices:
B.C. Icewine

Mascarpone

Made by Salerno Dairy Products

6	eggs, separated	6
6 tbsp	sugar	90 mL
1 lb	mascarpone cheese	500 g
2 tbsp	Tia Maria	25 mL
2	pkg (1 lb/500 g each) Savoiardi cookies	2
1½ cups	espresso coffee	375 mL
	Semisweet chocolate shavings (for garnish)	

1 In a large bowl, using a fork beat yolks with sugar until fluffy. Slowly beat in mascarpone and Tia Maria, beating until mixture is smooth. **2** Beat egg whites until stiff. Fold whites into cheese mixture; refrigerate for 5 minutes. **3** In a 10-inch (25 cm) pie plate, layer half the cookies dipped in espresso. Cover cookies with half the cheese mixture. Dip remaining cookies in espresso; layer over cheese mixture. Cover with remaining cheese mixture. Sprinkle with semisweet chocolate shavings. Refrigerate before serving.

CHOCOLATE CHEVRAI RASPBERRY TRUFFLE CAKE WITH MENNONITE CREAM

Chef Alex Begbie — London, Ontario

A CHEF AT SAY CHEESE since 1992, Alex Begbie created this spectacular dessert for this cookbook.

Raspberry Sauce:

1 cup	fresh raspberries	250 mL
½ cup	sugar	125 mL

Cake:

1 lb	semisweet chocolate	500 g
½ lb	butter	250 g
¼ lb	goat cheese (Chevrai)	125 g
6	eggs	6
½ cup	fresh raspberries	125 mL
1 cup	Mennonite cream OR whipping cream	250 mL

1 *To make raspberry sauce*, in a saucepan combine raspberries and sugar. Bring to a boil. Remove from heat; let cool. Strain sauce through a sieve. Chill. **2** *To make cake*, in the top of a double boiler set over simmering water, melt chocolate and butter. Beat in goat cheese until well mixed. Transfer mixture to a bowl. **3** In the cleaned top of the double boiler set over simmering water, beat eggs with a hand mixer until light and fluffy and tripled in volume. **4** Fold eggs into chocolate mixture, blending well. **5** Line the sides and bottom of an 8-inch (2 L) springform pan with parchment paper. Pour in half the batter. Sprinkle with raspberries. Pour remaining batter over raspberries. Smooth top with a spoon. **6** Half fill a shallow pan with warm water. Set springform pan into water. Bake at 425°F (220°C) for 5 minutes. **7** Cover springform pan with a sheet of buttered foil; do not let foil touch top of cake. Bake another 10 minutes. Cake will firm as it cools. **8** Let cake cool for 3 hours before removing sides. **9** Beat Mennonite cream until fluffy. Serve cake at room temperature with a pool of raspberry sauce and a generous dollop of Mennonite cream.

London Wines Cream Port

London, Ontario

Aged for 10 years in small oak barrels, this full-bodied tawny port is an excellent choice for all chocolate-based desserts. This decadent cake is no exception.

Other Choices:

B.C. port

Chevrai

Made by Woolwich Dairy

NEWFOUNDLAND PARTRIDGEBERRY TARTLETS WITH MASCARPONE CREAM

MAKES TWELVE   Shari Darling — Toronto, Ontario

Filling:

1 cup	fresh or frozen partridgeberries*	250 mL
¾ cup (approx)	sugar	250 mL

Pastry:

2 cups	all-purpose flour	500 mL
½ tsp	salt	2 mL
1 cup	cold butter	250 mL
⅔ cup	cold cream cheese	150 mL

Topping:

¾ cup	mascarpone cheese	175 mL
¼ cup	whipping cream	50 mL

Partridgeberries are also called mountain cranberries or foxberries. You will find them in Newfoundland specialty shops. You can substitute cranberries.

1 *To make filling,* in a saucepan combine partridgeberries with sugar. Add more sugar to taste, if needed. Over low heat, simmer until berries are jam consistency, about 1 hour. Let cool. **2** *To make pastry,* in a bowl mix together flour and salt. Cut in butter and cream cheese to form a soft dough. (Chill dough if it is too soft for rolling.) **3** On a lightly floured work surface, using half the dough at a time, roll out pastry to 1/8 inch (3 mm) thick. Using a 4-inch (10 cm) cookie cutter, cut out rounds; press in tart pan, making 12 tart shells. **4** Bake at 375°F (190°C) until golden. Cool on a rack. **5** *To make topping,* in a bowl whip together mascarpone cheese and cream. **6** Fill each tartlet with partridgeberry jam and top with a generous dollop of mascarpone cream.

Reif Estate Vidal Icewine

Niagara-on-the-Lake, Ontario

Though the mascarpone cheese adds a touch of sweetness to this dessert, the partridgeberries are extremely tart and so require a dessert wine with plenty of sweetness for balance. Icewine is the perfect choice. Reif's Icewine is full bodied and perfectly balanced, with a rich bouquet and palate of apricots, peaches and ripe honey melon.

Other Choices:

B.C. Icewine

Mascarpone

Made by Salerno Dairy Products

SWEET EXPRESSIONS WITH FIVE CHEESES

SERVES FOUR   Chef Clayton Folkers — Edmonton, Alberta

A RECIPE FOR THOSE serious cooks who find joy in spending a few hours in the kitchen preparing masterpieces. This masterpiece was created by chef Clayton Folkers of the Edmonton Convention Centre for the Dairy Bureau of Canada.

Château des Charmes Champagne Brut

Niagara-on-the-Lake, Ontario
Available in Alberta (The Bacchus Group, 403-484-5419)

This wine was made from Chardonnay and Pinot Noir grapes and done in the traditional méthode champenoise (second fermentation in the bottle). With a golden robe and firm Chardonnay fruit overlaid by creamy, vanilla flavours, this sparkler complements all the tasty treats in this dessert.

Other Choices:
B.C. Canadian champagne

Quark Bavarois:

1 tsp	unflavoured gelatin	5 mL
2	small eggs, separated	2
3 tbsp	sugar	50 mL
²/₃ cup	Quark cheese	150 mL
	Juice of ¹/₂ lemon	
4 tsp	orange juice concentrate	20 mL
¹/₂ cup	whipping cream	125 mL

Neufchatel and Blackberry Pudding:

³/₄ cup	fresh blackberries	175 mL
4 tsp	marzipan	20 mL
2 tsp	butter	10 mL
2 tsp	vodka	10 mL
¹/₃ cup	Neufchatel cheese with Strawberries (Delicreme with Strawberries)	75 mL
8	slices white bread, crusts removed	8

Emmenthal and Pine Nut Crusts:

2 tsp	sugar	10 mL
2 tsp	butter	10 mL
1	egg yolk	1
2 tsp	shredded Emmenthal cheese	10 mL
1 tsp	cake-and-pastry flour	5 mL
1 tbsp	finely chopped roasted pine nuts	15 mL

Cheddar Cheese Chips:

4 tsp	whipping cream	20 mL
1 tsp	sugar	5 mL
1	egg, beaten	1
1 tbsp	shredded mild Cheddar cheese	15 mL
³/₄ tsp	cornstarch	4 mL

Pinch	cardamom	Pinch

Cream Cheese Pistachios:

¼ cup	cream cheese	50 mL
4 tsp	butter	20 mL
1 tbsp	pistachio paste	15 mL
	Rind of ½ lemon	
2 tbsp	honey	25 mL

	Assorted fresh berries (for garnish)	

1 *To make Quark Bavarois,* line a baking sheet with plastic wrap; set aside. **2** Dissolve gelatin in 3 tbsp (50 mL) cold water; set aside. **3** Separate eggs. (Reserve egg whites for Cheddar Cheese Chips). In a medium bowl, beat egg yolks with sugar. Stir in Quark cheese, lemon juice and orange juice concentrate. **4** Whip cream until smooth and soupy. Fold whipped cream into Quark cheese. **5** Pour mixture onto the baking sheet. Cover with plastic wrap; refrigerate for 4 to 6 hours or overnight. (Freeze for 30 minutes before using.) **6** *To make Neufchatel and Blackberry Pudding,* in a food processor or blender purée blackberries. Press through a strainer to remove seeds; set aside. **7** In a bowl, rub together marzipan and butter. Slowly blend in vodka. Slowly blend in Neufchatel. Blend in 3 tbsp (50 mL) blackberry purée. **8** Using a round (2-inch/5 cm) cookie cutter, cut eight circles from bread. Dip four circles in blackberry purée; line the bottoms of four shallow (3.5-inch/9 cm) custard cups with dipped bread. **9** Spoon one-quarter of the cheese mixture into each custard cup, leaving a 1/2-inch (1 cm) space at top. Dip last four bread circles in blackberry purée; cover each pudding with bread. Reserve remaining blackberry purée. **10** Cover custard cups with plastic wrap; set on a baking sheet. Set another baking sheet on top of cups; weight the top. Refrigerate for at least 4 hours or overnight. **11** *To make Emmenthal and Pine Nut Crusts,* in a bowl rub together sugar, butter and egg yolk until smooth. Mix in Emmenthal and flour; do not overmix. Fold in pine nuts. Refrigerate, covered, for 30 minutes. **12** When set, on a lightly floured work surface roll out dough into a rectangle 2 inches (5 cm) wide and 5 inches (12 cm) long. Set on a buttered baking sheet. Bake at

400°F (200°C) for 8 to 10 minutes or until golden. Let cool slightly. While still warm, cut rectangle into four smaller rectangles. Set aside. **13** *To make Cheddar Cheese Chips*, in a bowl whip cream until almost stiff. In another bowl beat reserved egg whites with sugar until stiff; fold into cream. Fold beaten egg into cream mixture. Fold half the Cheddar, cornstarch and cardamom into cream mixture. **14** Using a teaspoon, drop eight circles of batter onto a buttered baking sheet. Using back of spoon, smooth circle out to very thin wafers. Bake at 400°F (200°C) for 6 to 7 minutes or until chips are golden. Cool on a rack. **15** *To make Cream Cheese Pistachios*, in a bowl blend cream cheese with butter until smooth. Mix in pistachio paste. Slowly add lemon juice and honey, stirring constantly until mixture is smooth. **16** Fit a piping bag with a #6 tip and fill bag with cream cheese mixture. Pipe a rosette onto each Cheddar Chip. Refrigerate.
17 *To assemble dessert*, using a heart-shaped cookie cutter, cut out 2 hearts from frozen Quark Bavarois. Slice hearts in half lengthwise. Set a half-heart on each plate. Arrange assorted berries on each half-heart. Place one Emmenthal and Pine Nut Crust beside each half-heart. Spoon one-quarter of reserved blackberry purée beside each crust. Dip Neufchatel Pudding cups in warm water; unmould beside the purée. Set one Cheddar Chip beside each pudding.

Rocky Mountain brand Quark

Made by Neapolis Dairy Products

Delicreme with Strawberries

Made by Agropur

Jersey Supreme mild Cheddar

Made by Neapolis Dairy Products

Anco Emmenthal

Made by Agropur

Parisee Cream Cheese

Made by Neapolis Dairy Products

WINNIPEG CHEESECAKE

SERVES SIX TO EIGHT Co-op Dairies/Dairyworld Foods — Winnipeg, Manitoba

CO-OP DAIRIES, ESTABLISHED IN 1925, is one of Manitoba's most renowned producers of cream cheese. What makes their cream cheese superior is its full flavour and smooth texture, achieved through a method of production called cold packing. Cold-packed cream cheese has a shorter shelf life — 20 to 30 days — because it is free of stabilizers and preservatives. In other words, it's natural: its only ingredients are milk, cream, enzyme culture and salt. Considered a specialty item, Co-op Dairies' cream cheese can be found only in fine food and gourmet shops, independent supermarkets and small delis. Ontarians can discover this delicacy under the President's Choice label "Memories of Winnipeg."

This recipe was developed by Heather Cram for Co-op Dairies.

*Cave Spring
Cellars
Chardonnay*

Jordan, Ontario
Available in Manitoba (L.C.C.)

Any wine but a light, fruity white would overpower this simple cheesecake. Cave Spring's Chardonnay offers apple character with ample acidity to counter the rich taste of the cream cheese and sweet crust.

Other Choices:
B.C. Chardonnay

Winnipeg Cream Cheese

Made by Co-Op Dairies

Crust:

3/4 cup	graham wafer crumbs	175 mL
1/3 cup	brown sugar	75 mL
	Grated rind of 1 lemon	
1/4 tsp	ground cardamom	1 mL
1/3 cup	butter, melted	75 mL

Filling:

1 1/4 cups	cream cheese	300 mL
4	eggs	4
3/4 cup	sugar	175 mL
	Juice of 1/2 lemon	
1 tsp	vanilla	5 mL

1 *To make crust,* in a large bowl combine wafer crumbs, brown sugar, lemon rind, cardamom and melted butter; mix thoroughly. Press into bottom and sides of a buttered 9-inch (23 cm) pie plate or 9-inch (2.5 L) springform pan pressing 1 1/4 inches (3 cm) up sides. **2** *To make filling,* in the cleaned bowl combine cream cheese, eggs, sugar, lemon juice and vanilla; beat thoroughly until smooth. Pour into crust. **3** Bake at 350°F (180°C) for 35 minutes or until filling is firm. Turn off oven, prop open oven door and let cheesecake stand in oven for 1 hour. Refrigerate for several hours before serving.

INDEX OF RECIPES AND WINERIES